NATIONALIST THOUGHT AND
THE COLONIAL WORLD

In this book a leading Indian political philosopher criticises Western theories of Third World nationalism – both liberal and Marxist. He demonstrates how Western theorists, with their emphasis on the power of reason, the primacy of the hard sciences and the dominance of the empirical method, have assumed that their presuppositions are universally valid, and, through the impact of Western education, have imposed concepts of nationalism on non-Western peoples to the detriment, if not destruction, of their own world-views. The author explores the central contradiction that nationalism in Africa and Asia has consequently experienced: setting out to assert its freedom from European domination, it yet remained a prisoner of European post-Enlightenment rationalist discourse.

Using the case of India, Professor Chatterjee goes on to show how Indian nationalism did effect significant displacements in the framework of modernist thinking imbibed from the West. Yet, despite constituting itself as a different discourse, it remained dominated by the very structure of power it sought to repudiate. And so the historical outcome generally has been the transformation of Third World nationalism by ruling classes into a state ideology legitimising their own rule, appropriating the life of the nation, and propelling it along the path of 'universal modernisation'. But the spurious ideological unity proclaimed by these classes, and their failure to subsume completely the life of the nation in the life of their new states, raises the historical prospect that a critique of state nationalism will emerge.

This profound exercise in political philosophy questions the legitimacy of the currently predominant formulations of nationalist ideology in the Third World. It anticipates a new generation of popular struggles that will redefine the content of Afro-Asian nationalism and the kinds of society people wish to build.

For scholars, it will make uncomfortable reading because of its radical attack on the fundamentals of Western bourgeois thought, an attack always couched, however, in the rational tones of Western scholarship.

To
Ranajit Guha
and
Asok Sen
from whom I have learnt the most

PARTHA CHATTERJEE

NATIONALIST THOUGHT AND THE COLONIAL WORLD

A Derivative Discourse

and a self-consciously political, "polemical" project (52)

The inherent contradiction of nationalist thought – p. 38
Bourgeoisie is constrained in its response to colonialism – seeks meliorism rather than a "war of maneuver" (ie direct confrontation) w/ the state – p. 45

3 moments: (1) departure (2) manoeuvre – "appropriation of the present" (p. 81)

MINNESOTA

University of Minnesota Press

Minneapolis

Gramsci on the interventionist capitalist state – p. 47

Nationalist Thought and the Colonial World: A Derivative Discourse
was first published on behalf of the United Nations University,
Tokyo, by Zed Books Ltd in 1986.

Copyright © United Nations University, 1986

Second Impression 1993

Published in the United States of America by the University of
Minnesota Press, 2037 University Avenue Southeast,
Minneapolis, MN 55455 and in the rest of the world
by Zed Books Ltd, 57 Caledonian Road,
London N1 9BU, United Kingdom.

Cover design by Andrew Corbett

Printed on acid-free paper and bound in the United Kingdom
by Biddles Ltd, Guildford and King's Lynn

Library of Congress Cataloging No. 92-42176

US ISBN 0-8166-2311-2 (pb)

The University of Minnesota is an equal-opportunity
educator and employer.

British CIP is available from the British Library.

UK ISBN 0 86232 553 6 (pb)

Contents

If there are obstacles the shortest line between two points may well be a crooked line.
Bertolt Brecht, *Life of Galileo*. scene 14

Preface

In the last scene of Bertolt Brecht's *Life of Galileo*, the scientist is quoted as having said, 'If there are obstacles the shortest line between two points may well be a crooked line.' Given the abstract neatness of the theoretical world of classical mechanics, the statement carries a ring of irony. In the much less well-ordered world of politics, however, it would seem to be a truism.

Yet it is remarkable how seldom political theorists have taken seriously the fact that 'politics' necessarily operates in an ideological world in which words rarely have unambiguous meanings; where notions are inexact, and have political value precisely because they are inexact and hence capable of suggesting a range of possible interpretations; where intentions themselves are contradictory and consequences very often unintended; where movements follow winding and unpredictable paths; where choices are strategic and relative, not univocal and absolute. And still, this inexact world of ambiguity and half-truth, of manipulation and deception, of dreams and illusions, is not wholly patternless, for here, too, objectives are realised, rules established, values asserted, revolutions accomplished and states founded.

This book is about a political revolution, but one whose course cannot be described by selecting from history two points of origin and culmination and joining them by a straight line. The critical viewpoint reveals that it is a revolution which at the same time, and in fundamental ways, is not a revolution. It is in the shifts, slides, discontinuities, the unintended moves, what is suppressed as much as what is asserted, that one can get a sense of this complex movement, not as so many accidental or disturbing factors but as constitutive of the very historical rationality of its process. And it is by examining the jagged edges that we can find clues to an understanding of the political relevance today of the ideological history of nationalism.

I wanted to call this book *Crooked Line*. But friends more knowledgeable than I in the ways of the publishing world have persuaded me that that would not be the best way to reach my potential readers. I have deferred to their judgment.

I began writing this book in the 1981-82 academic year which I spent at St Antony's College, Oxford. I am grateful to the Nuffield Foundation, London, for a travelling fellowship. I continued the work during my short stay in 1982-83 as a Visiting Fellow at the Research School of Pacific Studies, Australian

National University, Canberra, and completed it on my return to Calcutta. I am grateful to the staff of the Bodleian Library in Oxford, the ANU Library in Canberra, the National Library in Calcutta, the Department of History Library of the University of Calcutta and, of course, the Library of the Centre for Studies in Social Sciences, Calcutta, for their help.

Among those who have read and commented on earlier drafts of this book are Anouar Abdel-Malek, Shahid Amin, Jasodhara Bagchi, Dipesh Chakrabarty, John Dunn, Omkar Goswami, Ranajit Guha, Tapati Guha Thakurta, Sudipta Kaviraj, Rudrangshu Mukherjee, Gyan Pandey, Abhijit Sen and Asok Sen. I thank them all for their criticisms and suggestions.

I have presented and discussed different parts of this book in seminars at Algiers, Oxford, Canberra, Baroda, Paris and Calcutta. My thanks to all participants at those seminars.

I am grateful to Kinhide Mushakoji and Anouar Abdel-Malek of the United Nations University, Robert Molteno and Anna Gourlay of Zed Books, London, and Ravi Dayal and Rukun Advani of Oxford University Press, New Delhi, for their help in the publication of this book. My thanks also to May McKenzie and Margaret Hall for preparing the typescript.

Finally, I take this opportunity to record my gratitude to Gouri for her support and understanding.

Partha Chatterjee
Calcutta

December 1985

1. Nationalism as a Problem in the History of Political Ideas

> To trouble oneself with the task of dealing with something
> that has been adequately dealt with before is superfluous,
> a result of ignorance, or a sign of evil intent.
> Abu Bakr Muhammad Ibn Bajjah [Avempace],
> *Tadbīr al-mutawaḥḥid*

I

In one of his less celebrated articles, John Plamenatz has talked about 'two types' of nationalism:[1] in both, nationalism is 'primarily a cultural phenomenon' although it often takes a 'political form'. One type is 'western', having emerged primarily in Western Europe, and the other 'eastern', to be found in Eastern Europe, in Asia and Africa, and also in Latin America. Both types depend upon the acceptance of a common set of standards by which the state of development of a particular national culture is measured. In the first type, however, although there is the feeling that the nation is at a disadvantage with respect to others, it is nevertheless already 'culturally equipped' to make the attempt to remove those deficiencies. Thus, although the new global standard of progress may have been set for the rest of the world by France or Britain, they were based upon a set of ideas 'about man, morals and society' which, in their social and intellectual origins, were West European generally. Britain and France may have been the cultural, economic and political pace makers, and may have been envied or admired for this reason, but simultaneous with the process of their emergence as world leaders, there had emerged a 'comity of nations' in Western Europe 'which had already learned to think of itself as ahead of all the others'. Consequently, when nationalism emerged in the other countries of the West, despite the fact that it was the product of a sense of disadvantage with respect to the standards of progress set by the pace makers, there was no feeling that the nation was not culturally equipped to make the effort to reach those standards. Germans or Italians, for instance, already had the necessary linguistic, educational and professional skills that were deemed necessary for a 'consciously progressive civilisation'. They had therefore 'little need to equip themselves culturally by appropriating what was alien to them'. That is to say, although the acceptance of a universal standard of progress had produced an awareness of disadvantage, that universal standard itself was not seen in any fundamental way as being alien to the national culture.

'Eastern' nationalism, on the other hand, has appeared among 'peoples recently drawn into a civilisation hitherto alien to them, and whose ancestral cultures are not adapted to success and excellence by these cosmopolitan and increasingly dominant standards'. They too have measured the backwardness of their nations in terms of certain global standards set by the advanced nations of Western Europe. But what is distinctive here is that there is also a fundamental awareness that those standards have come from an alien culture, and that the inherited culture of the nation did not provide the necessary adaptive leverage to enable it to reach those standards of progress. The 'Eastern' type of nationalism, consequently, has been accompanied by an effort to 're-equip' the nation culturally, to transform it. But it could not do so simply by imitating the alien culture, for then the nation would lose its distinctive identity. The search therefore was for a regeneration of the national culture, adapted to the requirements of progress, but retaining at the same time its distinctiveness.

The attempt is deeply contradictory: 'It is both imitative and hostile to the models it imitates . . .' It is imitative in that it accepts the value of the standards set by the alien culture. But it also involves a rejection: 'in fact, two rejections, both of them ambivalent: rejection of the alien intruder and dominator who is nevertheless to be imitated and surpassed by his own standards, and rejection of ancestral ways which are seen as obstacles to progress and yet also cherished as marks of identity'. This contradictory process is therefore deeply disturbing as well. 'Eastern nationalism is disturbed and ambivalent as the nationalisms of Herder and Mazzini were not.'

Unlike much of his other work, this article by Plamenatz is neither rigorously argued nor particularly profound. But in making the distinction between the two types of nationalism, it states with sufficient clarity the premises of what may be called the liberal-rationalist dilemma in talking about nationalist thought. The same dilemma can be seen in the standard liberal histories of nationalism, most notably in the work of Hans Kohn.[2] This historiography accepts nationalism as an integral part of the story of liberty. Its origin is coeval with the birth of universal history, and its development is part of the same historical process which saw the rise of industrialism and democracy. In its essential aspects, therefore, nationalism represents the attempt to actualize in political terms the universal urge for liberty and progress. And yet the evidence was undeniable that it could also give rise to mindless chauvinism and xenophobia and serve as the justification for organized violence and tyranny. Seen as part of the story of liberty, nationalism could be defined as a rational ideological framework for the realization of rational, and highly laudable, political ends. But that was not how nationalism had made its presence felt in much of recent history. It has been the cause of the most destructive wars ever seen; it has justified the brutality of Nazism and Fascism; it has become the ideology of racial hatred in the colonies and has given birth to some of the most irrational revivalist movements as well as to the most oppressive political regimes in the contemporary world. The evidence was indeed overwhelming that nationalism and liberty could often be quite irreconcilably opposed.

The distinction between the two types of nationalism is an attempt to come to terms with this liberal dilemma. Indeed, Kohn also made a distinction of this sort, between 'western' and 'non-western' nationalisms,[3] and later between 'good' nationalism and 'evil' nationalism.[4] The distinction is designed to explain how a profoundly liberal idea could be so distorted as to produce such grossly illiberal movements and regimes. It does this by constructing a dichotomy, between a normal and a special type. The normal is the classical, the orthodox, the pure type. This type of nationalism shares the same material and intellectual premises with the European Enlightenment, with industry and the idea of progress, and with modern democracy. Together they constitute a historical unity, defined with a fair degree of clarity in both geographical and chronological terms. This gives the liberal-rationalist his paradigmatic form in which nationalism goes hand-in-hand with reason, liberty and progress. The special type emerges under somewhat different historical circumstances. It is, therefore, complex, impure, often deviant; it represents a very difficult and contradictory historical process which can be very 'disturbing'. There is nothing in it, the liberal-rationalist would argue, that is necessarily illiberal. But being a special type, operating in unfavourable circumstances, it can often be so. 'No doubt,' says Plamenatz, 'nationalists have quite often not been liberals, but this, I suggest, is largely because they have so often been active in conditions unpropitious to freedom, as the liberal understands it. I see no logical repugnance between nationalism and liberalism.' Indeed, the very fact that nationalists of the 'eastern' type accept and value the ideal of progress — and strive to transform their inherited cultures in order to make them better suited for the conditions of the modern world — means that archaic forms of authority are destroyed, conditions are created for the growth of a certain degree of individual initiative and choice, and for the introduction of science and modern education. All this cannot but be liberating in a fundamental historical sense. Consequently, even when this kind of nationalism appears in the form of revivalist movements or oppressive regimes, it still represents an urge for progress and freedom.

> We must see this nationalism as part of a social, intellectual and moral revolution of which the aspirations to democracy and personal freedom are also products. It is connected with these aspirations, and even serves to strengthen them and to create some of the social conditions of their realisation, even though it so often also perverts them.

Thus the liberal-rationalist saves the purity of his paradigm by designating as deviant all those cases which do not fit the classical form. Even in these deviant cases, he would argue, one can still discern the basic historical urge to attain the classical ideals. The deviations themselves are to be explained by the special circumstances in which this attempt has to be made in countries where conditions are 'unpropitious to freedom'. That is to say, the deviations are to be explained *sociologically*, by grouping and classifying the various empirical cases and then constructing coherent sets of sociological conditions which may be said to be the cause for each particular type of deviation.[5]

The argument could then start, to take one example,[6] by recognizing first of all the world-wide sweep of 'the tidal wave of modernisation', but distilling its essence in the awareness of man's 'capacity to contribute to, and to profit from, industrial society'. It would then proceed to describe the erosion of the 'structure' of traditional society, conceived as a system of role relationships, and its replacement by the 'culture' of industrial society, in which the classification of people by culture is the classification by nationality. The argument would then take in the fact of the notorious 'unevenness' of the process of industrialization, in terms of geographical and cultural regions. Not only does industrialization disrupt traditional society, it disrupts it unevenly. But now there is also a common standard by which the states of advancement of different regions can be compared. The perception of uneven development creates the possibility for nationalism; it is born when the more and the less advanced populations can be easily distinguished in cultural terms. 'Nationalism is not the awakening of nations to self-consciousness: it invents nations where they do not exist — but it does need some pre-existing differentiating marks to work on . . .' The two crucial social groups which carry the struggle forward are the proletariat and the intelligentsia. The intellectuals 'will exchange second-class citizenship for a first-class citizenship plus greater privileges based on rarity'. The proletarians will exchange 'hardships-with-snubs for possibly greater hardships with national identification'. The dilemma of a choice between imitation and identity? 'Superficially', the intellectuals

> always face the crucial dilemma of choosing between 'westernising' and a *narodnik* tendency . . . But the dilemma is quite spurious: ultimately the movements invariably contain both elements, a genuine modernism and a more or less spurious concern for local culture . . . By the twentieth century, the dilemma hardly bothers anyone: the philosopher-kings of the 'underdeveloped' world all act as westernisers, and all talk like *narodniks*.

Thus the liberal dilemma is circumvented by a positive sociology. The urge for modernization is a positive fact of contemporary history. If the struggles in the backward parts of the world 'to lift onself by one's own shoelaces, economically', mean a certain repressive attitude, that too is a sociological fact, to be understood and explained. But it is on the whole a good thing that these struggles are being conducted within a framework of nationalism. There are, first of all, the 'psychological blessings' of dignity and self-respect, of the elimination of inferior grades of citizenship. There is also the fortunate consequence that these political convulsions 'do not need to be re-imported into the developed, previously imperial, territories'. They can be fought out at a distance, with a certain degree of autonomy. If the liberal conscience of the West adopts the right moral attitude of sympathy and non-interference, these backward nations will find their own chosen paths to independence, freedom and progress.

An elaboration of this sociological understanding of the phenomenon of nationalism would then inevitably proceed towards a teleology, i.e. a theory of political development. And once this step is taken, the empirical relation between nationalism and illiberal regimes can even be justified by a theory of the stages of development. Thus, it could be argued that given the very special sociological circumstances in which the new nations have to struggle to modernize themselves, it might be a perfectly rational strategy for them, in a sense, to postpone the democratic consummation of their efforts until the economic structures of their society are sufficiently industrialized and their social institutions modernized.[7] An empiricist sociology can do wonderful things to resolve the moral dilemmas of a liberal conscience.

Indeed, armed with his sociological explanation of the 'conditions' which give rise to nationalist movements, the liberal theorist can even assert that nationalism poses only a very trivial problem for the history of political ideas. 'It is not so much,' runs the self-complacent judgment of Ernest Gellner,

> that the prophets of nationalism were not anywhere near the First Division, when it came to the business of thinking . . . It is rather that these thinkers did not really make much difference. If one of them had fallen, others would have stepped into his place . . . The quality of nationalist thought would hardly have been affected much by such substitutions. Their precise doctrines are hardly worth analysing.[8]

Why? Because given the 'conditions' in which nationalism made its appearance, there was little scope for genuine doctrinal innovation or philosophical defence. Or more precisely, the necessary philosophizing had already been done, in a different context — that of the rise of 'industrialism'. (Gellner quaintly refers to Hume and Kant as the ones who 'explored, with unparalleled philosophical depth . . . the general logic of the new spirit . . .'[9]) By the time nationalism came on the scene, mankind was 'irreversibly committed to industrial society, and therefore to a society whose productive system is based on cumulative science and technology'. This commitment necessarily meant coming to terms with the requirements of industrial society, namely a cultural homogeneity and its convergence with a political unit. Cultural homogeneity was an essential concomitant of industrial society, 'and we had better make our peace with it. It is not the case . . . that nationalism imposes homogeneity; it is rather that a homogeneity imposed by objective, inescapable imperative eventually appears on the surface in the form of nationalism.'[10]

Thus nationalist thought did not even need to investigate 'the general logic' of the kind of society it was trying to build: that logic was given to it objectively. It did, of course, have to confront the problem of selecting from pre-existing cultures in agrarian society some of the distinctive elements of this new homogeneous national culture. Nationalism 'uses some of the pre-existent cultures, generally transforming them in the process, but it cannot possibly use them all'.[11] It often defines itself in the name of some putative folk culture. But this is a myth, a piece of self-deception; that is not what it really does. In reality,

> nationalism is, essentially, the general imposition of a high culture on society, whose previously low cultures had taken up the lives of the majority, and in some

cases of the totality, of the population. It means that generalized diffusion of a school-mediated, academy-supervised idiom, codified for the requirements of reasonably precise bureaucratic and technological communication. It is the establishment of an anonymous, impersonal society, with mutually substitutable atomized individuals, held together above all by a shared culture of this kind, in place of a previous complex structure of local groups, sustained by folk cultures reproduced locally and idiosyncratically by the micro-groups themselves. That is what *really* happens.[12]

What if the new high culture happens to be the product of an alien imposition? Can it then effectively supersede the various folk cultures and become a truly homogeneous national culture? Is there not a problem of incommensurability and inter-cultural relativism which the new national culture must overcome? Gellner recognizes that there is a problem here, but it is not one which he thinks needs to be taken seriously. The fact is that with the universal acceptance of the imperative of industrialism, every national culture does manage to overcome incommensurability and relativism.

> The question concerning just *how* we manage to transcend relativism is interesting and difficult, and certainly will not be solved here. What is relevant, however, is that we somehow or other do manage to overcome it, that we are not hopelessly imprisoned within a set of cultural cocoons and their norms, and that for some very obvious reasons (shared cognitive and productive bases and greatly increased inter-social communication) we may expect fully industrial man to be even less enslaved to his local culture than was his agrarian predecessor.[13]

Nationalist thought, in other words, does not pose any special problems for either epistemology or political philosophy. All its problems can be reduced to the sociological requirements of industrial society whose universal sway provides the context for the understanding of nationalism.

It is by a recourse to sociology, in fact, that the liberal-rationalist can first identify in positive terms, and then 'sympathetically' understand, the difficult conditions under which the poor and oppressed nations of the world have to strive in order to attain those universal values of reason, liberty and progress which the latter have, at last, learnt to cherish. There is unfortunately a great historical lag which they must make up. The knowledge of backwardness is never very comforting. It is even more disturbing when its removal means a coming to terms with a culture that is alien. But that is the historical destiny of the backward nations. There can be no merit, as Plamenatz gently chides 'Western critics of nationalism', in expressing distaste for the failings of these backward peoples. 'In a world in which the strong and rich people have dominated and exploited the poor and the weak peoples, and in which autonomy is held to be a mark of dignity, of adequacy, of the capacity to live as befits human beings, in such a world this kind of nationalism is the inevitable reaction of the poor and the weak.'[14]

II

'Guilt!' an unrepentant critic of nationalism like Elie Kedourie will say: '. . . guilt, indignation, and moral passion'; '. . . powerful and corrosive feelings of guilt'.[15] This merciless self-accusation has been propagated in recent years by European publicists, and their audience, always so keen to be fair and considerate to the underdogs, have accepted the charge without protest. The very idea of nationalism being a rational and self-conscious attempt by the weak and poor peoples of the world to achieve autonomy and liberty is demonstrably false. Nationalism as an ideology is irrational, narrow, hateful and destructive. It is not an authentic product of any of the non-European civilizations which, in each particular case, it claims as its classical heritage. It is wholly a European export to the rest of the world. It is also one of Europe's most pernicious exports, for it is not a child of reason or liberty, but of their opposite: of fervent romanticism, of political messianism whose inevitable consequence is the annihilation of freedom.

Kedourie's is a severe indictment of nationalism, and one against which liberal defenders of the doctrine have been hard put to it to state their case. Of course, Kedourie's own brand of conservative politics, the ground from which he has launched his powerful attack, could easily be dismissed as archaic and irrelevant. For instance he states his belief in the essential fairness and nobility of the true principles of empire. He believes that those who rule and those who are ruled are 'different species of men' and that it is most conducive for political order when those distinctions are clearly maintained. He believes in a style of politics in which emotions and passions are kept to a minimum, where interests are not given the illusory form of moral principles, where governance is not compromised by the fickle determinations of a plebiscite. These ideas may seem quaint or bizarre, depending on one's particular taste for such old-world wisdoms. But they can be dismissed quite easily.

Why, then, the continuing debate with Kedourie, and the hesitant, almost timid, defence of the liberal's case? Anthony Smith, for instance, objects that Kedourie's description of the consequences of nationalism is a one-sided misrepresentation.[16] It overlooks 'the advantages and blessings of nationalist revivals': Dvořák and Chopin, for example, or Césaire, Senghor, 'Abduh and Tagore. Nationalism has often had a great humanizing and civilizing influence. Besides, it is misleading to portray nationalist politics merely as secret conspiracy and terrorism or nihilism and totalitarianism.

> Nobody would dispute that these have been features of some nationalisms . . . But it is only fair to recall the extreme situations in which they operated . . . Kedourie forgets the uses of nationalism in developing countries, the way in which they can legitimate new regimes desirous of maintaining political stability and keeping a fissiparous population under a single and viable harness. He forgets too the examples of nationalism providing an impetus to constitutional reforms, as in India or Ottoman Turkey, not to mention its uses in legitimising sweeping social change and modernisation . . .

This, of course, is a rather feeble rejoinder, conceding at the very start a great deal of empirical ground: 'Nobody would dispute that these have been features of *some* nationalisms . . .', but *not of all*. Smith then goes on to construct a defensible case by stating a 'core doctrine of nationalism', itself 'incomplete' and 'unstable', but capable of being rounded out by 'specific' theories that can encompass particular sets of empirical cases of movements conventionally called nationalist. The core doctrine 'fuses three ideals: collective self-determination of the people, the expression of national character and individuality, and finally the vertical division of the world into unique nations each contributing its special genius to the common fund of humanity'.[17] As such, this doctrine can be regarded 'as a not unreasonable application of Enlightenment principles to the complexities of modern politics and societies . . . it constitutes a necessary condition for the search for realistic conditions of liberty and equality, not to mention democracy, in an already divided world'.[18] About the 'specific' theories which are additionally necessary to encompass the many particular cases of nationalist movements, Smith's submission is that they are the products of very specific historical circumstances and are therefore 'morally highly variegated', and it would be wrong to make 'a *simpliste* ascription of all these concrete manifestations to the *unmediated* effects of "nationalism" '.

The problem of the 'specific', or rather the 'deviant', cases is thus consigned to the domain of the historically contingent, to be explained by a suitable sociological theory, and therefore not requiring a moral defence. The core doctrine, however, does assert a moral claim, made up of three separate but related parts: self-determination, expression of national character, and each nation contributing its special genius to the common fund of humanity. This is how the often contentious claim to national autonomy is reconciled with the ideal of universal liberty and fraternity. But in specifying this application of Enlightenment principles to the conditions of modern politics, the liberal defender of nationalism must invariably play straight into Kedourie's hand. For this specification will have to be in terms of the idea of progress, of the spread of science and rationality, of modernization and industrialization, and probably equality and democracy as well. And this will immediately destroy the central moral claim of the 'core doctrine' of nationalism, namely, the autonomy of national self-consciousness.

Now Kedourie can retort by beginning from the very first sentence of his book: 'Nationalism is a doctrine invented in Europe at the beginning of the nineteenth century.'[19] Every part of the nationalist doctrine, he will argue, can be taken apart and shown to have been derived from some species of European thought. It is totally alien to the non-European world: 'it is neither something indigenous to these areas nor an irresistible tendency of the human spirit everywhere, but rather an importation from Europe clearly branded with the mark of its origin'.[20] For the non-European world, in short, nationalist thought does not constitute an autonomous discourse.

Once that position has been surrendered, Kedourie can fire volley after volley directed at the spurious claims of a liberal doctrine of nationalism. The argument that culture, and more specifically, language, uniquely defines a nation is an invention of 19th century European writers, particularly Herder, Schlegel, Fichte and Schleiermacher, which has been subsequently taken up by nationalist intellectuals of the East. The emphasis, again, on history as a distinct mode of thought in which the life of the nation can be represented and indeed experienced is also a European innovation subsequently absorbed into the intellectual life of the new nationalisms. 'Nationalist doctrine . . . decrees that just as nations exist, so nations by definition must have a past.'[21] So every nationalism has invented a past for the nation; every nationalism speaks through a discourse, 'historical in its form but apologetic in its substance', which claims to demonstrate the rise, progress and efflorescence of its own particular genius. Modern European intellectual fashion not only decrees that a nation must have a past, it also demands that it have a future. Have faith in the historical progress of man, it preaches, and history will not let you down. The idea of progress, once again a European invention, 'is a secularized and respectable version of the medieval millennium'.[22] It goes hand in hand with an extremist, millennial style of politics, made respectable all over the world in the years following the French Revolution. 'This frenzied meliorism, which in its religious form was long suppressed and disreputable, in its secular form became the dominant strand of the political tradition first of Europe and then of the whole world.'[23] The antipathy which one often notices in nationalist revivals in Asia and Africa, the superficial rejection of things Western, is not really a rejection at all. It is part and parcel of this extremist style of politics, where the leaders of the revolution will use any means available to reach their goals, including 'conscious and deliberate manipulation of what [is], in their eyes, primitive superstition'.[24] Thus, when Bipin Chandra Pal glorifies Kālī, the dark goddess of destruction with a garland of human heads round her neck, blood dripping from the severed heads, he is 'in a line of succession from Robespierre's conjunction of virtue and terror'. '. . . the mainspring of nationalism in Asia and Africa is the same secular millennialism which had its rise and development in Europe and in which society is subjected to the will of a handful of visionaries who, to achieve their vision, must destroy all barriers between private and public'.[25] Yet another element of this extremist style of politics exported from Europe is the 'pathetic fallacy', known and demonstrated as false in the classical texts on power in every non-European civilization, which asserts 'that a government is the same as the subjects and is flesh of their flesh' and 'that the aims and interests of government are the very same as those for which the governed work and struggle'.[26] The new claimants to power in the nations of Asia and Africa constantly and profitably use this fallacy in a 'rhetoric of the heart', a fervent, impassioned, romantic, and inherently false, discourse.

'Resentment and impatience, the depravity of the rich and the virtue of the poor, the guilt of Europe and the innocence of Asia and Africa, salvation through violence, the coming reign of universal love':[27] those are the elements of nationalist thought. Each of them is an export from Europe, like the printing press, the radio, and television. Nationalist opposition to European rule is driven by a faith in a theory. Yet the theory itself, and indeed the very attitude of faith in a theory, are the gifts of Europe to the rest of the world. Nationalism sets out to assert its freedom from European domination. But in the very conception of its project, it remains a prisoner of the prevalent European intellectual fashions.

III

The last sentence is not really a paraphase of Kedourie, because he does not pose the problem in those terms. But it would be a logical implication of his critique of the liberal doctrine of nationalism if it was situated in the context of a different theoretical problem. What Kedourie does not see, and his liberal antagonists do not recognize, are the far-reaching implications of the argument that nationalist thought does not, and indeed cannot, constitute an autonomous discourse. Kedourie merely uses the argument as a convenient stick with which to beat the liberals, by showing that nationalism is an inauthentic and misguided attempt to reach illusory ideals that can never be reached and that its only consequence is violence, destruction and tyranny. The liberal, on the other hand, can object, quite justifiably, that this characterization of nationalism as something essentially irrational and illiberal is unwarranted. He then points to the specific socio-historical conditions in which most of these nationalist movements occur and suggests that one adopt a charitable view and try to understand these movements as more or less rational attempts made under difficult conditions to pursue the now universally accepted ideals of enlightenment and progress. If the conditions are right, there is reason enough to believe that these nationalisms would succeed in finding their way towards that goal. The liberal-rationalist, in other words, refuses to pose the lack of autonomy of nationalist discourse as a theoretical problem.

Indeed, to put it plainly, the Enlightenment view of rationality and progress and the historical values enshrined in that view are shared by both sides in the debate. But starting from this premise the conservatives argue, whether explicitly like Kedourie or in the form of a more implicit structure of assumptions as in a great deal of European historiography on nationalist movements in the colonial world — which sees them as a congeries of factions, patron–client relationships, traditional loyalties clothed in the garb of modern political organizations, etc. — that the non-European peoples are culturally incapable of acquiring the values of the Enlightenment. The liberals, on the other hand, assert that these irrational and regressive features are only a hangover from the past, that these countries too are involved in the historical task of modernization, and once the conditions which are detrimental to progress are removed there is no reason why they should not also proceed to approximate the values that have made the West what it is today. But neither side can pose the problem in a form in which the question can be asked: why is it that non-European colonial countries have no historical alternative but to try to approximate the given attributes of modernity when that very process of approximation means their continued subjection under a world order which only sets their tasks for them and over which they have no control?

I will now argue that it is not possible to pose this theoretical problem within the ambit of bourgeois-rationalist thought, whether conservative or liberal. For to pose it is to place thought itself, including thought that is supposedly rational and scientific, within a discourse of *power*. It is to question the very universality, the 'givenness', the sovereignty of that thought, to go to its roots and thus radically to criticize it. It is to raise the possibility that it is not just military might or industrial strength, but thought itself, which can dominate and subjugate. It is to approach the field of discourse, historical, philosophical and scientific, as a battleground of political power.

From such a perspective, the problem of nationalist thought becomes the particular manifestation of a much more general problem, namely, the problem of the bourgeois-rationalist conception of knowledge, established in the post-Enlightenment period of European intellectual history, as the moral and epistemic foundation for a supposedly universal framework of thought which perpetuates, in a real and not merely a metaphorical sense, a colonial domination. It is a framework of knowledge which proclaims its own universality; its validity, it pronounces, is independent of cultures. Nationalist thought, in agreeing to become 'modern', accepts the claim to universality of this 'modern' framework of knowledge. Yet it also asserts the autonomous identity of a national culture. It thus simultaneously rejects and accepts the dominance, both epistemic and moral, of an alien culture. Is knowledge then independent of cultures? If not, can there be knowledge which is independent of power? To pose the problem thus is to situate knowledge itself within a dialectic that relates culture to power.

In order to show a little more clearly the generality of this problem, it will be worth our while to digress into a recent debate about the cognitive status of anthropology as a science of cross-cultural understanding.[28] The problem is posed most sharply within the discipline of anthropology because here, as one participant in the debate puts it, the scientist consciously 'sets himself to understand a culture which is not his own'.[29] The anthropologist, consequently, must answer the question whether, and in what ways, culture differences affect cognition.

The most familiar problem which the Western anthropologist faces when trying to understand non-Western cultures is when beliefs held by other peoples turn out to be manifestly irrational and false when judged in terms of Western criteria of rationality or truth. The question then arises: how is one to interpret the fact that large numbers of people collectively hold beliefs that are false? Is it fair, or legitimate, or valid, to proceed by designating such beliefs as false and then to try and find out why, or how, such irrational beliefs are communally held? Would that not involve the bias of ethnocentrism? Several alternative answers have been proposed to this question. One of them seeks to apply what is called 'the principle of charity', derived from a proposal put forward by the philosopher Donald Davidson[30] which suggests that when confronted by large sets of communal beliefs which apparently seem false by our standards of rationality, we should be charitable in our interpretation and 'take it as given that most beliefs are correct'. Among the set of alternative interpretations of these beliefs, then, we (in this case, the anthropologist) should select the one which makes the largest possible number of beliefs true; that is to say, the strategy of interpretation should be to maximize the area of agreement between the anthropologist and the people he is studying. The underlying assumption is, of course, that it is only when such an area of agreement exists that interpretation becomes possible.

The pragmatic argument in favour of this principle is that even when other cultures seem vastly different from our own, the principle of charity can make large areas of those cultures open to interpretation in terms of the specific social circumstances in which those people live, especially in the area of beliefs which inform practical activity. The reason is that for any community with an ongoing social process, it is very unlikely that their everyday practical activities will be guided by large-scale communal error. There is, therefore, or so it is argued, good reason to think that the principle of charity (or its variants such as the 'principle of humanity'[31]) may yield fairly satisfactory results in at least those areas of cross-cultural understanding which involve practical activity.

Already we notice the parallels between the debate on nationalism and this one on anthropology, including a profusion of such enchantingly liberal sentiments as 'charity' and 'humanity'. The difficulty with these principles is, first of all, to decide what it means to specify adequately the social circumstances in which a community lives. Can this be done at all? Second, can we identify the particular outcomes which the community desires when it engages in particular acts, so that we can judge whether those acts, or the beliefs informing them, are rational or not? Most practising anthropologists do not seem to think that either of these is feasible. The dominant orientations in the discipline do not therefore explicitly subscribe to either of these principles. Instead they are in favour of either rejecting any search for rationality or proclaiming that there can be several alternative rationalities.

An influential approach which asserts the irrelevance of rationality in cross-cultural understanding is functionalism. Here the object of understanding is not to judge whether particular beliefs or actions are rational or not, but to discover in what ways they contribute to the functioning and persistence of the social system as a whole. Thus, whether or not particular acts are intelligible to us in terms of the avowed objectives for which they are performed, their continued performance may still be satisfactorily explained in terms of the (perhaps unintended) consequences of those acts which promote the maintenance of the social system.

The second anthropological approach which also denies the usefulness of looking for rational explanations of behaviour is the one which claims that apparently strange behaviour should be interpreted as symbolic acts: their meaning should be sought for in terms of their place within an entire symbolic pattern, whose fundamental structure may also be latent in consciousness, by which man's perception of nature, of his relations with nature and with other men, are ordered. The anthropologist's task is to discover this latent structure of the symbolic order, which will then make particular beliefs or actions meaningful in relation to other beliefs or actions within that order.

Many substantive problems have been raised about the validity and the usefulness of both functionalist and symbolist (structuralist) explanations in anthropology, but these need not concern us here. We are more interested in what the 'rationalists' have to say about these approaches. Their main argument is that both functionalism and symbolism skirt around the crucial question: why do people continue to hold beliefs which seem to us to be patently false? What, in other words, are the reasons for their acting in this apparently absurd way? And if those reasons can indeed be attributed to the specific social circumstances in which the beliefs are held, and not merely explained away by referring to the functional requirements of a social system or the internal logic of the symbolic order, then why should we not be justified in holding on to the superior cognitive status of the criteria of scientific rationality and attempting to interpret other cultures from that cognitive position?

Here there is a clear division within the rationalist camp, because one group has replied that what seems to us as an intelligible reason for acting may not be so for others. That is to say, although the actions of others may not seem rational to us, they may be perfectly rational according to entirely different criteria of rationality. The radical assertion then is: the notion of rationality may not be cross-cultural; other cultures may have their own, and equally valid because incommensurable, standards of rationality. By trying to judge other cultures according to our criteria of rationality and pronouncing them irrational, we are being unjustifiably ethnocentric, because there is no single cross-culturally valid standard of rationality: rationality is relative.

Now, there can be a strong argument of relativism which insists that each culture could have its own distinctive categorical scheme for ordering reality and its own distinctive system of logic which would make the beliefs held by people living in that culture thoroughly incommensurable with beliefs held in other cultures. This, of course, would invalidate any attempts at cross-cultural understanding, because no interpretation from outside a culture would be justified. However, the argument also depends crucially on our being able to determine the cognitive boundaries of a culture, and this is by no means a straightforward procedure. If the thought-system of a culture is indeed incommensurably different from those of others, we would not even have the background of consensus necessary to recognize the differences. This would make relativism completely unintelligible. Further, the argument applies not only to cases of judging cultures from the outside. If cognitive boundaries of cultures are indeterminate, we cannot reliably know whether we are inside or outside a culture when we attempt to interpret it. In other words, a strictly relativist position would have to be based on a holistic conception of cultures which would make any kind of interpretation, whether from within or without a culture, impossible, because our own perception of the full cognitive map of a culture — even the one which we belong to — can only be partial, and in many respects individually specific.

But most of those who have argued for a 'relativist' position on the matter of cross-cultural understanding do not seem to favour so strong an interpretation of their case. And curiously enough, many of those who think that a strictly relativist philosophical position would destroy any viable basis for a scientific understanding of society, also assert that weakly interpreted, as a basis for a sympathetic and imaginative understanding of other cultures, the relativist case says a lot of important things about an undogmatic, non-ethnocentric methodology of the social sciences. We are back, it would seem, to some kind of 'principle of charity', however formulated.

This leaves us with a somewhat paradoxical view of the debate. The 'relativist' argument originates in a critique of 'rationalist' methods of interpretation in which the main attack is directed against exaggerated claims of universal validity for those standards of evaluating social beliefs which are only specific to modern industrial society in the West. The 'relativist' thus accuses the 'rationalist' of holding an essentialist view of his own culture as a result of which he uses elements of his own belief-system to judge beliefs held in other cultures and pronounces the latter, either explicitly or by implication, to be erroneous or inferior, overlooking the fact that his own beliefs are the product of a specific socio-historical context which is different from the contexts of other cultures. This constitutes the unjustifiable ethnocentric bias in 'rationalist' attempts at cross-cultural understanding. On the other hand, the 'non-relativist' argues that relativism, in so far as it can claim a distinctive philosophical foundation, itself rests on an essentialist conception of cultures which militates against the validity of any scientific attempt at cross-cultural understanding. Each side, it would appear, ends up by accusing the other of the same crime: ahistorical essentialism.[32]

I will argue that this paradoxical situation is in fact an accurate reflection of the spurious philosophical premises on which the debate has been conducted in Anglo-American social science. A cultural essentialism has been germane to the very way in which the sciences of society have developed in the West in the post-Enlightenment period, at least since the early 19th century. It is an essentialism which is much more deep-rooted than the obvious cultural arrogance of colonial anthropology or the inept policy prescriptions of neo-Weberian modernization theory. It is indeed an aspect of the post-Enlightenment view of the world in which the idea of rational knowledge assumes a very definite form. The sciences of nature become the paradigm of all rational knowledge. And the principal characteristic of these sciences as they are now conceived is their relation to an entirely new idea of man's *control* over nature — a progressive and ceaseless process of the appropriation of nature to serve human 'interests'. By extension, a notion of 'interests' also enters into the conception of the new sciences of society. The rational knowledge of human society comes to be organized around concepts such as wealth, productive efficiency, progress, etc. all of which are defined in terms of the promotion of some social 'interests'. Yet 'interests' in society are necessarily diverse; indeed, they are stratified in terms of the relations of power. Consequently, the subject–object relation between man and nature which is central to the new conception of the sciences of nature is now subtly transferred, through the 'rational' conception of society, to relations between man and man. Thus, the sciences of society become the knowledge of the Self and of the Other. Construed in terms of rationality, it necessarily also becomes a means to the *power* of the Self over the Other. In short, knowledge becomes the means to the domination of the world.

And yet, the notion of rationality which is involved in the problem of universality and relativism is not a simple problem of positive science. If the question is 'Are the beliefs held by particular groups of people true or false?' a reasonable approach would seem to be to answer the question by reference to the currently accepted methods, procedures and theories in the particular scientific discipline to which the belief relates. Thus, the question of whether Kalabari beliefs about the curative properties of particular herbs are true or not can be answered within the theoretical knowledge currently provided by medical science, including considerations of possible psychosomatic effects of the particular procedures by which the drugs are administered in Kalabari society. However, it is clear that not all beliefs in society will admit a meaningful scientific answer as to whether they are true or not. There are large classes of beliefs for which the criteria true/false make little sense in terms of science as we know it today. However, to the extent that questions of this sort are at all answerable within currently established scientific theories, ethnicity or culture will be in principle an irrelevant consideration.

But, by pointing out that answers to such questions are only meaningful within 'currently accepted' scientific methods or theories, or that they can or cannot be answered only in terms of science 'as we know it today', we are acknowledging the historicity of scientific methods themselves — the fact that they rest only on the currently prevailing consensus among scientists, with a broad penumbra where they are subjects of varying degrees of contention, that even currently accepted methods are subject to change, including paradigmatic changes of the Kuhnian type, and that they too are affected (assuming we are not prepared to go so far as to say 'determined') by the socio-historical processes in the societies in which they appear. Again, when we say that in answering questions of this sort, ethnicity or culture are 'in principle' irrelevant, we recognize the possibility that this may not actually be the case in every instance of scientific practice. There can be, for example, a major problem of determining precisely *what* a particular belief is, because it may involve a complicated and not unproblematical exercise of trying to unravel the *meaning* of particular utterances or acts or behaviour of particular people. Here, the question of culture may well be considered crucial, and a host of problems would have to be sorted out before we can say that we have identified a belief which is held by a particular group of people. But these are problems which arise *before* the stage where we can ask whether a belief is true or not.

The second way in which ethnicity becomes relevant to scientific practice concerns the social structure of scientific research itself, in this case in the international or inter-cultural dimension. It could be argued that a given structure of the scientific profession — its pattern of funding, its assignment of research priorities, its very choice of problems for investigation and, inevitably, therefore, its judgment of what does or does not constitute a legitimate or worthwhile subject for scientific research — may be so biased in geographical, and hence cultural, terms that it overlooks, ignores· or dogmatically rejects insights into the nature of the physical or social world which may have been developed in supposedly 'non-scientific' cultures. These insights may form a part of the technological practices of various people in various parts of the world; or of the expressive or symbolic ordering of their relations with nature and with one another; or of their pre-theoretical practical guides to the activities of everyday life; or of their speculative philosophies about the nature of the world; or (who knows?) of their theoretical formulations about specific physical or social processes which have been overlooked or ignored by the currently dominant international structure of science because they were embedded within larger speculative systems of philosophy that were deemed irrational, archaic or morally repugnant. In this sense, ethnocentrism does affect the development of scientific knowledge.

But when one raises the question of whether people in other cultures are rational or not, one does not simply mean whether their beliefs are true in relation to currently accepted scientific theories. Anyone with even a modicum of awareness of the philosophical problems involved in answering the question 'Is such and such a statement scientifically true?' will realize that it is only in very rare cases that one can obtain even a reasonably unambiguous answer in the affirmative. If this was the meaning of the concept of rational belief, then the problem of rationality in sociological theory would be reduced to one of very minor importance, because very few beliefs held in societies anywhere in the world, including the contemporary Western world, would, by this definition, qualify as rational. No, rationality as the notion is used in current debates is wider than mere scientific truth. It is seen as incorporating a certain way of looking at the properties of nature, of ordering our knowledge of those properties in a certain consistent and coherent way, of using this knowledge for adaptive advantage vis-à-vis nature. It is, as Max Weber would have put it – and it does not matter if present-day votaries of rationality do not agree with his definition of its precise content — an ethic. Rationality becomes the normative principle of a certain way of life which is said to promote a certain way of thinking, namely, science. Hence, the question of culture does become relevant.

It is important to note, however, that the stricter definition of scientific truth is now contained within the wider notion of rationality as an ethic. So much so that the ethic of rationality is now seen to be characteristic of 'scientifically-oriented' or 'theoretically-oriented' cultures. And thus, by a conceptual sleight of hand, the epistemic privilege which is due to 'scientific truth' is appropriated by entire cultures. What results is an *essentialism*: certain historically specific correspondences between certain elements in the structure of beliefs in European society and certain, albeit spectacular, changes in techno-economic conditions of production are attributed the quality of essences which are said to characterize Western cultures as a whole. It is an essentialism which, when imposed on historical time, divides up the history of Western society into pre-scientific and scientific, and casts every other culture of the world into the darkness of unscientific traditionalism. Initially, this essentialism enjoys a straightforwardly ethnic privilege: the superiority of the European people. Later, it is given a moral privilege, encompassing as in the post-Enlightenment theories of progress — positivism, utilitarianism, Weberian sociology — a historically progressive philosophy of life. And finally, when all of these privileged positions are challenged with the spread of anti-colonial movements, it is the epistemic privilege which has become the last bastion of global supremacy for the cultural values of Western industrial societies. It is a privilege which sanctions the assertion of cultural supremacy while assiduously denying at the same time that it has anything to do with cultural evaluations. Relativist or rationalist, each one is keen to outdo the other in the radicalness of his stand against ethnocentric bias.

It is not trivial to point out here that in this whole debate about the possibility of cross-cultural understanding, the scientist is always one of 'us': he is a Western anthropologist, modern, enlightened and self-conscious (and it does not matter what his nationality or the colour of his skin happens to be). The objects of study are 'other' cultures — always non-Western. No one has raised the possibility, and the accompanying problems, of a 'rational' understanding of 'us' by a member of the 'other' culture — of, let us say, a Kalabari anthropology of the white man. It could be argued, of course, that when we consider the problem of relativism, we consider the relations between cultures in the abstract and it does not matter if the subject–object relation between Western and non-Western cultures is reversed: the relations would be isomorphic.

But it would not: that is precisely why we do not, and probably never will, have a Kalabari anthropology of the white man. And that is why even a Kalabari anthropology of the Kalabari will adopt the same representational form, if not the same substantive conclusions, as the white man's anthropology of the Kalabari. For there is a relation of power involved in the very conception of the autonomy of cultures. That is, in fact, why the problem of nationalist thought is only a particular manifestation of this much more general problem. If nationalism expresses itself in a frenzy of irrational passion, it does so *because* it seeks to represent itself in the image of the Enlightenment and *fails* to do so. For Enlightenment itself, to assert its sovereignty as the universal ideal, needs its Other; if it could ever actualize itself in the real world as the truly universal, it would in fact destroy itself. No matter how much the liberal-rationalist may wonder, the Cunning of Reason has not met its match in nationalism.[33] On the contrary, it has seduced, apprehended and imprisoned it: that is what this book is all about.

IV

So far I have argued that the problems of a liberal doctrine of nationalism can be traced back to a much more fundamental question about the moral and epistemic status of a bourgeois-rational conception of universal history. However, I cannot hope to settle the matter simply by designating it as a problem of 'bourgeois' knowledge. For we see much the same sorts of problems appearing in Marxist discussions of nationalism as well.

I will not go into the issue of what Marx himself had to say about nationalism.[34] However, what can be said quite definitely on this subject is that in his own work Marx never directly addressed himself to nationalism as a theoretical problem. Much of the debate on this question is about the implications of his general theoretical scheme, or about inferences from the various comments he made on the subject during a very active literary and political career. We are more concerned here about the more influential interpretations of Marxism addressed to what has come to be called 'the national question', and more particularly the problem of nationalism in the non-European world where it has taken the compendium form of 'the national *and* colonial question'.

The question was long debated in the Second and Third Internationals.[35] The most remarkable contribution came from Lenin who, working out his ideas from the immediate practical problems facing the revolution in a huge multi-ethnic empire, highlighted the central question of political democracy as the keystone of Marxist analyses of nationalism. It was this emphasis which led him to formulate his famous thesis on the rights of nations to self-determination.[36] But Lenin's proposals were not directed towards the construction of a general theoretical paradigm for the study of nationalism, and in the tumultuous period of national liberation movements since the 1930s, Marxists have continued to argue about the question.

Horace B. Davis has recently attempted a summarization of several of these arguments.[37] He too acknowledges that there are two types of nationalism,[38] one the nationalism of the Enlightenment which 'was by and large rational rather than emotional', and the other 'based on culture and tradition', developed by German romantic writers such as Herder and Fichte, which asserted that the nation was a natural community and therefore 'something sacred, eternal, organic, carrying a deeper justification than the works of men'. But even this second type was European in origin. 'This idea of the nation as preceding the state and eventually leading to its formation is very distinctly European; it has no relevance to the problems of newly formed nations such as most of those in Africa, where the state preceded the nation and conditioned its whole existence.'[39]

What then about nationalism in the non-European world? The national question here is, of course, historically fused with a colonial question. The assertion of national identity was, therefore, a form of the struggle against colonial exploitation. Yet an assertion of traditional cultural values would often be inconsistent with the conditions of historical progress. There is thus a very real dilemma: 'whether to consider nationalism a rationalist, secular, modern movement, or whether to emphasize the more distinctively national elements, many of which are frankly atavistic and irrelevant to modern conditions'.[40] But no matter how tormenting the dilemma for those in the thick of the struggle, the outcome itself was historically determined. Between the modern and the traditional trends within nationalism, 'the one that wins out in the end is the modernizing, Westernizing element, but it may be only after a prolonged struggle'.[41]

The question therefore was not one of taking a moral position with respect to nationalism qua nationalism, but one of judging its probable historical consequences. 'Nationalism, then, is not in itself irrational, but it may be irrationally applied. Atavistic nationalism cannot be condemned out of hand; when considered as part of a movement for a people to regain its pride and self respect, it has a constructive aspect. But belligerent, aggressive, chauvinistic nationalism is a menace and thus irrational from the point of view of humanity as a whole.'[42] Nationalism had to be looked at in its instrumental aspect: whether or not it furthered the universal movement of historical progress. 'Nationalism', Davis says,

> is not a thing, even an abstract thing, but a process, an implement ... One does not take a position for or against a hammer, or a can opener, or any other implement. When used for murder, the hammer is no doubt a weapon; when used for building a house, it is a constructive tool. Nationalism considered as the vindication of a particular culture is morally neutral; considered as a movement against national oppression, it has a positive moral content; considered as the vehicle of aggression, it is morally indefensible.[43]

This book by Davis may be a particularly unsubtle example of Marxist thinking on the subject of nationalism. If so, let us take a more recent, and in every way more sophisticated, treatment of the subject and see where it gets us: I have in mind Benedict Anderson's *Imagined Communities*.[44] Anderson's intervention is highly unorthodox, because far from following the dominant tendency in Marxist discussions on the 'national question', typically represented by Stalin's oft-quoted formulation,[45] he refuses to 'define' a nation by a set of external and abstract criteria. On the contrary, he fundamentally subverts the determinist scheme by asserting that the nation is 'an imagined political community'. It is not uniquely produced by the constellation of certain objective social facts; rather, the nation is 'thought out', 'created'.

At first glance, this may seem to be fairly close to Gellner's position: 'Nationalism is not the awakening of nations to self-consciousness: it invents nations where they do not exist.' But Anderson is quick to mark the difference. For Gellner 'invent' means 'fabrication' and 'falsity', a piece of historical disingenuousness; he cannot regard the thinking out of a nation as genuine creation.[46] What does 'creation' mean? Let us follow Anderson's argument.

Historically, the political community of nation superseded the preceding 'cultural systems' of religious community and dynastic realm. In the process there occurred 'a fundamental change ... in modes of apprehending the world, which, more than anything else, made it possible to "think" the nation'.[47] It was the 'coalition of Protestantism and print-capitalism' which brought about this change. 'What, in a positive sense, made the new communities imaginable was a half-fortuitous, but explosive, interaction between a system of production and productive relations (capitalism), a technology of communications (print), and the fatality of human linguistic diversity.'[48] The innumerable and varied ideolects of pre-print Europe were now 'assembled, within definite limits, into print-languages far fewer in number'. This was crucial for the emergence of national consciousness because print-languages created 'unified fields of exchange and communications' below Latin and above the spoken vernaculars, gave a new fixity to language, and created new kinds of 'languages-of-power' since some dialects were closer to the print-languages and dominated them while others remained dialects because they could not insist on their own printed form.

Once again historically, three distinct types or 'models' of nationalism emerged. 'Creole nationalism' of the Americas was built upon the ambitions of classes whose economic interests were ranged against the metropolis. It also drew upon liberal and enlightened ideas from Europe which provided ideological criticisms of imperialism and *anciens régimes*. But the shape of the new imagined communities was created by 'pilgrim creole functionaries and provincial creole printmen'. Yet as a 'model' for emulation, creole nationalism remained incomplete, because it lacked linguistic communality and its state form was both retrograde and congruent with the arbitrary administrative boundaries of the imperial order.

The second 'model' was that of the linguistic nationalisms of Europe, a model of the independent national state which henceforth became 'available for pirating'.

But precisely because it was by then a known model, it imposed certain 'standards' from which too-marked deviations were impossible . . . Thus the 'populist' character of the early European nationalisms, even when led, demagogically, by the most backward social groups, was deeper than in the Americas: serfdom had to go, legal slavery was unimaginable — not least because the conceptual model was set in ineradicable place.[49]

The third 'model' was provided by 'official nationalism' — typically, Russia. This involved the imposition of cultural homogeneity from the top, through state action. 'Russification' was a project which could be, and was, emulated elsewhere.

All three modular forms were available to third world nationalisms in the 20th century. Just as creole functionaries first perceived a national meaning in the imperial administrative unit, so did the 'brown or black Englishman' when he made his bureaucratic pilgrimage to the metropolis. On return,

the apex of his looping flight was the highest administrative centre to which he was assigned: Rangoon, Accra, Georgetown, or Colombo. Yet in each constricted journey he found bilingual travelling companions with whom he came to feel a growing communality. In his journey he understood rather quickly that his point of origin — conceived either ethnically, linguistically, or geographically — was of small significance . . . it did not fundamentally determine his destination or his companions. Out of this pattern came that subtle, half-concealed transformation, step by step, of the colonial-state into the national-state, a transformation made possible not only by a solid continuity of personnel, but by the established skein of journeys through which each state was experienced by its functionaries.[50]

But this only made possible the emergence of a national consciousness. Its rapid spread and acquisition of popular roots in the 20th century are to be explained by the fact that these journeys were now made by 'huge and variegated crowds'. Enormous increases in physical mobility, imperial

'Russification' programmes sponsored by the colonial state as well as by corporate capital, and the spread of modern-style education created a large bilingual section which could mediate linguistically between the metropolitan nation and the colonized people. The vanguard role of the intelligentsia derived from its bilingual literacy. 'Print-literacy already made possible the imagined community floating in homogeneous, empty time . . . Bilingualism meant access, through the European language-of-state, to modern Western culture in the broadest sense, and, in particular, to the models of nationalism, nation-ness, and nation-state produced elsewhere in the course of the nineteenth century.'[51]

Third-world nationalisms in the 20th century thus came to acquire a 'modular' character. 'They can, and do, draw on more than a century and a half of human experience and three earlier models of nationalism. Nationalist leaders are thus in a position consciously to deploy civil and military educational systems modelled on official nationalism's; elections, party organizations, and cultural celebrations modelled on the popular nationalisms of 19th century Europe; and the citizen–republican idea brought into the world by the Americas.' Above all, the very idea of 'nation' is now nestled firmly in virtually all print-languages, and nation-ness is virtually inseparable from political consciousness.

'In a world in which the national state is the overwhelming norm, all of this means that nations can now be imagined without linguistic communality — not in the naive spirit of *nostros los Americanos*, but out of a general awareness of what modern history has demonstrated to be possible.'[52]

Anderson's chief contribution to the Marxist debate on the national question is to emphatically pose the ideological creation of the nation as a central problem in the study of national movements. In doing this he also highlights the social process of creation of modern language communities. Yet, instead of pursuing the varied, and often contradictory, *political* possibilities inherent in this process, Anderson seals up his theme with a sociological determinism. What, if we look closely, are the substantive differences between Anderson and Gellner on 20th century nationalism? None. Both point out a fundamental change in ways of perceiving the social world which occurs before nationalism can emerge: Gellner relates this change to the requirements of 'industrial society', Anderson more ingeniously to the dynamics of 'print-capitalism'. Both describe the characteristics of the new cultural homogeneity which is sought to be imposed on the emerging nation: for Gellner this is the imposition of a common high culture on the variegated complex of local folk cultures, for Anderson the process involves the formation of a 'print-language' and the shared experience of the 'journeys' undertaken by the colonized intelligentsia. In the end, both see in third-world nationalisms a profoundly 'modular' character. They are invariably shaped according to contours outlined by given historical models: 'objective, inescapable imperative', 'too-marked deviations . . . impossible'.

Where in all this is the working of the imagination, the intellectual process of creation? For Gellner the problem does not arise, because even when nations are 'invented', it is out of necessity: some distinguishing cultural marks simply have to be chosen in order to identify the nation, and it is not a particularly interesting problem for him to study the intellectual process by which this is done. But Anderson? He too confines his discussion to the 'modular' character of 20th century nationalisms, without noticing the twists and turns, the suppressed possibilities, the contradictions still unresolved. Consequently, in place of Gellner's superciliousness, Anderson has to conclude on a note of unmitigated political pessimism: 'No one imagines, I presume, that the broad masses of the Chinese people give a fig for what happens along the border between Cambodia and Vietnam. Nor is it at all likely that Khmer and Vietnamese peasants wanted wars between their peoples, or were consulted in the matter. In a very real sense these were "chancellery wars" in which popular nationalism was mobilized after the fact and always in a language of self-defence.'[53] Thus, it is all a matter of a vanguard intelligentsia coming to state power by 'mobilizing' popular nationalism and using the 'machiavellian' instruments of official nationalism. Like religion and kinship, nationalism is an anthropological fact, and there is nothing else to it.

Marxists have found it extremely hard to escape the liberal dilemma we described in the previous section. More often than not, they have adopted exactly the same methods as those of the liberals — either a resort to *sociologism*, i.e. fitting nationalism to certain universal and inescapable sociological constraints of the modern age, or alternatively, reducing the two contending trends within nationalism, one traditional and conservative and the other rational and progressive, to their sociological determinants, or invoking a *functionalism*, i.e. taking up an appropriate attitude towards a specific nationalism by reference to its consequences for universal history. The problem can be even better illustrated if we shift our sights from general theoretical treatments to the analysis of particular nationalist movements. I will refer to a debate about India, a country where Marxist historiography has had to establish itself by trying to confront a nationalist intellectual orthodoxy.

V

To start with, Marxist historians in India had taken their cue from a well-known remark by Marx in his 1853 article on 'British Rule in India':

> England, it is true, in causing a social revolution in Hindustan, was actuated only by the vilest interests, and was stupid in her manner of enforcing them. But that is not the question. The question is, can mankind fulfil its destiny without a fundamental revolution in the social state of Asia? If not, whatever may have been the crimes of England she was the unconscious tool of history in bringing about that revolution.[54]

Here too, as in the liberal history of nationalism, history becomes episodic, marked by one Great Event which is in every sense the watershed, dividing up historical time into past and future, tradition and modernity, stagnation and development — and inescapably, into bad and good: despotism and liberty, superstition and enlightenment, priestcraft and the triumph of reason. For India, the Great Event was the advent of British rule which terminated centuries of despotism, superstition and vegetative life and ushered in a new era of change — of 'destruction' as well as 'regeneration', destruction of antiquated tradition and the emergence of modern, secular and national forces.

A whole generation of Marxist historians of India,[55] despite the many political differences among them, agreed that the intellectual history of India in the 19th and 20th centuries was a history of the struggle between the forces of reaction and those of progress. The approach was both sociological and functional. There was the attempt to reduce 'traditional-conservative' and 'rational-modernist' ideas to their social roots, i.e. to 'reactionary' and 'progressive' classes, respectively. At the same time, there was the attempt to judge the effectivity of these ideas in terms of their consequences, i.e. whether or not they furthered the national democratic struggle against colonial domination and exploitation. And the results of these two simultaneous inquiries often turned out to be contradictory. The national was not always secular and modern, the popular and democratic quite often traditional and even fanatically anti-modern.

The 1970s saw several attempts to question the earlier applications of Marxism to Indian intellectual history. In 1972 official celebrations were held to mark the bicentenary of the birth of Rammohun Roy (1772-1833), the first great 'modernizer' and father of the 19th century 'renaissance' in Indian thought. A volume of critical essays[56] brought out on the occasion contained several contributions in the earlier genre, but there were others which questioned the whole premise of the characterization of the 'renaissance' and even the categories of tradition/modernity. The main theoretical ground on which these critiques were located was a reassessment of the nature of the relationship between culture and structure or, to use an orthodox Marxist terminology which already in the very thrust of the critique seemed to lose some of its theoretical value, between superstructure and base. It was all very well, these critics argued, to pick out the many undoubtedly modern elements in the thought of the 19th century social reformers and ideologues, but what significance do these elements of modernity acquire when looked at in the context of the evolving colonial economy of the same period, of massive deindustrialization and destitution, of unbearable pressures on the land leading to a virtually irreversible process of regressive rent-exploitation and stagnation in levels of productivity, of the crushing of peasant resistance, of the growing social gulf rather than bonds of alliance between a modernized, western-educated, urban elite and the rest of the nation? In what sense can this modernity be reconciled with any meaningful conception of the national–popular?

These questions were posed from within a Marxist framework, but earlier Marxist formulations on the 19th century renaissance were severely criticized. Sumit Sarkar,[57] for instance, showed that Indian Marxists in interpreting the evolution of Indian thought as a conflict between two trends, 'westernist' or 'modernist' on the one hand and 'traditionalist' on the other, had, notwithstanding the many analytical intricacies, wholeheartedly plumped for westernism as the historically progressive trend. He then argued: 'An unqualified equation of the "westernizers" . . . with modernism or progress almost inevitably leads on to a more positive assessment of British rule, English education, and the nineteenth-century protagonists of both . . .' In fact, the entire 'tradition–modernization' dichotomy served as a cover under which 'the grosser facts of imperialist political and economic exploitation [were] very often quietly tucked away in a corner'. As facts stand, Rammohun Roy's break with tradition was 'deeply contradictory', accommodating within the same corpus of thinking numerous compromises with orthodox, Hindu-elitist and, by his own enlightened standards, clearly irrational ways of thought and practice, and in any case it was a break only 'on the intellectual plane and not at the level of basic social transformation'. In his economic thinking, he accepted *in toto* the then fashionable logic of free trade and seemed to visualize 'a kind of dependent but still real bourgeois development in Bengal in close collaboration with British merchants and entrepreneurs'. This was an utterly absurd illusion, because colonial subjection would never permit full-blooded bourgeois modernity but only a 'weak and distorted caricature'.[58]

The argument was therefore that while there were elements of modernity in the new cultural and intellectual movements in 19th century India, these cannot become meaningful unless they are located in their relation, on the one hand, to the changing socio-economic structure of the country, and on the other, to the crucial context of power, i.e. the reality of colonial subjection. When thus located, the achievements of early 19th century 'modernizers' such as Rammohun seemed limited within a Hindu-elitist, colonial, almost comprador, framework.

This argument was stated at much greater length in Asok Sen's study[59] of the career of another 19th century social reformer of Bengal, Iswar Chandra Vidyasagar (1820-1891). Sen placed the problem in the theoretical context of Antonio Gramsci's discussion of the relation of intellectuals to more fundamental forces of social transformation. The mere acceptance of new ideas or their original structure of assumptions and implications did not in themselves mean much; major changes in thought and attitude were, in fact, brought about 'by the capacity of nascent social forces to achieve goals of transformation [often] not entirely clarified in the original postulates of reasoning or speculation'.[60] What was crucial, therefore, was a fundamental class striving for class hegemony and advance of social production. Without such a class, 'the cultural influence of intellectuals is reduced to an essentially abstract phenomenon giving no consistent direction of significant social renewal; their influence is limited to tiny intellectual groups who have no creative bonds with a broader social consensus'.[61]

In the specific context of 19th century Bengal, the middle class was not a fundamental class in this sense, nor were its intellectuals organic to any fundamental project of social transformation or conquest of hegemony. The new middle class was a product of English education. But in an economy under direct colonial control, in which there was little prospect for the release of forces of industrialization, the attempt 'to achieve through education what was denied to the economy' was utterly anomalous.

The new intelligentsia was stirred by various elements of western thought — the ideas of liberal freedom, rational humanism and scientific advance. But the learned aspirations of the middle class were undone by its dysfunctional role in the process of production; the former called for goals which the latter necessarily precluded. Hence, modernity could hardly be a force of objective social achievement . . . For a middle class with no positive role in social production, the theories of Locke, Bentham and Mill acted more as sources of confusion about the nature of the state and society under colonial rule . . . the middle class had neither the position, nor the strength to mediate effectively between polity and production. There lay the travesty of imported ideas of individual rights and rationality.[62]

Vidyasagar's own attempts at social reform, for instance, placed great reliance upon liberal backing by the colonial government. The failure of those attempts showed that his hopes were misplaced. On the other hand, he did not find any effective support for his schemes from within his own class. When arguing for reform, Vidyasagar, despite his own professed disregard for the sanctity or reasonableness of the *śāstra*, felt compelled to look for scriptural support for his programmes. He did not think it feasible to attempt to create a 'nonconformism outside the bond of canonical orthodoxy'. In fact, this remained a major ideological anomaly in all 19th century attempts to 'modernize' religion and social practice — 'a spurious conciliation of Indian idealism and imported liberal sanctions' — which led to a major backlash after 1880 in the form of movements to 'revive tradition', movements that were openly hostile to the earlier decades of 'reason and enlightenment'.

Thus, a reformation with no entrenchment in conditions of mass hegemony failed not only to produce its Anabaptist complement, but the reaction, when it inevitably set in, hastened the reformation to its day of burial.[63]

In Sen, therefore, the argument becomes sharper. The 19th century intelligentsia may have genuinely welcomed the new ideas of reason and rationality, and some may even have shown considerable courage and enterprise in seeking to 'modernize' social customs and attitudes. But the fundamental forces of transformation were absent in colonial society. As a result, there was no possibility for the emergence of a consistently rational set of beliefs or practices. Liberalism stood on highly fragile foundations; 'reason dwindled to merely individual means of self-gratification without social responsibility'.[64] The half-heartedness and ambiguity was part of the very process of bourgeois development in a colonial country. ' . . . the dialectics of loyalty and opposition' did not permit 'a clear division among the native bourgeoisie or the entire middle class into two exclusive categories of collaborators and opponents of imperialism'.[65] In India, bourgeois opposition to imperialism was always ambiguous.

The attempt to relate developments in thought to the evolving socio-economic structure of a colonial country inevitably led, therefore, to the problem of power: the subjection of a colonial country and the question of loyalty or opposition to the imperial power. And once put in that perspective, the modern and the national seemed to diverge in fundamental ways.

It is the problem of power which is placed at the centre of another critique of the 19th century 'renaissance' — Ranajit Guha's analysis of a play on the 1860-61 Indigo Uprising in Bengal by the playwright Dinabandhu Mitra.[66] This play has always been regarded in nationalist circles in Bengal as a remarkably bold indictment of the depredations of English planters in the Indian countryside and as a classical portrayal of the bravery and determination of the peasantry in their resistance to colonialism. But Guha shows the innately liberal-humanitarian assumptions underlying Dinabandhu's criticism of the planters, assumptions he shared with virtually the whole of the new intelligentsia of the 19th century. Thus, underlying the criticism of the lawlessness of the planters and of the action of a few foolish and inconsiderate English officials, there was an abiding faith in the rationality and impartiality of English law and in the good intentions of the colonial administration taken as a whole. Never did the thought occur in the minds of these newly enlightened gentlemen, despite their fondness for justice and liberty, to question the legitimacy of British rule in India. In fact, it was the very existence of British power in India that was regarded as the final and most secure guarantee against lawlessness, superstition and despotism. Not only that, the image of the resolute peasant defending his rights against the predatory planter, as represented in élite accounts such as Dinabandhu's *Nīl Darpan*, is that of an enlightened liberal, conscious of his rights as an individual, willing to go to great lengths to defend those rights against recalcitrant officials, even succumbing to 'brief, intermittent bursts' of violence, but all the while believing in the fundamental legitimacy of the social order. This was a far cry from any truly revolutionary appreciation by a progressive intelligentsia of the strength of peasant resistance to colonialism and of its potentials for the construction of a new 'national–popular' consciousness. What the play does reveal is, in fact, an attitude of collaboration, between a colonial government and its educated native collaborators, sealed by the marriage of law and literacy. The sympathy of the intelligentsia for the victims of violence of indigo planters and the support by large sections of the rich and middling sorts of people in town and countryside for the cause of the peasants are explained by a specific conjuncture of interests and events. In the overall estimate, such opposition only opened up

> an immense hinterland of compromise and reformism into which to retreat from a direct contest for power with the colonial masters . . . And, thus, 'improvement', that characteristic ideological gift of nineteenth-century British capitalism, is made to pre-empt and replace the urge for a revolutionary transformation of society.

The formulation of the problem now encompasses a great deal of complexity in the relations between thought, culture and power. First of all, there is the question of the effectiveness of thought as a vehicle of change. If the imperatives, conditions and consequences of change have been thought out within an elaborate and reasonably consistent framework of knowledge, does this itself indicate that the social potentials exist for the change to occur? The assumption here would be that if the conditions did not exist at least potentially, then the theory could not have been thought. Or is the more crucial element the existence of determinate social forces, in the form of a class or an alliance of classes, which have the will and strength to act as agents of transformation, perhaps even without the aid of an elaborately formulated theoretical apparatus to think out the process of change? The sociological determinist would say that the conditions for the emergence of a nationalist ideology for the transformation of an agrarian into an industrial society are present universally. The only point of interest for particular nationalisms is the specific cultural demarcation of a national identity which wills for itself a distinct political unit. Yet the historical evidence marshalled in the above debate suggests that the social forces which could be said to have favoured the transformation of a medieval agrarian society into a rational modern one were not unambiguously nationalist, while those that were opposed to colonial domination were not necessarily in favour of a transformation.

Second, there is the question of the relation of thought to the existing culture of the society, i.e. to the way in which the social code already provides a set of correspondences between signs and meanings to the overwhelming mass of the people. What are the necessary steps when a new group of thinkers and reformers seek to substitute a new code in the place of the old one? Do they set up a radical group of nonconformists, or do they gradually 'modernize' the tradition? If such a cultural transformation does take place, what is the role of an ideological leadership — a vanguard intelligentsia — in bringing it about?

Third, there is the question of the implantation into new cultures of categories and frameworks of thought produced in other — alien — cultural contexts. Is the positive knowledge contained in these frameworks neutral to the cultural context? Do they have different social consequences when projected on different socio-cultural situations? Even more interestingly, do the categories and theoretical relations themselves acquire new meanings in their new cultural context? What then of the positivity of knowledge?

Fourth, when the new framework of thought is directly associated with a relation of dominance in the cross-cultural context of power, what, in the new cultural context, are the specific changes which occur in the original categories and relations within the domain of thought? That is to say, if relations of dominance and subordination are perceived as existing *between* cultures, which is what happens under colonial rule, what are the specific ways in which frameworks of thought conceived in the context of the dominant culture are received and transformed in the subordinate culture?

Finally, all of the above relations between thought and culture have a bearing on still another crucial question — the changing relations of power *within* the society under colonial domination. And here, even if we grant that the social consequences of particular frameworks of thought produced in the metropolitan countries would be drastically different in the colonized culture, i.e. the historical correspondence between thought and change witnessed in the age of Enlightenment in the West would not obtain in the colonized East, we would still have to answer the question, 'What are the specific relations between thought and change which do obtain in those countries?'

Unlike the sociological determinist who is satisfied with the supposedly empirical 'fact' that all nationalist leaderships manage 'somehow or other' to transcend the problems of cross-cultural relativism inherent in the colonial situation, we will need to pose this as a matter of fundamental significance for an understanding, first, of the relationship between colonialism and nationalism, and second, of the specific structure of domination which is built under the aegis of the post-colonial national state.

The critique of the 1970s seriously damaged the old structure of assumptions about the Indian 'renaissance'. It emphasized at numerous points the impossibility of making the distinction between a progressive and a conservative trend within the 19th century intelligentsia. It showed, in fact, that on most fundamental questions virtually the whole intelligentsia shared the same presuppositions. But those presuppositions were neither unambiguously modern, nor unambiguously national. Liberal, secular and rational attitudes were invariably compromised by concessions to scriptural or canonical authority or, even more ignominiously, by succumbing to pressures for conformity or to enticements of individual material advancement. On the other hand, sentiments of nationality flowed out of an unconcealed faith in the basic goodness of the colonial order and the progressive support of the colonial state. All this reflected the absence of a fundamental social class infused by a revolutionary urge to transform society and to stamp it with the imprint of its own unquestioned hegemony. The Indian 'renaissance' had no historical links with the revolutionary mission of a progressive bourgeoisie seeking to create a nation in its own image.

Interestingly, however, even in their critique of the 'renaissance' argument, the historians of the 1970s did not relinquish the analogy with European history as their basic structure of reference. Indeed, the critique was possible only by reference to that analogue. The point of the critique was, in fact, to show that if modern Europe is taken as the classic example of the progressive significance of an intellectual revolution in the history of the emergence of the capitalist economy and the modern state, then the intellectual history of 19th century India did not have this significance. As the harbinger of a bourgeois and a national revolution, the Indian 'renaissance' was partial, fragmented; indeed, it was a failure. Thus, what was meant to be modern became increasingly alienated from the mass of the people. What seemed to assert greater ideological sway over the nation were newer forms of conservatism. And yet those seemingly conservative movements in thought were themselves premised on the same presuppositions — 'modern' presuppositions — as those of the 'renaissance'.

VI

The Indian debate has brought up these questions within the ambit of Marxist theory, but more specifically within the relations between culture and politics suggested in the writings of Antonio Gramsci. In so doing, it has brought to the foreground of the discussion several problems with the conventional Marxist approach to the 'national and colonial question'. Recent European discussions on Gramsci have highlighted the importance of his ideas not merely in the context of revolutionary politics in Europe, but for problems such as the national and colonial questions or the nature of the post-colonial state in the countries of Asia, Africa and Latin America. Leonardo Paggi, for instance, has argued:

> If, beginning in 1924, Gramsci's position is characterised by an emphasis on the specificity of the Western European situation with regard to czarist Russia, his contribution cannot be reduced to the recognition of this specificity . . . The most favourable conditions do not always necessarily exist in those countries where the development of capitalism and industrialism has reached the highest level . . . To theorise this possibility was not merely a matter of claiming the existence of conditions favourable to a revolutionary development *even* in countries which have not yet reached capitalist maturity, but also, and more importantly, to have completely changed the analytical tools. It meant primarily the abandonment of the traditional interpretation of historical materialism which had shown itself inadequate not only in the East, but also in the West . . . In the East as well as the West, marxism had to reject the interpretative scheme based on the relation of cause and effect between structure and superstructure. It had to reintroduce the concept of the social relations of production in political science, according to Gramsci's analysis of power relations.[67]

It is Gramsci's conception of the state as 'coercion plus hegemony' and of the struggle for power as 'domination plus intellectual–moral leadership' which enabled the Indian critics to examine afresh the so-called 'renaissance' in 19th century India in terms of the aspirations of a new class to assert its intellectual–moral leadership over a modernizing Indian nation and to stake its claim to power in opposition to its colonial masters. But the examination also demonstrated how, under the specific conditions of the economy and polity of a colonial country, this domination necessarily rests on extremely fragile foundations and the intellectual–moral leadership of the dominant classes over the new nation remains fragmented.

Even more specifically, Gramsci's writings provide another line of enquiry which becomes useful in the understanding of such apparently deviant, but historically numerous, cases of the formation of capitalist nation-states. In his famous 'Notes on Italian History',[68] Gramsci outlines an argument about the 'passive revolution of capital'. Contrasting the history of the formation of the Italian state in the period of the Risorgimento with the classic political revolution in France in 1789, Gramsci says that the new claimants to power in Italy, lacking the social strength to launch a full-scale political assault on the old dominant classes, opted for a path in which the demands of a new society would be 'satisfied by small doses, legally, in a reformist manner — in such a way that it was possible to preserve the political and economic position of the old feudal classes, to avoid agrarian reform, and, especially, to avoid the popular masses going through a period of political experience such as occurred in France in the years of Jacobinism, in 1831, and in 1848.'[69] Thus in situations where an emergent bourgeoisie lacks the social conditions for establishing complete hegemony over the new nation, it resorts to a 'passive revolution', by attempting a 'molecular transformation' of the old dominant classes into partners in a new historical bloc and only a partial appropriation of the popular masses, in order first to create a state as the necessary precondition for the establishment of capitalism as the dominant mode of production.

Gramsci's ideas provide only a general, and somewhat obscurely stated, formulation of this problem. To sharpen it, one must examine several historical cases of 'passive revolutions' in their economic, political and ideological aspects. On the face of it, the Indian case seems a particularly good example, but the examination of modern Indian history in terms of this problematic has only just begun. What I will outline here is an analytical framework in which the ideological history of the Indian state can be studied. The framework attempts to locate, within a historical context of 'passive revolution', the problem of the autonomy of nationalist discourse as a discourse of power..

Nationalist texts were addressed both to 'the people' who were said to constitute the nation and to the colonial masters whose claim to rule nationalism questioned. To both, nationalism sought to demonstrate the falsity of the colonial claim that the backward peoples were culturally incapable of ruling themselves in the conditions of the modern world. Nationalism denied the alleged inferiority of the colonized people; it also asserted that a backward nation could 'modernize' itself while retaining its cultural identity. It thus produced a discourse in which, even as it challenged the colonial claim to political domination, it also accepted the very intellectual premises of 'modernity' on which colonial domination was based. How are we to sort out these contradictory elements in nationalist discourse?

Notes

1. John Plamenatz, 'Two Types of Nationalism' in Eugene Kamenka, ed., *Nationalism: The Nature and Evolution of an Idea* (London: Edward Arnold, 1976), pp.23-36.
2. Hans Kohn, *The Idea of Nationalism* (New York: Macmillan, 1944); *The Age of Nationalism* (New York: Harper, 1962); *Nationalism, Its Meaning and History* (Princeton, NJ: Van Nostrand, 1955).
3. For a discussion of this distinction in Kohn, see Aira Kemiläinen, *Nationalism* (Jyväskylä: Jyväskylä: Kasvatusopillinen Korkeakoulu, 1964), pp.115ff.
4. See Ken Wolf, 'Hans Kohn's Liberal Nationalism: The Historian as Prophet', *Journal of the History of Ideas*, 37, 4 (October-December 1976),

pp.651-72. Carlton Hayes, the American historian of nationalism, proposed a theory of the 'degeneration' of nationalism from a liberal, humanitarian and peaceful form to a reactionary, egoistic and violent form. Carlton J.H. Hayes, *The Historical Evolution of Modern Nationalism* (New York: R.R. Smith, 1931) and *Nationalism: A Religion* (New York: Macmillan, 1960). More recently, Seton-Watson has written a comparative history of nationalist movements based on a distinction between 'old' and 'new' nations. 'The old are those which had acquired national identity or national consciousness before the formulation of the doctrine of nationalism'. Such nations were the English, Scots, French, Dutch, Castilians, Portuguese, Danes, Swedes, Hungarians, Poles and Russians. 'The new are those for whom two processes developed simultaneously: the formation of national consciousness and the creation of nationalist movements. Both processes were the work of small educated political elites.' Hugh Seton-Watson, *Nations and States: An Enquiry into the Origins of Nations and the Politics of Nationalism* (London: Methuen, 1977).

5. Thus for example, Karl W. Deutsch, *Nationalism and Social Communication* (Cambridge, Mass: MIT Press, 1966); or Anthony D. Smith, *Theories of Nationalism* (London: Duckworth, 1971); or most recently, John Breuilly, *Nationalism and the State* (Manchester: Manchester University Press, 1982).

6. Ernest Gellner, *Thought and Change* (London: Weidenfeld and Nicholson, 1964), pp.147-78.

7. Thus, for example, David E. Apter, *The Politics of Modernization* (Chicago: University of Chicago Press, 1965); Samuel P. Huntington, *Political Order in Changing Societies* (New Haven, Conn: Yale University Press, 1969).

8. Ernest Gellner, *Nations and Nationalism* (Oxford: Basil Blackwell, 1983), p.124.

9. Ibid., p.20.

10. Ibid., p.39.

11. Ibid., p.48.

12. Ibid., p.57. Gellner's typology of nationalism, despite a rather elaborate attempt at model-building, coincides with the 'two types' of Plamenatz, with the addition of a third type, that of 'diaspora nationalism'.

13. Ibid., p.120.

14. John Dunn is somewhat less gentle:

if nationalism as a political force is in some ways a reactionary and irrationalist sentiment in the modern world, its insistence on the moral claims of the community upon its members and its emphasis that civic order and peace is not a force but an achievement which may well have to be struggled for again is in many ways a less superstitious political vision than the intuitive political consciousness of most capitalist democracies today.

It is in this sense broadly true that the populations of most if not all capitalist democracies today espouse a relaxed and peaceful economic nationalism but shrink back rather from the stridencies and the violence of those whose nations still appear to them to require liberation, to be still *unfree*. And it is natural for them to see the former versions of nationalism as harmless and the latter as purely damaging, fit conduct for Palestinians. Yet both of these more or less reflex judgements are disastrously inadequate. The relaxed economic nationalism of operating states, although it is a natural outcome of the dynamics of the world economy, poses a real threat to the future of the species, while the terrorist politics of national liberation, unprepossessing though it certainly is in itself, is premised upon very deep truths about the human political condition which it is wildly imprudent for us to ignore.

Western Political Theory in the Face of the Future (Cambridge: Cambridge University Press, 1979), p.71.

15. 'Introduction' in Elie Kedourie, ed., *Nationalism in Asia and Africa* (London: Weidenfeld and Nicolson, 1970), p.2.

16. Anthony Smith, *Theories of Nationalism*, pp.12-24.

17. Ibid., p.23.

18. Ibid., p.15.

19. *Nationalism* (London: Hutchinson, 1960), p.9.

20. *Nationalism in Asia and Africa*, p.29.

21. Ibid., p.36.

22. Ibid., p.103.

23. Ibid., p.105.

24. Ibid., p.76.

25. Ibid., p.106.

26. Ibid., p.135.

27. Ibid., pp.146-7.

28. A representative selection of the different arguments in this debate can be found in Bryan R. Wilson, ed., *Rationality* (Oxford: Basil Blackwell, 1970).

29. Martin Hollis, 'Reason and Ritual', *Philosophy*, 43 (1967), 165, pp.231-47.

30. Davidson's argument is that the idea that there can be two 'conceptual schemes', both largely true but not translatable from one to the other, rests on a holistic theory of meaning, viz., that to give the meaning of any sentence or word in a language we need to give the meaning of every sentence or word in that language. This is false. If so, then Davidson shows that there can be no intelligible basis for saying that another scheme is different from our own in the sense of being untranslatable. And if we cannot say schemes are different, neither can we intelligibly say they are the same. Hence, the only intelligible procedure would be to maintain that most of the beliefs in a scheme are true and that every other language is in principle translatable into our own. Donald Davidson, 'On the Very Idea of a Conceptual Scheme', *Proceedings of the American Philosophical Association*, 17 (1973-4), pp.5-20.

31. The 'principle of humanity' suggests that instead of attempting to maximize agreement, one should try to minimize disagreement, specifically in those cases in which we find the beliefs apparently unintelligible. Here the underlying assumption is that of the unity of human nature, from which basis it is argued that, except for a small number of bizarre cases, it should be possible to explain most cross-cultural differences in beliefs or actions in terms of the varying circumstances in which other peoples live. That is to say, one assumes a certain universal instrumental rationality for all human beings and then asks: are the particular beliefs according to which a particular group of people act in a certain way in order to achieve certain outcomes rational *within* their specific social circumstances? If so, then their beliefs and behaviour would become intelligible to us. We would then in effect be saying that had we been placed in exactly the same circumstances, we would have held the same beliefs.

32. Consider for instance, the following exchange:

Alasdair MacIntyre: . . . at any given date in any given society the criteria in current use by religious believers or by scientists will differ from what they are at other times and places. Criteria have a history . . . It seems to me that one could only hold the belief of the Azande rationally *in the absence* of any practice of science and technology in which criteria of effectiveness, ineffectiveness and kindred notions have been built up. But to say this is to recognize the appropriateness of scientific criteria of judgment from our standpoint. The Azande do not intend their belief either as a piece of science or as a piece of non-science. They do not possess those categories. It is only *post eventum*, in the light of later and more sophisticated understanding, that their belief and concepts can be classified and evaluated at all.

This suggests strongly that beliefs and concepts are not merely to be evaluated by the criteria implicit in the practice of those who hold and use them.

Alasdair MacIntyre, 'Is Understanding Religion Compatible with Believing?' in Wilson, ed., *Rationality*, pp.62-77.

Peter Winch: . . . far from overcoming relativism, as he claims, MacIntyre himself falls into an extreme form of it. He disguises this from himself by committing the very error of which, wrongly as I have tried to show, he accuses me: the error of overlooking the fact that 'criteria and concepts have a history'. While he emphasizes this point when he is dealing with the concepts and criteria governing action in particular social contexts, he forgets it when he comes to talk of the criticism of such criteria. Do not the criteria appealed to in the criticism of existing institutions equally have a history? MacIntyre's implicit answer is that it is in ours; but if we are to speak of difficulties and incoherencies appearing and being detected in the way certain practices have hitherto been carried on in a society, surely this can only be understood in connection with problems arising *in* the carrying on of that activity. Outside that context we could not begin to grasp what was problematical . . . MacIntyre criticizes, justly, Sir James Frazer for having imposed the image of his own culture on more primitive ones; but that is exactly what MacIntyre himself is doing here. It is extremely difficult for a sophisticated society to grasp a very simple and primitive form of life: in a way he must jettison his sophistication, a process which is itself perhaps the ultimate sophistication. Or, rather, the distinction between sophistication and simplicity becomes unhelpful at this point.

Peter Winch, 'Understanding a Primitive Society', *American Philosophical Quarterly*, 1 (1964), pp.307-24.
33.

Nationalism is the starkest political shame of the twentieth century . . . The degree to which its prevalence is still felt as a scandal is itself a mark of the unexpectedness of this predominance, of the sharpness of the check which it has administered to Europe's admiring Enlightenment vision of the Cunning of Reason. In nationalism at last, or so it at present seems, the Cunning of Reason has more than met its match.

John Dunn, *Western Political Theory*, p.55.
34. There exists a set of notebooks by Marx, which Engels called the 'Chronological Notes', containing Marx's researches in the years 1881-2 into the history of the emergence of the bourgeoisie, the formation of nation-states and peasant rebellions in Europe in the period of transition. There has been little discussion on these notes. The only account I know is in Boris Porshnev, 'Historical Interest of Marx in his Last Years of Life: The Chronological Notes' in

E.A. Zeluvoskaya, L.I. Golman, V.M. Dalin and B.R. Porshnev, eds., *Marks Istorik* (Moscow: Academy of Sciences, 1968), pp.404-32. A Bengali translation of this article is available in *Baromas*, 7, 1 (Autumn 1985), pp.1-12.

35. For a short review, see Michael Löwy, 'Marxists and the National Question', *New Left Review*, 96 (March-April 1976), pp.81-100. Also see the remarkable note by Roman Rosdolsky, 'Worker and Fatherland: A Note on a Passage in the *Communist Manifesto*', *Science and Society*, 29 (1965), pp.330-7.

36. See in particular, V.I. Lenin, 'Critical Remarks on the National Question', *Collected Works* (Moscow: Progress Publishers, 1964), vol.20, pp.17-54; 'The Right of Nations to Self-determination', *Collected Works*, vol.20, pp.393-454; 'The Socialist Revolution and the Right of Nations to Self-determination', *Collected Works*, vol.22, pp.143-56; 'The Discussion on Self-determination Summed Up', *Collected Works*, vol.22, pp.320-60.

37. *Toward a Marxist Theory of Nationalism* (New York: Monthly Review Press, 1978).

38. Ibid., p.29.

39. Ibid.

40. Ibid., p.24.

41. Ibid., p.25.

42. Ibid.

43. Ibid., p.31.

44. *Imagined Communities: Reflections on the Origin and Spread of Nationalism* (London: Verso, 1983).

45. J.V. Stalin, 'Marxism and the National Question', *Works*, vol.2 (Calcutta: Gana-Sahitya Prakash, 1974), pp.194-215. Stalin's definition runs as follows:

> A nation is a historically constituted, stable community of people, formed on the basis of a common language, territory, economic life, and psychological make-up manifested in a common culture . . . none of the above characteristics taken separately is sufficient to define a nation. More than that, it is sufficient for a single one of these characteristics to be lacking and the nation ceases to be a nation.

46. *Imagined Communities*, p.15.

47. Ibid., p.28.

48. Ibid., p.46.

49. Ibid., pp.78-9.

50. Ibid., p.105.

51. Ibid., p.107.

52. Ibid., p.123.

53. Ibid., p.146.

54. Karl Marx, 'The British Rule in India' in K. Marx and F. Engels, *The First Indian War of Independence 1857-1859* (Moscow: Foreign Languages Publishing House, 1959), p.20.

55. See, for instance, R.P. Dutt, *India Today* (Bombay: People's Publishing House, 1949); S.C. Sarkar, *Bengal Renaissance and Other Essays* (New Delhi: People's Publishing House, 1970); A.R. Desai, *Social Background of Indian Nationalism* (Bombay: Popular Book Depot, 1948); Bipan Chandra, *The Rise and Growth of Economic Nationalism in India* (New Delhi: People's Publishing House, 1966); Arabinda Poddar, *Renaissance in Bengal: Search for Identity* (Simla: Indian Institute of Advanced Study, 1977).

56. V.C. Joshi, ed., *Rammohun Roy and the Process of Modernization in*

India (Delhi: Vikas, 1975).

57. Sumit Sarkar, 'Rammohun Roy and the Break with the Past', ibid., pp.46-68.

58. Similar arguments were put forward in three other articles in the same volume: Asok Sen, 'The Bengal Economy and Rammohun Roy'; Barun De, 'A Biographical Perspective on the Political and Economic Ideas of Rammohun Roy'; and Pradyumna Bhattacharya, 'Rammohun Roy and Bengali Prose'; and in Sumit Sarkar, 'The Complexities of Young Bengal', *Nineteenth Century Studies*, 4 (1973), pp.504-34; Barun De, 'A Historiographical Critique of Renaissance Analogues for Nineteenth-Century India' in Barun De, ed., *Perspectives in the Social Sciences I: Historical Dimensions* (Calcutta: Oxford University Press, 1977), pp.178-218.

59. Asok Sen, *Iswar Chandra Vidyasagar and his Elusive Milestones* (Calcutta: Riddhi-India, 1977).

60. Ibid., p.75

61. Ibid., p.86.

62. Ibid., pp.152, 155-6.

63. Ibid., pp.106-7.

64. Ibid., p.157.

65. Ibid., p.xiii.

66. Ranajit Guha, 'Neel Darpan: The Image of the Peasant Revolt in a Liberal Mirror', *Journal of Peasant Studies*, 2, 1 (October 1974), pp.1-46.

67. Leonardo Paggi, 'Gramsci's General Theory of Marxism' in Chantal Mouffe, ed., *Gramsci and Marxist Theory* (London: Routledge and Kegan Paul, 1979), pp.113-67.

68. Antonio Gramsci, *Selections from the Prison Notebooks*, tr. Q. Hoare and G. Nowell Smith (New York: International Publishers, 1971), pp.44-120.

69. Ibid., p.119.

2. The Thematic and the Problematic

Do not conduct a war before studying the layout of
the land — its mountains, forests, passes, lakes, rivers, etc.
The Art of War, a treatise on Chinese military science
compiled about 500 BC

I

In his book *Orientalism*,[1] Edward W. Said has shown how the post-Enlightenment age in Europe produced an entire body of knowledge in which the Orient appeared as a 'system of representations framed by a whole set of forces that brought the Orient into Western learning, Western consciousness, and later, Western empire'. As a style of thought, Orientalism is 'based upon an ontological and epistemological distinction made between "the Orient" and (most of the time) "the Occident" '. On this basis, an 'enormously systematic discipline' was created 'by which European culture was able to manage — and even produce — the Orient politically, sociologically, militarily, ideologically, scientifically, and imaginatively during the post-Enlightenment period'. Orientalism *created* the Oriental; it was a body of knowledge in which the Oriental was '*contained* and *represented* by dominating frameworks' and Western power over the Orient was given the 'status of scientific truth'. Thus, Orientalism was 'a kind of Western projection onto and will to govern over the Orient'.

The central characteristics of this dominating framework of knowledge have been described by Anouar Abdel-Malek as follows,[2] and this characterization has been adopted by Said. Abdel-Malek identified the *problematic* in Orientalism as one in which the Orient and Orientals were

an 'object' of study, stamped with an otherness — as all that is different, whether it be 'subject' or 'object' — but of a constitutive otherness, of an essentialist character . . . This 'object' of study will be, as is customary, passive, non-participating, endowed with a 'historical' subjectivity, above all, non-active, non-autonomous, non-sovereign with regard to itself: the only Orient or Oriental or 'subject' which could be admitted, at the extreme limit, is the alienated being, philosophically, that is, other than itself in relationship to itself, posed, understood, defined — and acted — by others.

At the level of the *thematic*, on the other hand, there was an

> essentialist concept of the countries, nations and peoples of the Orient under study, a conception which expresses itself through a characterized ethnist typology . . .
>
> According to the traditional orientalists, an essence should exist — sometimes even clearly described in metaphysical terms — which constitutes the inalienable and common basis of all the beings considered; this essence is both 'historical', since it goes back to the dawn of history, and fundamentally a-historical, since it transfixed the being, 'the object' of study, within its inalienable and non-evolutive specificity, instead of defining it as all other beings, states, nations, peoples, and cultures — as a product, a resultant of the vection of the forces operating in the field of historical evolution.
>
> Thus one ends with a typology — based on a real specificity, but detached from history, and, consequently, conceived as being intangible, essential — which makes of the studied 'object' another being with regard to whom the studying subject is transcendent; we will have a homo Sinicus, a homo Arabicus (and why not a homo Aegypticus, etc.), a homo Africanus, the man — the 'normal man', it is understood — being the European man of the historical period, that is, since Greek antiquity.

Abdel-Malek does not elaborate on the precise meaning of his distinction between the problematic and the thematic. Presumably, he uses them in the sense in which the terms *problématique* and *thématique* (or *thétique*) have been used in post-War French philosophy, especially in the 'phenomenological' writings of Jean-Paul Sartre or Maurice Merleau-Ponty. However, it is worth pursuing the possibilities opened up by his distinction of 'levels' within the structure of a body of knowledge, because this could give us a clue to the formulation of our problem in which nationalist thought appears to oppose the dominating implications of post-Enlightenment European thought at one level and yet, at the same time, seems to accept that domination at another.

Let us then recall that in Aristotelian logic, the term 'problematic' is used to indicate the mode or modality of a proposition. A problematic proposition is one that asserts that something is possible; it will contain modal terms like 'possible' or 'may'. We need not, of course, restrict ourselves to the syllogistic framework of Aristotelian logic. But let us open our analytic towards the ground for play that this definition offers. We also know the sense in which the term 'problematic' has been used in contemporary philosophy of science, viz. to indicate the common thrust or direction of theoretical inquiry implied by the posing of a whole group or ensemble of problems in a particular scientific discipline. Finally, we have the sense in which Louis Althusser has used the term, to mean the theoretical or ideological framework in which a word or concept is used, to be recovered by a 'symptomatic reading' of the relevant body of texts.[3]

The term 'thematic', on the other hand, has been used in widely varying senses. In Greek logic, 'themata' are rules of inference, i.e. rules which govern the construction of arguments out of arguments. In contemporary linguistics, the 'theme' or the 'thematic' is used in the analysis of sentences (or, by extension, of discourse) to refer to the way in which the 'relative importance' of the subject-matter of a sentence (or discourse) is identified. In Sartre or Merleau-Ponty, the 'thematic' is that which poses something as an intentional object of mental activity, whether implicitly in a non-reflective mode or explicitly in the reflective mode of thought. But these are merely fragments from the history of this philosophical term, which we can cite so as to indicate the range of meaning it can suggest; we need not be bound by any of the stricter definitions of the term as they occur in particular logical or theoretical systems.

Our present concern is to make a suitable distinction by which we can separate, for analytical purposes, that part of a social ideology, consciously formulated and expressed in terms of a formal theoretical discourse, which *asserts* the existence, and often the practical realizability, of certain historical possibilities from the part which seeks to *justify* those claims by an appeal to both epistemic and moral principles. That is to say, we wish to separate the claims of an ideology, i.e. its identification of historical possibilities and the practical or programmatic forms of its realization, from its justificatory structures, i.e. the nature of the evidence it presents in support of those claims, the rules of inference it relies on to logically relate a statement of the evidence to a structure of arguments, the set of epistemological principles it uses to demonstrate the existence of its claims as historical possibilities, and finally, the set of ethical principles it appeals to in order to assert that those claims are morally justified. The former part of a social ideology we will call its *problematic* and the latter part its *thematic*. The thematic, in other words, refers to an epistemological as well as ethical system which provides a framework of elements and rules for establishing relations between elements; the problematic, on the other hand, consists of concrete statements about possibilities justified by reference to the thematic.

By applying this distinction to our material, we will find that the problematic in nationalist thought is exactly the reverse of that of Orientalism. That is to say, the 'object' in nationalist thought is still the Oriental, who retains the essentialist character depicted in Orientalist discourse. Only he is not passive, non-participating. He is seen to possess a 'subjectivity' which he can himself 'make'. In other words, while his relationship to himself and to others have been 'posed, understood and defined' by others, i.e. by an objective scientific consciousness, by Knowledge, by Reason, those relationships are not acted by others. His subjectivity, he thinks, is active, autonomous and sovereign.

At the level of the thematic, on the other hand, nationalist thought accepts and adopts the same essentialist conception based on the distinction between 'the East' and 'the West', the same typology created by a transcendent studying subject, and hence the same 'objectifying' procedures of knowledge constructed in the post-Enlightenment age of Western science.

There is, consequently, an inherent contradictoriness in nationalist thinking, because it reasons within a framework of knowledge whose representational structure corresponds to the very structure of power nationalist thought seeks to repudiate. It is this contradictoriness in the domain of thought which creates the possibility for several divergent solutions to be proposed for the nationalist

38

problematic. Furthermore, it is this contradictoriness which signifies, in the domain of thought, the theoretical insolubility of the national question in a colonial country, or for that matter, of the extended problem of social transformation in a post-colonial country, within a strictly nationalist framework.

II

At first sight, the distinction between the thematic and the problematic might seem analogous to the distinction in structural linguistics between *langue* and *parole*, where the former refers to the language system shared by a given community of speakers while the latter is the concrete speech act of individual speakers. It might also appear analogous to the distinction in the analytical philosophy of language between an understanding of meaning in terms of the subjective *intentions* that lie behind particular speech acts and meaning as codified in linguistic *conventions*. Thus, it might seem that what we are trying to suggest about the lack of autonomy of nationalist discourse is simply that it puts forward certain propositions about society and politics whose syntactic and semantic structure — more generally, whose meaning — is fully governed by the rules of the 'language' of post-Enlightenment rational thought. In other words, nationalist texts are 'meaningful' only when read in terms of the rules of that larger framework of thought; the former, therefore, merely consists of particular utterances whose meanings are fixed by the lexical and grammatical system provided by the latter. Alternatively, it may be supposed that what we are trying to establish at the level of the problematic are the subjective 'reasons' behind particular assertions made in nationalist texts, to establish *why* nationalist writers wrote what they wrote, the 'meaning' of those assertions, of course, being established only in terms of the 'conventions' laid down at the level of the thematic, i.e. the theoretical framework of post-Enlightenment rational thought.

These are not, however, the sort of problems we will need to tackle here. Our particular distinction between the thematic and the problematic must serve a purpose which the seemingly analogous distinctions in other fields are not designed to serve.

First of all, a strictly linguistic study will be premature if we have not adequately delineated the particular conceptual or theoretical field in which our nationalist texts are located. Given the sort of problems we have raised in the previous chapter, it is obvious we will need to find our preliminary answers by looking directly in the field of political–ideological discourse. Although this field will be constituted for us by the material provided in a variety of ideological texts, a linguistic study of these texts cannot immediately be of much use for us. That is to say, even if we assume that we can give to a body of ideological texts a reasonable macro-structural semantic form (which itself is a very large assumption because the linguistic study of discourse is still concerned with short sequences of sentences[4]), a strictly linguistic study can only give us the general syntactic and semantic conditions determining to what extent this discourse is well-formed or interpretable. But before one can proceed to that level of textual analysis, one must first constitute the discursive field in its own theoretical terms, viz. in the terms of a *political* theory. That, therefore, is the first requirement which our proposed analytical framework must fulfil.

Second, to address ourselves to the interpretation of nationalist texts as a body of writings on political theory necessarily means to explore their meaning in terms of their implicit or explicit reference to things, i.e. their logical and theoretical implications. It means, in other words, to conduct our analysis not at the level of language, but at the level of *discourse*. It would not do to prejudge the issue by declaring straightaway that since this discourse is only a product of ideology, its content must be purely tautological and thus unworthy of being studied as content. On the contrary, it is precisely the relation between the content of nationalist discourse and the kind of politics which nationalism conducts which will be of central concern to us.

What will be required, therefore, is an explicitly critical study of the *ideology* of nationalism. Both sociological determinism and functionalism have sought to interpret nationalist ideology by emptying it of all content — as far as nationalist politics is concerned, their assumption is that 'thinkers did not really make much difference'. Our position, however, is that it is the content of nationalist ideology, its claims about what is possible and what is legitimate, which gives specific shape to its politics. The latter cannot be understood without examining the former.

Indeed, our approach in this study admits an even stronger formulation: nationalist ideology, it will be evident, is inherently polemical, shot through with tension; its voice, now impassioned, now faltering, betrays the pressures of having to state its case against formidable opposition. The polemic is not a mere stylistic device which a dispassioned analyst can calmly separate out of a pure doctrine. It is part of the ideological content of nationalism which takes as its adversary a contrary discourse — the discourse of colonialism. Pitting itself against the reality of colonial rule — which appears before it as an existent, almost palpable, historical truth — nationalism seeks to assert the feasibility of entirely new political possibilities. These are its political claims which colonialist discourse haughtily denies. Only a vulgar reductionist can insist that these new possibilities simply 'emerge' out of a social structure or out of the supposedly objective workings of a world-historical process, that they do not need to be thought out, formulated, propagated and defended in the battlefield of politics. As a matter of fact, it is precisely in the innovative thinking out of political possibilities and the defence of their historical feasibility that the unity is established between nationalist thought and nationalist politics. The polemical content of nationalist ideology *is* its politics.

It is this aspect that we seek to identify at the level of what we have called the problematic. It is the level, let us recall, where nationalist discourse makes certain claims regarding the historical possibilities which it thinks are feasible; it also makes claims regarding the practical forms through which those possibilities could be realized. *Historical* possibilities, *practical* realization. The claims of the ideology are directly located on the terrain of politics, the field of contest for power, where its claims are challenged by others emanating from an opposite discourse. It is at the level of the problematic then that we can fix the specifically historical and the specifically political character of nationalist discourse. It is there that we can connect the ideology to its 'social bases', relate its theoretical claims to the state of the social structure and its dynamics, to the 'interests' of various social classes, their opposition as well as their coming together. It will also become evident that the problematic need not remain fixed and unchanging. As 'historical conditions' change, so are new political possibilities thought out; the problematic undergoes a transformation within the same structure of discourse. With the help of the problematic, then, we seek to establish the political location as well as the historicity of nationalist discourse.

But political–ideological discourse does not consist only of claims: those claims also have to be justified by appeal to logical, epistemological and above all ethical principles. In politics, people have to be persuaded about not only the feasibility but also the legitimacy and desirability of ends and means. Consequently, along with its claims, political–ideological discourse also has its structures of justification. It must present credible evidence in support of its political claims, build a logical structure of argument to show how that evidence supports the claims, and try to convince that the claims are morally justified.

It is at this level that we can consider the content of nationalist discourse as having logical and theoretical implications. The sociological determinist, of course, ignores this aspect of nationalist ideology altogether, dogmatically asserting that in this respect its logical principles and theoretical concepts are wholly derived from another framework of knowledge — that of modern Western rational thought. It will be a major task of this study to show that this dogmatic refusal to take seriously the content as well as the logical and theoretical forms of nationalist thought not only leads one to miss out on the fascinating story of the encounter between a world-conquering Western thought and the intellectual modes of non-Western cultures, it also results in a crucial misunderstanding of the true historical effectivity of nationalism itself.

At the level of the thematic we will be necessarily concerned with the relation between nationalist discourse and the forms of modern Western thought. But this, we will show, is not a simple relation of correspondence, even of derivation. First of all, nationalist thought is selective about what it takes from Western rational thought. Indeed it is deliberately and necessarily selective. Its political burden, as we have said, is to oppose colonial rule. It must therefore reject the immediate political implications of colonialist thought and argue in favour of political possibilities which colonialist thought refuses to admit. It cannot do this simply by asserting that those possibilities are feasible; the quarrel with colonialist thought will be necessarily carried into the domain of justification. Thus nationalist texts will question the veracity of colonialist knowledge, dispute its arguments, point out contradictions, reject its moral claims. Even when it adopts, as we will see it does, the modes of thought characteristic of rational knowledge in the post-Enlightenment age, it cannot adopt them in their entirety, for then it would not constitute itself as a *nationalist* discourse.

Taken together, in its dialetical unity, the problematic and the thematic will enable us to show how nationalism succeeds in producing a *different* discourse. The difference is marked, on the terrain of political–ideological discourse, by a political contest, a struggle for power, which nationalist thought must think about and set down in words. Its problematic forces it relentlessly to demarcate itself from the discourse of colonialism. Thus nationalist thinking is necessarily a struggle with an entire body of systematic knowledge, a struggle that is political at the same time as it is intellectual. Its politics impels it to open up that framework of knowledge which presumes to dominate it, to displace that framework, to subvert its authority, to challenge its morality.

Yet in its very constitution as a discourse of power, nationalist thought cannot remain only a negation; it is also a *positive* discourse which seeks to replace the structure of colonial power with a new order, that of national power. Can nationalist thought produce a discourse of order while daring to negate the very foundations of a system of knowledge that has conquered the world? How far can it succeed in maintaining its difference from a discourse that seeks to dominate it?

A different discourse, yet one that is dominated by another: that is my hypothesis about nationalist thought. It is, on the face of it, a paradoxical formulation. But surely that is what ought to emerge from a critical study of a body of ideological doctrine which claims for itself a certain unity and autonomy. The object of the critique is not to produce a new 'theory' which presumes to explain nationalist ideology by reducing it to something else. Rather, the object is to ask: 'What does nationalist discourse presuppose? Where is it located in relation to other discourses? Where are the cracks on its surface, the points of tension in its structure, the contrary forces, the contradictions? What does it reveal and what does it suppress?' These are the types of questions with which I propose to conduct this study, not with a positive sociological theory.

There is a second reason why the relation between nationalist thought and the framework of colonialist knowledge cannot be a simple one. This reason has to do with the very historicity of thought. Like all other systems of ideological doctrine, nationalist thought has evolved over time. Hence, there is a *historical* process through which nationalist discourse constitutes itself. At the level of the problematic, the political opposition to colonial rule goes through specific programmatic phases, marked by innovations in political objectives, in strategy and tactics, in selecting the types of issues on which to focus its ideological sights and concentrate its polemical attack. Shifts at the level of the problematic may well call for a reconsideration of the logical or theoretical underpinnings of the ideology. It could lead to a change in the sorts of theoretical ideas which nationalist thought had borrowed from Western rationalism, giving up older theories and adopting, even devising, new ones. There could be new theoretical resources which become available at the level of the thematic, for like nationalist thought Western rationalism too has a continuing history. On the other hand, the very logical and theoretical structure of the thematic may influence the formulation of the problematic, constrain the identification of political possibilities, make some possibilities appear more desirable or feasible than others. Indeed, the thematic will tend to apply a closure on the range of possibilities, and many possibilities will be ignored and some not even recognized. At the same time, this process of mutual influence between the thematic and problematic of nationalist discourse — the periodic dissociations and coming together — could even produce at critical junctures a thoroughgoing critique of the thematic itself, points at which nationalist thought will seem to be on the verge of transcending itself.

The complexity in the relation between nationalist and colonialist thought therefore must also be tackled in terms of a theory of *stages* in the constitution of a nationalist discourse — not necessarily chronological stages, but rather a logical sequence in the evolution of its full ideological structure. But is a theory of stages not one which assumes a certain linearity of evolution, a certain teleology? We need to face this question, because it has to do quite centrally with the way in which we propose to relate a political theory of nation-state formation with the ideological history of that state.

III

We have already introduced at the end of the previous chapter Gramsci's concept of 'passive revolution'. Since this is the central concept around which we will build our political analysis of 20th century nationalism, it is necessary to explore the location of this concept within the Marxist theory of state and revolution, and its possible uses in our field of inquiry. In particular, we will need to show how, given the contradictions between the problematic and the thematic of nationalism, passive revolution becomes the historical path by which a 'national' development of capital can occur without resolving or surmounting those contradictions.

Antonio Gramsci himself locates this concept on the theoretical ground defined by two propositions stated by Marx in his Preface to *The Critique of Political Economy*: 'No social order ever perishes before all the productive forces for which there is room in it have developed; and new, higher relations of production never appear before the material conditions of their existence have matured in the womb of the old society itself. Therefore mankind always sets itself only such tasks as it can solve . . .'[5] Gramsci applies the two propositions to the history of bourgeois-national movements in late 19th century Europe, particularly the history of the Italian Risorgimento, and is led to the identification, in all their concreteness, of two inseparably related aspects of those movements: one, the historical impediments to bourgeois hegemony, and two, the possibilities of marginal change within those limits.

What are these limits? Gramsci analyses them in terms of three moments or levels of the 'relation of forces'.[6] The first is that of the objective structure, 'independent of human will'. In countries such as Italy in the second half of the 19th century, the level of the development of the material forces of production and the relative positions and functions of the different classes in production were not such as to favour the rapid emergence of a fully developed system of capitalist production. The political position of the older governing classes; a backward agrarian economy; the weakness of the national capitalist class in relation to the advanced levels of productive organization in the world capitalist economy — all of these were constraints at the level of the 'objective structure'.

The second moment is the relation of political forces, 'the degree of homogeneity, self-awareness and organization attained by the various social classes'. Here the question of ideology and organization is not simply that of the economic–corporate organization of particular productive groups or even the solidarity of interests among all members of a social class. The crucial level is the 'most purely political' one where 'one becomes aware that one's own corporate interests, in their present and future development, transcend the corporate limits of the purely economic class, and can and must become the interests of other subordinate groups too'. It is at this level that

> previously germinated ideologies become 'party', come into confrontation and conflict, until only one of them, or at least a single combination of them, tends to prevail, to gain the upper hand, to propagate itself throughout society — bringing about not only a unison of economic and political aims, but also intellectual and moral unity, posing all the questions around which the struggle rages not on a corporate but on a 'universal' plane, and thus creating the hegemony of a fundamental social group over a series of subordinate groups. It is true that the State is seen as the organ of one particular group, destined to create favourable conditions for the latter's maximum expansion. But the development and expansion of the particular group are conceived of, and presented, as being the motor force of a universal expansion, of a development of all the 'national' energies. In other words, the dominant group is coordinated concretely with the general interests of the subordinate groups, and the life of the State is conceived of as a continuous process of formation and superseding of unstable equilibria (on the juridical plane) between the interests of the fundamental group and those of the subordinate groups — equilibria in which the interests of the dominant group prevail, but only up to a certain point, i.e. stopping short of narrowly corporate economic interests.[7]

This is the 'moment' to which Gramsci paid the greatest attention in his *Notebooks*, analyzing in concrete detail the political history of the Risorgimento to show how the ideology and organization of bourgeois hegemony in its twin aspects of coercive power embodied in the state and intellectual–moral leadership in society at large necessarily remained incomplete and fragmented.

The third 'moment' is that of the relation of military forces, consisting of the technical military configuration as well as what might be called the 'politico-military' situation. In the case of the direct political occupation of a country by a foreign armed power, for instance,

> this type of oppression would be inexplicable if it were not for the state of social disintegration of the oppressed people, and the passivity of the majority of them; consequently independence cannot be won with purely military forces, it requires

both military and politico-military. If the oppressed nation, in fact, before embarking on its struggle for independence, had to wait until the hegemonic State allowed it to organise its own army in the strict and technical sense of the word, it would have to wait quite a while . . . The oppressed nation will therefore initially oppose the dominant military force with a force which is only 'politico-military', that is to say a form of political action which has the virtue of provoking repercussions of a military character in the sense: 1. that it has the capacity to destroy the war potential of the dominant nation from within; 2. that it compels the dominant military force to thin out and disperse itself over a large territory, thus nullifying a great part of its war potential.[8]

In this aspect too Gramsci noted 'the disastrous absence of politico-military leadership' in the Italian Risorgimento.

Considering together all three 'moments' of the political situation, the conclusion becomes inescapable that in conditions of a relatively advanced world capitalism, a bourgeoisie aspiring for hegemony in a new national political order cannot hope to launch a 'war of movement' (or 'manoeuvre') in the traditional sense, i.e. a frontal assault on the state. For such a bourgeoisie, a full-scale, concentrated and decisive attack on the existing structure of political rule in the fashion of the French Revolution or the Revolutions of 1848 is impossible. Instead, it must engage in a 'war of position', a kind of political trench warfare waged on a number of different fronts. Its strategy would be to attempt a 'molecular transformation' of the state, neutralizing opponents, converting sections of the former ruling classes into allies in a partially reorganized system of government, undertaking economic reforms on a limited scale so as to appropriate the support of the popular masses but keeping them out of any form of direct participation in the processes of governance.

This is the 'passive revolution', a historical phase in which the 'war of position' coincides with the revolution of capital. But this 'interpretative criterion' Gramsci applies 'dynamically' to the history of the Italian Risorgimento. In the process, he is able to make some observations of great significance in the analysis of the emergence of nation-states in the period of a relatively advanced world capitalism.

Talking about the relationship between Cavour, a classic exponent of the 'war of position', and Mazzini who represented to a much greater extent the element of popular initiative or 'war of movement', Gramsci asks: 'are not both of them indispensable precisely to the same extent?'[9] The answer is: yes, but there is a fundamental asymmetry in the relation between the two tendencies. Cavour was aware of his own role; he was also aware of the role being played by Mazzini. That is to say, Cavour was not only conscious that the change he was seeking to bring about was a partial, circumscribed and strictly calibrated change, he was also conscious of how far the other tendency, that of a more direct challenge to the established order by means of popular initiative, could go. Mazzini, on the other hand, was a 'visionary apostle', unaware both of his own role and that of Cavour. As a result, the Mazzinian tendency was in a sense itself appropriated within the overall strategy of the 'war of position'. 'Out of the Action Party and the Moderates, which represented the real "subjective forces" of the Risorgimento? Without a shadow of doubt it was the Moderates, precisely because they were also aware of the role of the Action Party: thanks to this awareness, their "subjectivity" was of a superior and more decisive quality.'[10] On the other hand, if Mazzini had been more aware of Cavour's role and that of his own, 'then the equilibrium which resulted from the convergence of the two men's activities would have been different, would have been more favourable to Mazzinianism. In other words, the Italian State would have been constituted on a less retrograde and more modern basis.'[11] Instead, what happened was that the forces of 'moderation' succeeded in appropriating the results of popular initiative for the purposes of a partially reorganized and reformist state order. The dialectic was blocked, the opposition could not be transcended. The passive revolution allowed

> the 'thesis' to achieve its full development, up to the point where it would even succeed in incorporating a part of the antithesis itself — in order, that is, not to allow itself to be 'transcended' in the dialectical opposition. The thesis alone in fact develops to the full its potential for struggle, up to the point where it absorbs even the so-called representatives of the antithesis: it is precisely in this that the passive revolution or revolution/restoration consists.[12]

In exploring the relation between passive revolution and the 'war of position', therefore, Gramsci is not proposing some invariant, suprahistorical 'theory' of the formation of nation-states in the period of advanced world capitalism. Indeed, he begins from the premise that there are two contrary tendencies within such movements — one of gradualism, moderation, molecular changes controlled 'from the top', the other of popular initiative, radical challenge, war of movement. The equilibrium that would result from the struggle between these two tendencies was in no way predetermined: it depended on the particular 'moments' of the relation of forces, especially on the relative quality of the 'subjective forces' which provided political-ideological leadership to each tendency.

If we are to apply this 'interpretative criterion of molecular changes' to anti-colonial movements in the non-European parts of the world, movements seeking to replace colonial rule with a modern national state structure, we would be led into identifying at the level of the overall political-ideological strategy the two conflicting and yet mutually indispensable tendencies. The specific organizational forms in which the two tendencies appear in particular national movements, the manner in which the struggle takes place between them, the particular form of resolution of the struggle — all of these could be documented and analysed in order to provide a more varied and comprehensive treatment of the problem of the formation of national states in recent history. For the case of the Risorgimento, Gramsci illustrates the fundamental asymmetry between the two tendencies by noting that while conditions did not exist for the popular initiative to take the form of a 'concentrated and instantaneous' insurrection, it could not even exert itself in the 'diffused and capillary form of indirect pressure'.[13] Consequently, while there did exist 'the enormous importance of the "demagogic" mass movement, with its leaders thrown up by chance . . . it was nevertheless in actual fact taken over by the traditional organic forces — in other words, by the parties of long standing, with rationally-formed leaders . . .'[14] It would be an interesting exercise in itself to explore what form this relation between 'demagogic' and 'rationally-formed' leaderships takes in a non-Western cultural context in which the very notion of a 'rational' structure of political power is likely to be associated with the ideology of colonial rule.

But there is another aspect to this asymmetry between the 'subjective forces' in the passive revolution which is of even greater significance in understanding the ideological history of nation-state formation in colonial countries. Besides the relative quality of the two leaderships in the Risorgimento, Gramsci also relates the asymmetry to certain 'organic tendencies of the modern state' which seem to favour the forces which carry out a protracted, many-faceted and well-coordinated 'war of position' rather than those which think only of an instantaneous 'war of movement'. And it is at this level of his argument that Gramsci draws out the implications of his analysis of the Risorgimento in relation to the political struggle of the proletariat against the capitalist order.

These 'organic tendencies of the modern state' are set under historical conditions in which the question of socialism and the possibility of socialist revolution have been already raised and demonstrated. Thus, in a fundamental historical sense, the capitalist state can no longer retain the same character as before. What it does now is intervene in the process of production in a far more direct way than was the case under the classical liberal state. The state now 'finds itself invested with a primordial function in the capitalist system, both as a company . . . which concentrates the savings to be put at the disposal of private industry and activity, and as a medium and long-term investor . . .' Once the state assumes this function, it is then inevitably led

> to intervene in order to check whether the investments which have taken place through State means are properly administered . . . But control by itself is not sufficient. It is not just a question of preserving the productive apparatus just as it is at a given moment. It is a matter of reorganising it in order to develop it in parallel with the increase in the population and in collective needs.

Besides, there are other elements which also compel the state to become interventionist: 'increasing protectionism and autarkic tendencies, investment premiums, dumping, salvaging of large enterprises which are in the process, or in danger of going bankrupt; in other words, as the phrase goes, the "nationalisation of losses and industrial deficits" . . .'[15]

Gramsci of course discusses this interventionist capitalist state in the context of 'Americanism' and 'Fordism'. Here the state retains the formal character of a liberal state, 'not in the sense of a free-trade liberalism or of effective political liberty, but in the more fundamental sense of free initiative and of economic individualism which, with its own means, on the level of "civil society", through historical development, itself arrives at a regime of industrial concentration and monopoly.'[16] Gramsci then continues the argument about the

47

interventionist capitalist state into the stage where it attains the specific form of fascism.

We need not concern ourselves here with the debate on the relevance of Gramsci's analysis for an understanding of the state in the advanced capitalist countries of today. Instead, let us piece together some of these fragments of his analysis into an argument about the historical character of capitalist nation-states which have emerged from successful anti-colonial movements in countries of the non-European world.

First of all, at the level of the 'objective structure', an aspiring bourgeoisie in a colonial country faces the two-fold problem, now well known in the literature on 'underdevelopment', of a low level of development of the forces of production at home as well as the overwhelming dominance, both economic and political, of an advanced metropolitan capitalism. The problem takes on a particularly intractable structural form in countries with a large and backward agrarian economy. The principal task for a nationalist bourgeoisie in such a country becomes one in which it must find for itself sufficient room for a certain degree of relatively independent capitalist development. For this it must engage in a political struggle with the colonial power as well as with forces at home which impede the structural transformation of the domestic economy. How can it project this two-fold struggle as something going beyond the narrow corporate interests of the bourgeoisie and give to it the form of a 'national' struggle? That becomes its principal political-ideological task.

The task is still more formidable if at the 'politico–military' level the possibility of a 'concentrated and instantaneous' armed assault on the colonial state is remote. Thus if the 'politico–military' basis of the colonial state itself is strong enough not to permit the formation of a rival armed force, then the nationalist leadership will not have before it the viable option of a purely military solution. It must rely on a 'politico–military' strategy based on the coordinated, and perhaps protracted, action of very large sections of the popular masses against the colonial state.

The nationalist leadership in such situations cannot resort to a 'war of movement'; a 'war of position' becomes inevitable. To conduct this 'war of position' it must bring under the sway of a nationalist ideology and political programme the overwhelming part of the popular elements in the nation, and particularly the vast mass of peasants. It is here that the politico–ideological problem would get intertwined with a more fundamental cultural problem. The structural 'underdevelopment' of the agrarian economy would be associated with the cultural 'backwardness' of the peasantry — its localism, immobility, resistance to change, subjection to a variety of pre-capitalist forms of domination, etc. Will the 'war of position' be one in which a 'modernization' of these cultural institutions precedes the phase of independent capitalist development and formation of the nation-state, or is the replacement of the colonial state by a national one itself the precondition for capitalist development and 'modernization'?

The characteristic form of 'passive revolution' in colonial countries follows the second path. That is to say, the 'war of position' implies a political–ideological programme by which the largest possible nationalist alliance is built up against the political rule of the colonial power. The aim is to form a politically independent nation-state. The means involve the creation of a series of alliances, within the organizational structure of a national movement, between the bourgeoisie and other dominant classes and the mobilization, under this leadership, of mass support from the subordinate classes. The project is a reorganization of the political order, but it is moderated in two quite fundamental ways. On the one hand, it does not attempt to break up or transform in any radical way the institutional structures of 'rational' authority set up in the period of colonial rule, whether in the domain of administration and law or in the realm of economic institutions or in the structure of education, scientific research and cultural organization. On the other hand, it also does not undertake a full-scale assault on all pre-capitalist dominant classes; rather, it seeks to limit their former power, neutralize them where necessary, attack them only selectively, and in general to bring them round to a position of subsidiary allies within a reformed state structure. The dominance of capital does not emanate from its hegemonic sway over 'civil society'. On the contrary, it is its measure of control over the new state apparatus which becomes a precondition for further capitalist development. It is by means of an interventionist state, directly entering the domain of production as a mobilizer and manager of investible resources, that the foundations are laid for the expansion of capital. Yet the dominance of capital over the national state remains constrained in several ways. Its function of representing the 'national–popular' has to be shared with other governing groups and its transformative role moderated to reformist and 'molecular' changes. It is thus that the passive revolution acquires the dual character of 'revolution/restoration'.

IV

To be sure, there are many differences in the specific forms which the post-colonial state has taken in various countries of Asia, Africa and Central and South America. There also exists a large literature which explores these forms from the standpoint of political economy or political sociology. Even if one were to look at the character of the dominant ideologies associated with these state forms, one would find diverse mixes of free enterprise/state control, electoral democracy/authoritarianism and a variety of populist doctrines. An empirical description or classification of these forms would justify the comparative methods of study on which much of this sociological literature has been based.

What I propose here, however, is a study of the ideological history of the post-colonial state by taking as *paradigmatic* the most developed form of that state. That is to say, I give to nationalist thought its ideological unity by relating it to a form of the post-colonial state which accords most closely to the theoretical characterization I have made above of the passive revolution. I trace the historical constitution of this unity in terms of certain stages, which I will call *moments*, each having a specific form of combination of the thematic and the problematic and each bearing certain distinct historical possibilities in terms of the relation of 'subjective forces'. I use as my material certain nationalist texts from India, but the theoretical import of the argument is general.

In fact, to sustain my analytical framework, I will need to argue that 'passive revolution' is the *general* form of the transition from colonial to post-colonial national states in the 20th century. The various stages of movement in the realm of ideas which accompany the historical process of this passive revolution are also an aspect of this general argument. The precise historical location of the transitions from one stage to another, or even the specific ideological content of each stage, will of course need to be fixed separately for each particular nationalist movement. I do not even try to locate, in comparative terms, some of these specific variants even for illustrative purposes, because I do not have the same familiarity with nationalist texts from any other country. But the theoretical structure of my argument must stand or fall at the general level, as an argument about nationalist thought in colonial countries and not as an argument about Indian nationalism. That is one of the main theoretical uses to which I wish to put Gramsci's remarks on 'the organic tendencies of the modern state'.

The question of identifying the different ideological strands or 'subjective forces' in nationalist thought cannot, however, be answered by applying any simple criterion such as progressive/reactionary, elitist/populist or indirect/direct assault on the colonial state. In fact, even Gramsci's interpretative criterion of war of position/war of movement cannot be used to separate out two distinct and opposed ideological tendencies in all nationalist movements. In one of his stray remarks on India, for instance, Gramsci himself says: 'India's political struggle against the English . . . knows three forms of war; war of movement, war of position and underground warfare. Gandhi's passive resistance is a war of position, which at certain moments becomes a war of movement, and at others underground warfare.'[17] Here, therefore, a straightforward identification of the two 'subjective forces', as in the case of Cavour and Mazzini in the Italian Risorgimento, is not possible. We will consequently need to devise other, more general, analytical means to make sense of the various ideological ensembles we will encounter in our study of nationalist thought.

I tackle this problem by breaking up the presumed unity of nationalist thought into three stages or moments. I call these, respectively, the moments of departure, manoeuvre and arrival. The argument is that for nationalist thought to attain its paradigmatic form, these three are *necessary* ideological moments.

The *moment of departure* lies in the encounter of a nationalist consciousness with the framework of knowledge created by post-Enlightenment rationalist thought. It produces the awareness — and acceptance — of an essential cultural difference between East and West. Modern European culture, it is thought, possesses attributes which make the European culturally equipped for power and progress, while such attributes are lacking in the 'traditional' cultures of the East, thus dooming those countries to poverty and subjection. But the nationalist's claim is that this backwardness is not a character which is historically immutable: it can be transformed by the nation acting collectively, by adopting all those modern attributes of European culture. But would this not obliterate those very differences which mark the national culture as something distinct from Western culture? Nationalist thought at its moment of departure formulates the following characteristic answer: it asserts that the superiority of the West lies in the materiality of its culture, exemplified by its science, technology and love of progress. But the East is superior in the spiritual aspect of culture. True modernity for the non-European nations would lie in combining the superior material qualities of Western cultures with the spiritual greatness of the East. I illustrate this moment in the formation of nationalist thought by a study of the writings of Bankimchandra Chattopadhyay, an early nationalist thinker.

This ideal, however, necessarily implies an elitist programme, for the act of cultural synthesis can only be performed by the supremely refined intellect. Popular consciousness, steeped in centuries of superstition and irrational folk religion, can hardly be expected to adopt this ideal: it would have to be transformed from without. This is where the central political–ideological dilemma of capitalist transformation occurs in a colonial country, whose solution, as we have outlined above, is passive revolution. It requires the mobilization of the popular elements in the cause of an anti-colonial struggle and, at the same time, a distancing of those elements from the structure of the state. This is achieved at the *moment of manoeuvre*, a crucial moment with many contradictory possibilities. It combines in one inseparable process elements of both 'war of movement' and 'war of position'. It consists in the historical consolidation of the 'national' by decrying the 'modern', the preparation for expanded capitalist production by resort to an ideology of anti-capitalism — in other words, 'the development of the thesis by incorporating a part of the antithesis'. This moment I illustrate in the course of a discussion of the thought of Mohandas Karamchand Gandhi.

The *moment of arrival* is when nationalist thought attains its fullest development. It is now a discourse of order, of the rational organization of power. Here the discourse is not only conducted in a single, consistent, unambiguous voice, it also succeeds in glossing over all earlier contradictions, divergences and differences and incorporating within the body of a unified discourse every aspect and stage in the history of its formation. This ideological unity of nationalist thought it seeks to actualize in the unified life of the state. Nationalist discourse at its moment of arrival is passive revolution uttering its own life-history. I illustrate this final point in the argument with a study of the writings of Jawaharlal Nehru.

At each stage, I attempt to use the distinction between the level of the problematic and that of the thematic to point out the inherent contradictions in the structure of the ideology, the range of possibilities and the logic of the development towards the next moment. True enough, assertions and justifications lie intertwined in the same body of doctrine. Indeed, this is precisely what gives to an ideology its unity, for it is also a characteristic of ideological thinking that the solution is already thought of at the same time as a problem is formulated.

But, for that very reason, it is by following the disjunctures between the claims and their justifications that I propose to identify the ambiguities and contradictions in the doctrine of nationalism, show how the assertion of political possibilities conditions the choice of a structure of justification, how on the other hand the justificatory structure itself may condition the identification of possibilities, how some possibilities are emphasised, others erased, how the marks of disjuncture are suppressed and the rational continuity of a progressive historical development established.[18] The distinction between the thematic and the problematic will offer us a means of access into the internal structure of nationalist discourse and the relation between its theory and practice. It will also give us a standpoint for the critical analysis of the complex relation between nationalist thought and the discourse of colonialism.

This critique, as I have said before, is not one which stems from an alternative theory claiming to provide better answers to the problems which nationalism poses for itself. Rather, the object is to look into the manner in which those problems were posed by nationalist thought. In a sense, therefore, we too will need to locate texts in their own historical contexts, an interpretative procedure which some recent historians of political thought have recommended in opposition to the view that the classic texts of politics can be read as part of some timeless discourse of human wisdom.[19] But we will need to do more. We will not attempt to suppress the marks of our own engagement in a political–ideological discourse. The critical analysis of nationalist thought is also necessarily an intervention in a political discourse of our own time. Reflecting on the intellectual struggles of nationalist writers of a bygone era, we are made aware of the way in which we relate our own theory and practice; judging their assessment of political possibilities, we begin to ponder the possibilities open to us today. Thus, analysis itself becomes politics; interpretation acquires the undertones of a polemic. In such circumstances, to pretend to speak in the 'objective' voice of history is to dissimulate. By marking our own text with the signs of battle, we hope to go a little further towards a more open and self-aware discourse.

Notes

1. Edward W. Said, *Orientalism* (London: Routledge and Kegan Paul, 1978).
2. Anouar Abdel-Malek, 'Orientalism in Crisis', *Diogenes*, 44 (Winter 1963), pp.102-40.
3. Louis Althusser, *For Marx*, tr. Ben Brewster (London: Allen Lane, 1969); Louis Althusser and Étienne Balibar, *Reading Capital*, tr. Ben Brewster (London: New Left Books, 1970).
4. See for a survey of linguistic research on this subject, Teun A. van Dijk, *Text and Context: Explorations in the Semantics and Pragmatics of Discourse* (London: Longman, 1977).
5. Karl Marx, 'Preface to *A Contribution to the Critique of Political Economy*'

in K. Marx and F. Engels, *Selected Works*, vol.1 (Moscow: Progress Publishers, 1969), p.504.

6. Antonio Gramsci, *Selections from the Prison Notebooks*, pp.180-5. For discussions on Gramsci's concept of passive revolution, see Christine Buci-Glucksmann, 'State, Transition and Passive Revolution' in Mouffe, ed., *Gramsci and Social Theory*, pp.113-67; Buci-Glucksmann, *Gramsci and the State*, tr. David Fernbach (London: Lawrence and Wishart, 1980), pp.290-324; Anne Showstack Sassoon, 'Passive Revolution and the Politics of Reform' in Sassoon, ed., *Approaches to Gramsci* (London: Writers and Readers, 1982), pp.127-48.

7. Antonio Gramsci, *Selections from the Prison Notebooks*, pp.181-2.

8. Ibid., p.183.

9. Ibid., p.108.

10. Ibid., p.113.

11. Ibid., p.108.

12. Ibid., p.110.

13. Ibid., p.110.

14. Ibid., p.112.

15. Ibid., pp.314-5.

16. Ibid., p.293.

17. Ibid., p.227.

18. This kind of exercise in the history of ideas has now become much more acceptable than before in academic circles, not only because of the impact of hermeneutic philosophy and the writings of that diverse group of French intellectuals clubbed together under the ungainly label of 'post-structuralists', but also because of the many uncertainties even among Anglo-American professional philosophers regarding the 'givenness' of *a* scientific method. See for instance, Richard Rorty, *Philosophy and the Mirror of Nature* (Oxford: Basil Blackwell, 1980). It is only proper for me to acknowledge the influence on my thinking of the works of many of the former group of writers, in particular Hans-Georg Gadamer, Paul Ricoeur, Roland Barthes, Michel Foucault and Jacques Derrida. I cannot, of course, attempt here a systematic discussion of these writings or of the relation which they bear to the historical method of Marxism. But I must state that my intellectual attitude towards the relation between nationalism and the universalist claims of 'science' stems from a completely different source, namely, the cultural predicament of one whose practice of science means not only a separation from his own people but also invariably the intellectual legitimation of newer and ever more insidious forms of domination of the few over the many.

19. See, for instance, Quentin Skinner, 'Meaning and Understanding in the History of Ideas', *History and Theory*, 8 (1969), pp.3-53; Skinner, 'Some Problems in the Analysis of Political Thought and Action', *Political Theory*, 2 (1974), pp.277-303; John Dunn, 'The Identity of the History of Ideas' in P. Laslett, W.G. Runciman and Q. Skinner, eds., *Philosophy, Politics and Society*, Series IV (Oxford: Oxford University Press, 1972), pp.158-73; Dunn, 'Practising History and Social Science on "Realist" Assumptions' in C. Hookway and P. Pettit, eds., *Action and Interpretation: Studies in the Philosophy of the Social Sciences* (Cambridge: Cambridge University Press, 1978), pp.145-75.

3. The Moment of Departure: Culture and Power in the Thought of Bankimchandra

> ... the Bengali is a creature of his circumstances;
> circumstances do not come under his control.
> (*Kapālkuṇḍalā*, I, ch.8)

Bankimchandra Chattopadhyay (1838-94), novelist, satirist, and easily the most acclaimed man of letters in the Calcutta of his day,[1] was one of the first systematic expounders in India of the principles of nationalism. He was widely read in European literature, particularly in 19th century sociology and political economy, and was greatly influenced, according to his own admission, by positivism as well as utilitarianism. He wrote a great deal on social and political questions, using several literary forms. It makes no sense to try to present here anything like a fair assessment of the richness and complexity of his thought, often clothed in the colourful garb of banter and satire, subtly combining within a highly formal discursive prose the earthiness of popular colloquialisms, much of it quite untranslatable. All we can do here is concentrate on some of his essays dealing directly with the issues we have raised in the preceding chapters. Specifically, we look at the ways in which his thought relates culture to power in the particular context of a colonial country.

I

Let us begin with the question of power: why has India been a subject nation for such a long time? Bankim first considers one obvious answer to this question: because Indians lack physical strength and courage; because, as the Europeans always allege, the 'Hindoos' are 'effeminate'. Yet this answer is obviously false, because although the Hindus are notorious for their negligence in the writing of their own history, the accounts left behind by chroniclers accompanying the victorious Greek and Muslim armies speak of the bravery and strength of the Hindus. Even as recently as the early decades of the 19th century, the English had taken a beating from the Marathas and the Sikhs. The question is not, therefore, of the lack of strength or valour. There are two great reasons, Bankim thinks, for India being a subject nation. The first is that Indians lack a natural desire for liberty. Some Indians probably nurse a vague feeling that independence is better than subjection, but never has this feeling become a compelling desire; never have the majority of Indians fought for their liberty.

For more than three thousand years, Aryans have fought against Aryans, or Aryans against non-Aryans, or non-Aryans against non-Aryans — Magadh has fought Kanauj, Kanauj has fought Delhi, Delhi has fought Lahore, Hindus have battled against Pathans, Pathans against Mughals, Mughals against the English — all of these people have fought against one another and continually stoked the fires of war in this country. But all of these were battles among kings; the bulk of Hindu society has never fought for or against anyone. Hindu kings or the rulers of Hindustan have been repeatedly conquered by alien people, but it cannot be said that the bulk of Hindu society has ever been vanquished in battle, because the bulk of Hindu society has never gone to war.[2]

And this led directly to the second great reason for the subjection of India: the lack of solidarity in Hindu society. National solidarity, Bankim says, is crucially dependent on two kinds of attitudes. One is the conviction that what is good for every Hindu is good for me; that my opinions, my beliefs, my actions must be combined and made consistent with those of every other Hindu. The other attitude is a single-minded devotion to the interests of my nation, if necessary even at the cost of the interests of other nations. It is true that such an attitude leads to a lot of misery and bitter warfare, as the history of Europe clearly shows. But such are the realities of national feeling and the love of liberty. Hindus have always lacked this feeling and today, with diverse nationalities living in this country, separated by habitat, language, race and religion, national solidarity is completely absent.

However, argues Bankim, it is because of our contacts with the English that we have discovered for the first time the true basis of liberty and national solidarity. We know that the reason for our subjection does not lie in our lack of physical strength. We have seen in the examples of Shivaji and Ranjit Singh what can be achieved by the spirit of fraternity and united action. If only Hindus become desirous of liberty, if they can convince themselves of the value of liberty, they can achieve it.

Thus, Bankim's explanation of the subjection of India is not in terms of material or physical strength. It is an explanation in terms of *culture*. More specifically, it is an explanation which proceeds from a premise of cultural difference: an essential difference from all those attributes which make the European culturally equipped for power and for progress. Consequently, India, and the people of India, are defined as the 'Other' of the European. Sometimes it is the Bengali, sometimes the Hindu; sometimes Bankim is talking of the *bhāratvarṣīya*, the inhabitants of India. There is no attempt here to define the boundaries of the Indian nation *from within*. This definition of the Bengali, the Hindu or the Indian as the 'Other', the 'subject', is then extrapolated backwards into the historical past. In talking about the subjection of India, Bankim encapsulates into his conception of the cultural failure of the Indian people to face up to the realities of power a whole series of conquests dating from the first

55

Muslim invasions of India and culminating in the establishment of British rule. To Bankim, India has been a subject nation for seven centuries.

II

The crucial cultural attribute which, according to Bankim, stands out as the major reason for India's subjection is the Hindu attitude towards power. In a long essay on 'Sāṅkhya Philosophy',[3] he argues that the central philosophical foundation of the overwhelming part of religious beliefs in India, including Buddhism, lies in the philosophy of Sāṅkhya. And the chief characteristic of the philosophy is its emphasis on *vairāgya*.

> The present state of the Hindus is a product of this excessive other-worldliness. The lack of devotion to work which foreigners point out as our chief characteristic is only a manifestation of this quality. Our second most important characteristic — fatalism — is yet another form of this other-worldliness derived from the Sāṅkhya. It is because of this other-worldliness and fatalism that in spite of the immense physical prowess of the Indians, this land of the Aryans had come under Muslim rule. And it is for the same reason that India remains a subject country till this day. It is for the same reason again that social progress in this country slowed down a long time ago and finally stopped completely.[4]

Philosophically, the Sāṅkhya (which, incidentally, was the only system of Indian philosophy Bankim says he had studied in any depth up to this time in his life[5]) was 'perhaps the only system of belief known in the whole world which accepts a Revelation and rejects a God'. It was a thoroughly sceptical and atheistic philosophy which nonetheless asserted, perhaps not very sincerely, the ultimate authority of the Vedas. This specific combination of religion and philosophy had 'disastrous consequences'.

> These consequences must in every case be, that philosophy moving within the narrow circles of orthodoxy, would develop into systems of error; and the errors of national and sectarian creeds, which would otherwise die out of their own rottenness, would receive strength and life from the subtle and illusory arguments of philosophy. This mischievous tendency of an alliance between religion and philosophy, was never so conspicuous as in the case of the Sāṅkhya. The Sāṅkhya is remarkably sceptical in its tendency; many antiquated or contemporaneous errors were swept away by its merciless logic. Carried to its legitimate consequences, a wise scepticism might have contributed to the lasting benefit of the Hindú progress. And yet the Sāṅkhya is as great a mass of errors as any other branch of Hindú philosophy — even inferior, perhaps, to the Nyáya and Vaiśeshika in intrinsic worth. This was the result of its uniform display of a tendency to support the authority of the Vedas. God himself could be denied, but not the authority of the Vedas. There is every reason to believe that this veneration for the Vedas was by no means a very sincere feeling with the sceptical philosopher; but whether that feeling was sincere or hollow, the authority of the Vedas appears to have set the limits beyond which thought was not allowed to range.[6]

It is not as though the Sāṅkhya philosophers did not recognize the need for gaining a knowledge of the world. But the goal of knowledge was salvation.

'Knowledge is power': that is the slogan of Western civilisation. 'Knowledge is salvation' is the slogan of Hindu civilisation. The two peoples set out on the same road bound for two different goals. The Westerners have found power. Have we found salvation? There is no doubt that the results of our journeys have been dissimilar.

Europeans are devotees of power. That is the key to their advancement. We are negligent towards power: that is the key to our downfall. Europeans pursue a goal which they must reach in this world: they are victorious on earth. We pursue a goal which lies in the world beyond, which is why we have failed to win on earth. Whether we will win in the life beyond is a question on which there are differences of opinion.[7]

It will be noticed here that Bankim's critique of the state of religious beliefs in India during its period of subjection, and perhaps also the period of decline beginning a few centuries before its actual subjection, is founded on a specific conception of the relation between culture and power. Certain cultural values are more advantageous than others in the real-political world of power relationships. Those which are advantageous imply a certain rational evaluation of the importance of power in material life, and indeed of the material bases of power in society, and attempt to sustain and extend those bases. Other cultures do not make such a rational evaluation and are consequently thrown into subjection. The critique of Indian culture is here, in every way, a 'rationalist' critique, and so is the critique of Sāṅkhya philosophy.

The argument is further clarified in another article: here Bankim considers the allegation that the Bengalis are a weak people. Discussing several possible reasons as to why this should be so — the fertility of the land, the hot and humid climate, the food habits, customs such as child marriage, etc., Bankim does not find adequate scientific grounds for believing that these establish sufficient conditions for the continued physical weakness of a people. But whether or not these reasons are adequate, they can only point to the lack of physical strength of a people. Yet physical strength is not the same thing as force or power. Power, or the lack of it, is a social phenomenon; power results from the application on physical strength of four elements: enterprise, solidarity, courage and perseverance. The Bengalis as a people have always lacked these elements, which is why they are a powerless people. But these are cultural attributes; they can be acquired.

If ever (i) the Bengalis acquire a compelling desire for some national good, (ii) if this desire becomes compelling in every Bengali heart, (iii) if this compulsion becomes so great that people are prepared to stake their lives for it, and (iv) if this desire becomes permanent, then the Bengalis would certainly become a powerful people.[8]

The theoretical position implied in Bankim's discussion — and this is a position which recurs in much of his writing — involves, then, the following line of reasoning: 1) force or power is the basis of the state; 2) the liberty or subjection of a nation is ultimately a question of force or power; 3) but power is not something that is determined by material (environmental or technological) conditions; 4) power can be acquired by the cultivation of appropriate national–cultural values.

Let us stop for a moment and fix the location of this argument within our frame of reference. The entire mode of reasoning in Bankim involves an attempt to 'objectify'; the project is to achieve positive knowledge. The 'subject' is a scientific consciousness, distanced from the 'object' which is the Indian, the Bengali, the Hindu (it does not matter which, because all of them are defined in terms of the contraposition between the Eastern and the Western). The material is the archive — historical documents, literary texts, archaeological finds —and the archivist (helpless as he feels about this, there is nothing he can do about it!)[9] the Orientalist scholar — William Jones, H.H. Wilson, Thomas Colebrooke, Albrecht Weber, Friedrich Max Müller, and all the rest of them. Of course, he often quarrels with their interpretations — these Europeans do not really have a good enough knowledge of India — but when he does, it is always as another scientist with a superior command over the facts (or else, he is alleging that the European might have special reasons for misrepresenting the facts); he never questions the 'objectivity' of the facts themselves or that they could be 'objectively' represented. And the procedures for objective representation were, for him, laid down in the Great Science of Society of which the three greatest architects were Auguste Comte, John Stuart Mill and Herbert Spencer.

III

Bankim's method, concepts and modes of reasoning are completely contained within the forms of post-Enlightenment scientific thought. One major characteristic of this thought is its celebration of the principle of historicity as the essential procedure for acquiring 'objective' knowledge. The study of social institutions or beliefs, for instance, had to consist of a description of their own internal histories — of their origins and processes of evolution — just as the study of non-human or inanimate beings became the field of natural history. History, indeed, was seen as reflecting on its surface the scientific representation of the objective and changing world of being.

To Bankim this was axiomatic. In his mind, for instance, the self-awareness of a people consisted of the knowledge of its own history. One might indeed say that to him a nation existed in its history. Thus, his distress at what he saw as the ignorance of the Hindus of their own history, indeed their apathy towards it, and his anger at the 'falsifications' of Hindu history at the hands of foreign (including Muslim) historians, are hardly surprising. And his repeated exhortations to the Indian peoples for urgent efforts to 'discover' their true histories are entirely in keeping with this 'scientific' mode of thought.

When he attempted, for instance, to set down in one of his last books, *Krsnacaritra* (1886), a full statement of his ethical philosophy in the form of an appreciation of the character of Krishna, the first task he set for himself was to establish the historicity of the character. He accepted, of course, that Sanskrit literary texts consisted of an abundance of myths and legends, but this did not mean that they were entirely useless as historical sources. The accounts of Livy and Herodotus or Ferishta contained much that was patently mythical; yet they were still regarded as useful sources of history. And

> no matter what modern European critics may say, ancient Greeks or Romans did not regard Livy or Herodotus as unhistorical. On the other hand, there may well come a day when Gibbon or Froude will be dismissed as unhistorical. And despite the protests of modern critics, no history of Rome or Greece has yet been written without using Livy or Herodotus as sources.[10]

The fact was, of course, that the texts on the life of Krishna as handed down to the present day contained numerous additions, abridgements and recensions on the 'original', carried out by unknown and unidentifiable editors over a period of many hundreds of years. The first task, therefore, was to select out and brush aside these later alterations and reach the 'original historical account' of the life of Krishna. To do this Bankim devised several criteria, all of them strictly scientific and rational. Some of these criteria were formal and textual, having to do with continuity, stylistic consistency, uniformity of conception, and so on. But more important were the substantive criteria, because according to him, the formation of these texts as they now existed consisted of an original core of historical truth overlaid by subsequent layers of 'legends, fables and fantastic imaginings'. What is truly historical in a book such as the *Mahābhārata* must lie in its *original* text; the myths and fables were merely the dross of time. Therefore, if one followed the strict criterion of refusing to accept all 'unreal, impossible and supernatural events', it would become possible to extract the rationally acceptable historical core of the *Mahābhārata*.

It is a different matter altogether to judge whether Bankim performed this hermeneutic task with any reasonable degree of technical competence. The more important point is that he should have felt that a discourse on ethical principles, arguing in favour of the exemplariness of the character of Krishna as an ideal for modern man, *required* a demonstration of the historicity of Krishna. Equally important is the fact that all those attributes which, according to him, went to make the character of Krishna an ideal for modern man were the ones which he showed to be part of the 'original historical core' of the *Mahābhārata*, and all those which make the Krishna of folk belief 'an object of contempt and ridicule in the eyes of educated Indians and foreigners' the creations of fable-makers. History, to him, was the receptacle of rational truth; conversely, the validation of truth had to lie in a rational demonstration of its historicity.

It is also significant that when Bankim quarrels with the Orientalists about their assessment of the quality of the sources of Indian history and the way these should be used, he does so from a thoroughly rationalist position. From that position, he accuses his adversaries of ethnocentric bias and racial prejudices which, when they were not plain ignorant, deflected them from a strictly rational examination of the evidence. Albrecht Weber, for instance, had argued that the *Mahābhārata* could not have existed in the 4th century BC because Megasthenes did not mention it in his accounts. This, Bankim says, is 'deliberate fraud' on the part of Weber, because Weber knew perfectly well that only fragments of the original accounts of Megasthenes had survived, and in any case it was sheer prejudice to place such overwhelming reliance on Megasthenes's evidence merely because he was European.

> Many Hindus have travelled to Germany and have returned to write books about that country. We have not come across the name of Mr Weber in any of their accounts. Shall we conclude then that Mr Weber does not exist?[11]

In one of the episodes in *Kamalākānter Daptar*, that brilliant product of Bankim's penchant for 'nonsense [which] I can create ad libitum',[12] the narrator Kamalakanta, a sparkling combination of acerbic wit and opium-induced wisdom, talks to the Plateetud bird which had flown from Europe to the warm climes of Bengal in order to preach its profound rallying cry: 'Plateetud, plateetud!' The bird explains to Kamalakanta its own origins: how it used to live near the shores of the Black Sea; only then it was not a bird but a pig, wallowing in the swamps off the coast. And then some fierce two-legged beasts called humans arrived and mistook the pigs for eels. What follows must go down as one of the earliest rationalist critiques of structuralist anthropology, written fifty years before Lévi-Strauss was born!

> *I*. How could they mistake pigs for eels?
> *Bird*. Well, pigs scavenge in the swamps, so do eels. Therefore, pigs and eels are the same thing.
> I knew my Whateley's *Logic*. Immediately I objected, 'But that's a fallacy of the undistributed middle!' 'Tut, tut,' the bird said. 'Fallacy of the undistributed middle! That's logic! This is Antiquities! What does logic have to do with Antiquities? Study Antiquities for a few days, read the books of Mr Weber, and you'll never ask questions like that!'[13]

What Bankim identifies here as an incorrect or incomplete application of the principles of rational scientific investigation, he can explain only as a case of racial prejudice.

> It is impossible for one whose ancestors were only the other day barbarians roaming the forests of Germany to accept the reality of India's glorious past. Consequently, he is ever keen to prove that civilisation in India is only a recent phenomenon.[14]
> . . . These pundits of Europe and America . . . attempt to construct historical theories out of ancient Sanskrit texts, but they cannot accept that the subject and powerless people of India were ever civilised, or that this civilisation dates from very ancient times.[15]

Later in his life, he formulated the problem as one of an irreconcilable difference in points of view, arising out of the fact that Hindu scriptures or religious practices had a significance for European scholars that was fundamentally different from its significance for Indians.

European scholars, like Professor Max Müller, have been very eloquent on the importance of the study of the Vedas, but their point of view is exclusively the European point of view, and fails to represent the vastly superior interest Vedic studies possess of us, natives of the country. The Vedas are nothing less than *the basis of our entire religious and social organisation.*[16]

He even brought up the question of the fundamental impossibility of adequate translation in cross-cultural understanding.

Let the translator be the profoundest Sanskrit scholar in the world — let the translation be the most accurate that language can make it, still the disparity between the original and the translation will be, for practical purposes, very wide. The reason is obvious. You can translate a word by a word, but behind the word is an idea, the thing which the word denotes, and this idea you cannot translate, if it does not exist among the people in whose language you are translating. . . . And who is best qualified to expound the ideas and conceptions which cannot be translated — the foreigner who has nothing corresponding to them in the whole range of his thoughts and experiences, or the native who was nurtured in them from his infancy? . . . [A European] will fail in arriving at a correct comprehension of Hinduism, as — I say it most emphatically — *as every other European who has made the attempt has failed.*[17]

Thus, he would assert: 'A single hour of study of the Sakuntala by a Bengali writer, Baboo Chandranath Bose, is worth all that Europe has had to say on Kalidasa, not excepting even Goethe's well-known eulogy.'[18] Drawn into debate, Bankim was even prepared to question the sovereignty of European knowledge, to challenge

that monstrous claim to omniscience, which certain Europeans — an extremely limited number happily — put forward for themselves. No knowledge is to them true knowledge unless it has passed through the sieve of European criticism. All coin is false coin unless it bears the stamp of a Western mint. Existence is possible to nothing which is hid from their searching vision. Truth is not truth, but noisome error and rank falsehood, if it presumes to exist outside the pale of European cognisance.[19]

Yet, even at this point, Bankim's critique of Orientalist knowledge is not epistemological, or even methodological. His charge is still one of prejudice, from which 'certain Europeans — an extremely limited number happily' suffered. It does not occur to Bankim that these distortions in Orientalist knowledge might actually be a much more fundamental and systematic feature of the *content* of many of the theories which made up the rational sciences of society, even in those aspects not directly related to the subject of Indian civilization. His critique of Orientalist scholarship remains at the level of technical criteria, showing how *a priori* prejudices could vitiate a truly objective enquiry. It does not extend to questioning the cognitive or explanatory status of the framework of concepts and theoretical relations which defined the science of society. Here he accepted entirely the fundamental methodological assumptions, the primary concepts and the general theoretical orientation of 19th century positivist sociology and utilitarian political economy. He wholly shared the Enlightenment belief in the perfectibility of man and agreed with the positivist view of looking at the history of social institutions as evolving from less developed and imperfect forms to more developed and perfect ones. 'In worldly matters I accept the teachings of science in demonstrating that the world is evolving gradually from an incomplete and undeveloped state towards a complete and developed form.'[20]

He accepted, for instance, that free trade was a more developed form of economic organization than anything that had existed previously, including protectionism, because it represented a rational scheme of division of labour and was beneficial to all parties involved in economic exchange.

> The gravely erroneous theory of protectionism has been superseded by the modern theory of free trade, a feat for which Bright and Cobden will always be remembered in history. Napoleon III has now established this theory as the basis of official policy in France. Yet many in Europe still hold on to the earlier erroneous beliefs. Is it surprising then that ordinary people in our country should also believe in this mistaken theory? If you wish to learn what harm was caused to Europe by protection, read Buckle. If you wish to know why the theory is false, read Mill.[21]

Trade between Britain and India, he thought, had led to an expansion of agricultural activity in India.

> What we buy from England we pay for by exporting agricultural commodities, such as rice, silk, cotton, jute, indigo, etc. It goes without saying that as trade expands, the demand for such agricultural commodities will also increase by the same proportion. As a result, agriculture will expand in this country. Ever since the establishment of British rule, the trade of this country has increased, leading to a demand for more exportable agricultural products and hence to an expansion of agriculture.[22]

But had this not also meant a destruction of indigenous manufacturing, as many people in Bengal were already alleging? Perhaps, is Bankim's reply, but this did not necessarily mean that Indians were becoming less prosperous. If it was becoming difficult for Indian weavers to compete with imported textiles, the logical course to adopt would be for them to shift to those activities which were expanding as a result of this trade.

> The weaving trade may have collapsed, but why does not the weaver move to another occupation? . . . He may not be able to feed himself by weaving cloth, but there is no reason why he cannot do so by cultivating rice. Social theorists have shown that the rate of return from all productive activities is, on the average, equal. If the weaver had earned five rupees a month by weaving, he could do the same by cultivating rice instead.[23]

The real reason weavers were not seizing the opportunities opened up by expanded agricultural activities was cultural: the inertia of backward and outmoded social customs.

> People in our country are reluctant to give up their hereditary trades. This is unfortunate for our weavers, but it does not mean a loss of wealth for the country. The import of foreign cloth results in a corresponding increase in agricultural

incomes — this is inevitable. What happens is merely that this income goes not to the weaver but to somebody else. The misery of the weaver does not indicate a loss of national wealth.[24]

Thus, Bankim's devotion to what he regarded as the fundamental principles of a rational science of economics makes it impossible for him to arrive at a critique of the political economy of colonial rule, even when the evidence from which such a critique may have proceeded was, in a sense, perfectly visible to him. He could not, for instance, formulate a problem in which the axiomatic equality of all exchange relations may have been called into question, in spite of the fact that late in his life he admitted that substantial wealth was probably being transferred to Britain in the form of payments to colonial administrators for which India was getting nothing in return.[25] He was aware of the fact of deindustrialization, but did not possess, and could not construct for himself, a conceptual apparatus by which this could be interpreted in any way other than free trade, increasing specialization and division of labour, and hence inevitable progress and prosperity. It is indeed ironic that his infinitely less sophisticated and obviously prejudiced antagonists in the journal *Samājdarpan*, who thought that Bengal was being impoverished by the trade policies of the colonial government, were, in a quite unreflective perceptual sense, correct.

On agrarian matters, again, Bankim's keen and sympathetic perception of the poverty of the majority of Bengal's peasantry is made sensible to him only after it is filtered through the conceptual grid of 19th century political economy. It is the Permanent Settlement which he thinks is to blame, but only because it was made with a class of unproductive landlords.

> We consider the Settlement of Cornwallis erroneous, unjust and harmful, not because the English relinquished their rights to the land and gave it to the people of this country or because they gave up the right to increase the revenue — this we do not think can be criticised, because it was wise, just and conducive to social welfare. Our argument is that the Permanent Settlement should have been made not with the zamindar but with the tenant.[26]

It was a land settlement which could only have worked if the landlords were kind and sympathetic to their tenants, but this of course was an unrealistic expectation, and what had happened to the Bengal peasantry was only the result of the greed and rapacity of a certain section of landlords, instances of which he catalogued at great length in his essay on 'The Bengal Peasantry' and later incorporated into his book *Sāmya* [Equality]. It was idle, and perhaps impolitic, he thought, to now attempt to reverse the Permanent Settlement. The only course open was for landlords to mend their ways.

> We request the British Indian Association to pay heed to this task. If they can control the wicked landlords, they will do a service to the country which will be remembered in history for all time to come . . . If this is not done, there is no hope for the prosperity of Bengal.[27]

That is all he could suggest as a remedy for the poverty of Bengal's peasants.

Besides the rapacity of landlords who sought to skim off by force every available pice out of a submissive and helpless peasantry, the other great reason for the misery of the peasants was — and this again is part and parcel of Malthusian political economy — 'the increase in population'.[28] Bankim narrates an imaginary conversation with Ramdhan Pod, a typical Bengal peasant, who announces to him his plans for his son's marriage.

> I asked him, 'You cannot feed the mouths you've already collected around you. Why do you want to add more?' . . . Ramdhan got angry. He said, 'Who doesn't want to get his son married? Everyone does, whether he can feed himself or not'. I said, 'But is it good for someone who can't feed his family, to get his son married?' Ramdhan said, 'The whole world does it'. I said, 'Not the whole world, Ramdhan. Only in this country. There is no more ignorant country in the world'. Ramdhan replied, 'Why blame me when the whole country is at fault?' How do I convince someone as ignorant as this? I said, 'If the whole country hangs itself, will you do the same?'[29]

Reasoning from within his rational world of thought, made up of received concepts and objective criteria of validation, there was no way in which Bankim could arrive at anything other than a positive assessment of the overall social effects of British rule in India. Comparing the colonial order in India with a historical reconstruction of the Brahmanical order, he had to admit that British rule had established a fairer and more impersonal legal and judicial system, greater access — at least in principle — for the lower castes to positions of power and status, and had made available the means for Indians to acquire the benefits of Western science and literature. All this had regenerated the conditions for social progress. The position of the upper classes may have declined some-what because of the loss of liberty, but as far as the lower classes were concerned — well, 'for one who is oppressed, it makes no difference whether the oppressor is one's compatriot or whether he is foreign'.[30] If anything, the position of the lower classes in India had improved slightly under British rule.

> Some may become displeased with me and ask, 'Are you then saying that liberty or subjection makes no difference? Why then does every nation on earth fight for its liberty?' To these critics we can only reply, 'We are not engaged in settling that question. We are a subject people, and will remain that way for a long time to come: let us not get involved in fruitless debate. All that we set out to discuss was whether ancient Indians were in general better off because of their liberty than the people of modern India. We have concluded that the condition of the upper classes such as Brahmans and Kshatriyas has declined, but that of Sudras or ordinary people has improved.'[31]

IV

Bankim indeed undertakes the same classificatory project as the Orientalist, and arrives at precisely the same typologies under which the Oriental (the Hindu, the Bengali) is stamped with an essentialist character signifying in every aspect his difference from modern Western man.

What Bankim does not accept, however, is the immutability of this character.

There is, he argues, a subjectivity that can *will* a transformation of this culturally determined character. This is the National Will, which can be summoned into existence by the nation acting collectively. But how? How are these national–cultural values to be cultivated? One way is to imitate those who have demonstrated their capacities as powerful and freedom-loving nations. A perennial problem this has been in all nationalist thinking: how does one accept what is valuable in another's culture without losing one's own cultural identity? Rajnarayan Bose, in a public address entitled 'Then and Now' (1874), had castigated the newly educated classes of Bengal for aping English manners and life-styles. This was only one in a whole series of attacks on overt Westernization which was in the 19th century the staple of social satire in the popular literature and the visual and performing arts of Bengal. But Bankim's answer to the question is curiously half-hearted and ambiguous. 'Is all imitation bad?', he asks, in an uncharacteristically gentle rejoinder to Rajnarayan's speech.

> That cannot be. One cannot learn except by imitation. Just as children learn to speak by imitating the speech of adults, to act by imitating the actions of adults, so do uncivilised and uneducated people learn by imitating the ways of the civilised and the educated. Thus it is reasonable and rational that Bengalis should imitate the English.[32]

Of course, mere imitation can never produce excellence. That is the product of genius. But imitation is always the first step in learning. It is true that there have been nations such as the Greeks who have become civilised on their own, but that is a matter of protracted evolution. It is much quicker to learn from others who are more advanced.

> Such imitation is natural, and its consequences can be most beneficial. There are many who are angry at our imitating English habits in food and dress; what would they say of the English imitating the French in their food and dress? Are the English any less imitative than Bengalis? At least we imitate the rulers of our nation; who do the English imitate?[33]

But almost as soon as Bankim has made this characteristic thrust of logic, he feels compelled to backtrack: 'Of course, we agree that it may not be entirely desirable for the Bengalis to be as imitative as they now are.'[34]

We can see Bankim's predicament here. He accepts that the reasons for India's subjection, and those for her backwardness, are to be found in her culture. He accepts that there exist historically demonstrated models embodying superior cultural values. His project is to initiate 'progress' by transforming the backward culture of his nation. But does this not necessarily imply losing the essential character of his culture which, within the thematic of nationalism, is defined in opposition to Western culture? Bankim does not have an answer.

There did, however, exist an answer, and Bankim was to find it in the later years of his life. This is the answer which he spent many pages in explaining in his last books. It is also an answer which is characteristic of nationalist thought at its moment of departure.

The answer can be found within the thematic and problematic of nationalist thought. It does no violence to its theoretical framework where the thematic of

Orientalism is dominant, while it still provides a specific subjectivity to the East in which it is active, autonomous and undominated.

The superiority of the West was in the materiality of its culture. The West had achieved progress, prosperity and freedom because it had placed Reason at the heart of its culture. The distinctive culture of the West was its science, its technology and its love of progress. But culture did not consist only of the material aspect of life. There was the spiritual aspect too, and here the European Enlightenment had little to contribute. In the spiritual aspect of culture, the East was superior — and hence, undominated.

This answer did not conflict in any way with the fundamental classificatory scheme of Orientalist thought. All it did was to assert a cultural domain of superiority for the East and, in time, to tie this assertion with the national struggle against Western political domination.

Let us see how Bankim formulates this answer. In 1888 he wrote a long tract entitled *The Theory of Religion* in the form of a dialogue between a teacher and his pupil, in which he set out his concept of *anuśīlan* or practice. *Anuśīlan*, he said, was a 'system of culture', more complete and more perfect than the Western concept of culture as propounded by Comte or, more recently, by Matthew Arnold. The Western concept was fundamentally agnostic, and hence incomplete.[35] *Anuśīlan* was based on the concept of *bhakti* which, in turn, implied the unity of knowledge and duty. There were three kinds of knowledge: knowledge of the world, of the self and of God. Knowledge of the world consisted of mathematics, astronomy, physics and chemistry, and these one would have to learn from the West. Knowledge of the self meant biology and sociology, and these too one would have to learn from the West. Finally, knowledge of God, and in this field the Hindu *śāstra* contained the greatest human achievements — the *Upaniṣad*, the *darśana*, the *Purāṇa*, the *itihāsa,* but principally the *Gītā*.[36]

But mere knowledge would not create *bhakti*; for that, knowledge would have to be united with duty. Duty meant the performance of acts without the expectation of reward. To eat is a duty; so is the defence of one's country. But these acts had to be performed because they should be performed, not because they might produce beneficial results.[37] This non-possessive, non-utilitarian concept of duty was the core of *dharma* or religion.

Teacher. The day the European industries and sciences are united with Indian *dharma*, man will be god . . .
Pupil. Will such a day ever come in the life of man?
Teacher. It will if you Indians are prepared to act. It is in your hands. If you will it, you can become master and leader of the whole world. If you do not aspire to it, then all my words are in vain.[38]

In fact, that day was not far off.

Teacher. Soon you will see that with the spread of the doctrine of pure *bhakti*, the Hindus will gain new life and become powerful like the English at the time of Cromwell or the Arabs under Muhammad.[39]

Here then was a cultural ideal which retained what was thought to be distinctively Indian, while subsuming what was valuable in the culture of the West. The aim was to produce the complete and perfect man — learned, wise, agile, religious and refined — a better man than the merely efficient and prosperous Westerner.

But once again, the striking fact here is not so much the distinction between the material and the spiritual spheres of culture. What is remarkable is that this distinction should be defended on the most thorough rationalist grounds afforded by 19th century European philosophy. There are two planks on which Bankim builds his defence. One was the rationalist critique of Christianity which Bankim uses to demolish the claims of European religion as a suitable moral philosophy for man living in a modern scientific age and, by implication, to expose the irrationality of reformist attempts to 'Christianize' in some form or other the popular religious practices and beliefs in Indian society. The second referred to the contemporary philosophical debates in Europe about the finite limits of empirical science which Bankim employs to demonstrate the rational validity of a suitable philosophy of spirit and then to turn this argument around to show the much greater accordance of a purified Hindu philosophy of spirit with the rational scientific temper of the modern age. Bankim advances some strikingly ingenious arguments on both these points, and it is worth looking into some of them in detail in order to appreciate the subtle and immensely complex interplay between the thematic and the problematic in some of the philosophically most sophisticated variants of nationalist thought.

Bankim spelled out one part of the argument in an essay which was originally entitled 'Mill, Darwin and Hindu Religion' when it was first published in 1875 in *Baṅgadarśan*, and later changed to 'What Science Has to Say About the [Hindu] Trinity' when it was reprinted in his collected essays. Here Bankim considers the common Hindu conception of Brahmā, Viṣṇu and Maheśvara — Creator, Preserver and Destroyer — as the three distinct forms of the Divine, and asks how far this conception accords with the findings of modern scientific investigations. For a start, he takes the three posthumously published essays of J.S. Mill on religion[40] in which Mill assesses the validity of the 'intelligent creator' argument for the existence of an omnipotent, omniscient and all-merciful God. Mill argues that if the evidence for the existence of the omniscient creator lies in the massive intricacy of the skills involved in the act of creation, then the obvious imperfections of the products of creation — susceptibility to injury and pain, mortality, decay — would seem to militate against the creator's omniscience. Of course, it could be argued that it is not a lack of omniscience, but rather certain limits to his powers which result in these imperfections in God's creation. Here, Mill advanced two explanations, both of which he held in different periods of his life. The first is the argument that God was not a creator, but only a constructor, working on material which was already in existence, and it was the imperfection of those materials which have resulted in the imperfections in the final products of creation. This, therefore, saves both the omniscient and the omnipotent qualities of God, but reduces him from the role of creator to that of a mere constructor. The other argument is that there is another power distinct from God which acts as an impediment to his actions, and it is as an effect of this antagonistic power that imperfections appear in the acts of creation. Mills' arguments, therefore, raise considerable doubts about the existence of an omniscient and omnipotent creator; moreover, they indicate the existence of two distinct forces — one, the preserver, and the other, the destroyer.

But what about the creator? Here Bankim brings in the results of Darwin's researches on evolution. Darwin had shown that the powers underlying creation cannot ensure survival; many more creatures are born in nature than are able to survive. Hence a principle of natural selection had to operate in order to ensure that those who were the fittest would survive. This scientific principle could be interpreted to imply the existence of two distinct forces in nature — one, the creator, and the other, the preserver. It could, of course, be objected that this was not the implication at all. There was no need to think of the creator and the preserver as distinct entities. The principle of natural selection could easily be interpreted as the consequence of the acts of a destructive force which impeded the acts of the creator who was at the same time the preserver. But this argument is fallacious, because it requires one to believe in an omniscient creator–preserver who creates much more than he knows can be preserved. It is much more logical to conceive of a creator whose sole intention is to create, a preserver whose sole intention is to preserve, and a destroyer who seeks to destroy what has been created.

Having advanced this argument, Bankim then establishes very clearly what he thinks its cognitive status is in relation to an empiricist epistemology. In the first place, he says this argument does not prove the existence of God. It was, therefore, open to one to believe in God in the absence of an empirical proof either in favour or against his existence. If one did believe in God, however, the question would arise of the nature or form of the Divine. It is as a reply to this question that the argument establishes the logical accordance of the Hindu conception of the Trinity with the findings of modern science. Second, the argument does not assert that the founders of the Hindu religion had these scientific considerations in mind when they conceived of the Trinity. Third, although the argument establishes a natural basis for the religious belief in the Trinity, it does not purport to be a scientific proof of the existence of the Trinity, nor does it justify a belief in their existence in tangible physical forms. What the argument does imply, however is the following:

> it is true that there is no scientific proof of the existence of the Trinity. But it must be admitted that in comparison with Christianity, the religion followed by those great practitioners of science, the European peoples, the Hindu worship of the Trinity is far more natural and in accordance with scientific theories. The worship of the Trinity may not be founded in science, but it is not in opposition to it. On the other hand, Mill's arguments have shown conclusively that the Christian belief in an omnipotent, omniscient and all-merciful God is entirely contrary to scientific principles. The Hindu philosophies of *karma* or *māyā* are far more consistent with science.
>
> Science is showing at every step that there exists everywhere in this universe

an infinite, inconceivable and inscrutable power — it is the cause of all being, the inner spirit of the external world. Far be it for us to deny the existence of this great force; on the contrary, we humbly pay our respects to it.[41]

The second argument which Bankim uses to defend a rational philosophy of spirit is based on the notion of finite limits to positive knowledge. He develops this argument in the course of his commentary on the *Gītā*. Science, he says, admits of two sorts of proof: one, direct sense–perception and two, inference based on sense–perception. Neither is sufficient to prove the existence of the soul. Hence, empirical science is incapable of constructing a true philosophy of spirit.

It cannot, because it is beyond the power of science. One can only go as far as one is able. The diver tied by a rope to his boat can only search the bottom of the sea as far as his rope will permit him; it is beyond his powers to gather all the treasures which the sea holds. Science is tied to its epistemic leash; how can it find a philosophy of spirit which lies beyond its range of proof? Where science cannot reach, it has no privilege: it can consider itself beholden by resting on the lowest steps of that stairway which leads up to the higher reaches. To look for scientific proof where it cannot apply is a fundamentally mistaken search.[42]

Scientists could object here and say that since only empirical proof provides valid basis of knowledge, all we can say about the existence of the soul is that we neither know that it exists nor that it does not. Only a thoroughly agnostic position would be consistent with science.

To this, Bankim says, there can be two answers: one is provided in Indian philosophy which admits two other kinds of proof, namely, analogy and revelation. Analogy, we now know from the findings of science, is a very uncertain basis of knowledge and can lead to numerous errors. Revelation, if one accepts it as a valid basis of knowledge, can eliminate all uncertainty since, unlike human perception or inference, God can never be wrong. However, revelation can only be accepted by the believer; a scientist can hardly be expected to admit it as a method of proof. The second answer, however, has been given in German philosophy. Kant has argued that besides phenomenal knowledge arising out of sense–perception or inference based on perception, there is also a transcendental knowledge based on concepts which are true in themselves. Of course, Kant's philosophy is not universally accepted.

However, I am obliged to state here what I, in accordance with my own knowledge and beliefs, consider true. I firmly believe that if all one's mental faculties are suitably developed, the knowledge of this philosophy of spirit becomes transcendentally true.
 . . . I have engaged in this extended discussion because many use the findings of a limited and imperfect science to ridicule the philosophy of spirit. They ought to know that the philosophy of spirit is beyond the limits of Western science, not opposed to it.[43]

V

The contrast with Christianity also brings out another crucial aspect of Bankim's philosophical system: the centrality of a rational philosophy of *power* within an entire moral project of national regeneration. In *Kṛṣṇacaritra*, Bankim discusses the rival claims of Buddha, Christ and Krishna as ideal characters. It is true, he says, that Krishna's life does not show the same concern for redeeming the fallen as do the lives of Jesus or Gautama. But the latter were men whose sole occupation was the preaching of religion — a most noble occupation, and Gautama and Jesus both revealed themselves in that occupation as great human beings. But their lives could hardly serve as complete ideals for all men, because the truly ideal character must retain its ideal quality for all men of all occupations.

> The true fulfilment of human life consists of the fullest and most consistent development of all human faculties. He whose life shows this full and consistent development is the ideal man. We cannot see it in Christ; we can in Sri Krishna. If the Roman Emperor had appointed Jesus to govern the Jews, would he have succeeded? No, because the requisite faculties were not developed in him . . . Again, suppose the Jews had risen in revolt against Roman oppression and elected Jesus to lead them in their war of independence, what would Jesus have done? He had neither the strength nor the desire for battle. He would have said, 'Render unto Caesar what is due to Caesar', and walked away. Krishna too had little taste for war. But war was often justified in religion. In cases of just war, Krishna would agree to engage in it. When he engaged in war, he was invincible . . . Krishna is the true ideal for man. The Hindu ideal is superior to the Christian ideal . . .
>
> Krishna himself was householder, diplomat, warrior, law-giver, saint and preacher; as such, he represents a complete human ideal for all these kinds of people . . . We cannot appreciate the comprehensiveness of the Hindu ideal by reducing it to the imperfect standards of the Buddhist or Christian ideals of mercy and renunciation.[44]

What, in fact, had happened in Europe was a complete divorce between its religion and its political practice. Europe's religion idealizes the humble, peace-loving and merciful renunciator. Yet its politics is the battlefield of violent forces wholly dedicated to the amoral pursuit of worldly goods. A similar fall had occurred in Indian society too, from the supreme ideal represented by the Krishna of the *Mahābhārata* to the Krishna celebrated in popular cults and festivities. What was needed above all for a national regeneration in India was the re-establishment of a harmonious unity of religion and politics, harmony between a comprehensive ethical ideal and the practice of power.

Bankim then brings up what he thinks is the central problem in the field of law and politics: the establishment of a criterion based on a judicious combination of force and mercy. The two are opposed in their consequences. A show of mercy to all offenders would ultimately lead to the destruction of social life. On the other hand, a society based entirely on force would reduce human life to a state of unmitigated bestiality. Modern and civilized Europe had hardly succeeded in finding the right balance between the two. The politics of modern Europe had overwhelmed its religion, which is why mercy had disappeared from European life and force reigned supreme in every sphere. In the Udyogaparva of the *Mahābhārata*, however, Krishna raises precisely this question: the right combination of force and mercy. Faced with the dilemma, the strong prefer a solution based on force and the weak appeal for mercy. But what is the answer for one who is both powerful and compassionate? That would be the ideal answer, and Krishna provides it in the Udyogaparva.

Bankim's interpretation of these passages in the *Mahābhārata* strongly emphasises a concept of duty which embodies what Bankim regards as a rational as well as an ethical philosophy of power. One element here is the notion of moral right.

> I will not desire a paradise given to the pursuit of immoral pleasures. But at the same time, I will not relinquish to the swindler a single grain of what is morally due to me. If I do so, I may not harm myself too much, but I will be guilty of the sin of adopting a path that will bring ruin upon society.[45]

Another element consists of the notions of rightful self-defence and just war.

> It is moral to wage war in defence of myself and of others. To shy away from doing so is grave immorality. We, the people of Bengal, are bearing the consequences of our immorality for seven hundred years.[46]

But self-defence and just war are totally opposed to the European conceptions of conquest and glory.

> Apart from the bloodthirsty demons who pursue glory, anyone else will realise that there is only a small difference between *glorie* and theft: the conqueror is a great robber, others are petty thieves.[47]

And here Bankim adds with unconcealed disingenuousness:

> Of course, we are told that there exist other considerations when foreign lands are conquered for the good of the aliens. I am unable to judge this question, because I do not claim to be an expert in politics.[48]

In any case, moral philosophers would agree in principle that it is ethically right to defend oneself against small as well as big thieves.

> The English name for self-defence against petty theft is Justice, while defence against the great robber is called Patriotism. The Indian name for both is *dharma*.[49]

The third element is the concept of *ahiṃsā* or non-violence, but it is a concept entirely in keeping with the ideas of moral right, self-defence and just war. *Ahiṃsā* does not enjoin one to abhor violence at all times and under all circumstances. It is impossible to conduct even the ordinary acts of human living without in some form or other doing violence to other creatures. With every drink of water we gulp down a million microscopic germs; every step we take, we trample under our feet a thousand little creatures. If it is said that these are unintended acts of violence, then many other instances can be given where conscious violence is the only protection to life. When a tiger prepares to spring upon me, I must pull the trigger as quickly as possible because if I do not destroy it, it will destroy me. There are situations where violence is moral. The main consideration here is the following:

> the supreme moral duty is to refrain from violence except when it is demanded by *dharma*. To use violence to prevent one who does violence is not immoral; on the contrary, it is the highest moral duty.[50]

However, the duty of non-violence, i.e. refraining from violence except when morally justified, is a higher duty than considerations such as honesty or truth. That is to say, there are situations where it is moral to utter falsehood in order to avoid unjustified violence. Bankim is particularly harsh here on Westernized moralists who pretend that there can be nothing more precious than honesty and who regard any compromise with that principle a licence for chicanery and deviousness. In the first place, Bankim says, nowhere in the public life of Europe is honesty given that kind of privilege: the entire corpus of Western jurisprudence shows, for instance, that a murderer is treated as a much greater offender than a liar. Second, such adulation, whether hypocritical or merely sentimental, of honesty and plain-speaking is precisely the result of the divorce between religious ideals and political practice which is the hallmark of European civilization today.

> If there is any moralist who says, 'Kill if need be, but do not lie', then we say to him, 'Keep your religion to yourself. Let India remain unacquainted with such a hellish religion.'[51]

The fourth important element in the concept of duty is the principle of control over the senses. Bankim is very careful here to distinguish this principle from both asceticism and puritanism. The philosophy of *dharma* is not an ascetic philosophy. It does not advocate the renunciation of sensual pleasure. It is a worldly philosophy which makes it a duty to achieve control over the senses. On the other hand, unlike puritanism, it does not set up a moral ideal as a result of which human life is constantly torn by an unnatural, and irreconcilable, opposition between sensual pleasure and spiritual salvation. Puritanism is opposed to sensual pleasure: the *dharma* of the *Gītā* advocates neither desire nor abhorrence: '... no room for hypocrisy here'.[52]

Bankim's concept of *dharma* attempts to reconcile a philosophy of spirit with a rational doctrine of power. In the process, the interplay between the thematic and the problematic of nationalist thought results in a curious transposition of the supposed relation between a puritan ethic and the rationalization of social life in the modern age. Bankim's nationalism leads him to the claim that a purified and regenerated Hindu ideal is far superior as a rational philosophy of life than anything that Western religion or philosophy has to offer.

VI

We have in Bankim a reversal of the Orientalist problematic, but within the same general thematic. It is only in this sense that nationalist thought is opposed to colonialist (Orientalist) thought. Bankim then seeks a specific subjectivity for the nation, but within an essentialist typology of cultures in which this specificity can never be truly historical. Within the domain of thought thus defined, however, it seems a valid answer. The West has a superior culture, but only partially; spiritually, the East is superior. What is needed, now, is the creation of a cultural ideal in which the industries and the sciences of the West can be learnt and emulated while retaining the spiritual greatness of Eastern culture. This is the national–cultural project at its moment of departure.

An elitism now becomes inescapable. Because the act of cultural synthesis can, in fact, be performed only by a supremely cultivated and refined intellect. It is a project of national–cultural regeneration in which the intelligentsia leads and the nation follows. The national–cultural ideal of the complete and perfect man was to be aspired for and approximated by practice, that is, *anuśīlan*. And it was not likely that large masses of people would reach this perfection. Bankim states this quite clearly: 'I do not entertain much hope at this time that the ordinary Hindu would understand the religion of *anuśīlan*.' But, 'a national character is built out of the national religion . . . I do expect that if intellectuals accept this religion, a national character will finally be built.'[53]

Bankim's doctrine of power, in fact, drew him towards a singularly elitist project for a new national politics. Compared to the various forms of nationalist political movements in 20th century India, Bankim's ideas were, of course, much less clearly specified in organizational terms. There was little in them from which one could derive anything by way of a nationalist political programme. But in accordance with the fundamental unity in his conception of power between a doctrine of force and the need for an organic moral authority incorporated into a national religion or culture, he became an unsparing opponent of the principal form of elite-nationalist politics of his times, viz. social reform through the medium of the legislative institutions of the colonial state. It is not as though he disagreed with the reformers' critique of various Hindu customs and practices; in fact, he seldom did. But he vehemently questioned both the mode of reasoning employed by the reformers and their means for achieving the reform. Relentlessly, he poured scorn and ridicule on their attempts, on the one hand, to persuade British administrators to legislate on social questions by appealing to enlightened reason and rationality, and on the other, to neutralize conservative opinion by a highly selective interpretation of Hindu scriptures in order to show that the reforms were sanctioned by the *śāstra*. This he thought hypocritical, because it implied a wholly opportunistic ambivalence with regard to the moral foundations of reform — rationality for some, scriptural infallibility for others. Moreover, and somewhat paradoxically in the context of his general sympathy for utilitarian social theory, he had little faith in the efficacy of legislation to bring about a genuine reform of social institutions. Reform, in order to succeed, must flow from a new moral consensus in society. To the extent that this new morality was an inevitable consequence of changes in the basic economic and social conditions of living in the modern age, a new pattern of beliefs and practices would emerge on its own, and reform by legislation would become redundant. This was, for instance, Bankim's reading of the issue of polygamy. It was clear, he thought, that polygamy, to the extent that it was ever common in Hindu society, was rapidly on the decline. This decline had come about without state legislation or injunctions by religious leaders. Given the changes in social conditions, its ultimate disappearance was inevitable. Consequently, he thought there was little difference between the efforts of reformers like Vidyasagar and those of Don Quixote.[54]

More fundamentally, however, Bankim's conception of power, unlike the reformers' faith in the general accordance of British rule of law with the universal principles of reason and rationality, could hardly allow him to disregard the great and unbridgeable gulf which separated the colonial state from the rest of Indian society. The colonial state was founded on a superiority of force; its *raison d'être* lay in the maintenance and extension of British imperial power. In the process, many of the fundamental elements of the conditions of social life in India were undergoing rapid change. But the original superiority of force was the product of a superior culture which shaped and directed the British national project in the world. To match and overcome that superiority, Indian society would have to undergo a similar transformation. And the key to that transformation must lie in a regeneration of national culture embodying, in fact, an unrivalled combination of material and spiritual values. To Bankim, therefore, the remedy for cultural backwardness was not reform, but a total regeneration of national culture, or as he preferred to call it, the national religion. Indeed, mere reform negates the nationalist problematic itself, for it assumes that the Oriental (the Indian, the Hindu) is non-autonomous, passive, historically non-active, indeed for that very reason ahistorical, and therefore ever in need to be acted upon by others. Bankim's doctrine of power, as we have seen, is premised on a reversal of this historical relationship.

This autonomous subjectivity of the nation, now, would have to be provided by a new national religion. Its elements were all there. If religion, as Comte defined it, 'in itself expresses the state of perfect unity which is the distinctive mark of man's existence both as an individual and in society, when all the constituent parts of his nature, moral and physical, are made habitually to converge towards one common purpose', then Bankim's burden was to show that 'Hinduism is the greatest of all religions'.[55] All that was necessary was to 'sweep it clean of the dross that had accumulated over the centuries',[56] to interpret its tenets in the light of contemporary social conditions.

> For religion is universal, and its relation to society immanent. It cannot be in accordance with the intentions of God that his words must apply only to a particular society or to specific social conditions, and that if those conditions change they would not apply any more, and that, consequently, society must be kept static. As times change, it is necessary to reinterpret the words of God in accordance with the new social conditions and the advances in social knowledge.[57]

And to do this one would need to set up a new moral ideal to be accepted and followed by the intellectual leaders of society. Their practice of the national religion would lead to the establishment of the new national character.

> The national religion can bring under its fold and shape the lives even of those who understand nothing of religion. Few people ever understand the subtle intricacies of religious thought. Most merely accept and imitate the example set by those who do understand. That is how the national character is determined.[58]

Why this new national religion had to be based on a purified 'Hindu' ideal is, of course, an interesting question and one that has embarrassed 'secular nationalists' in 20th century India who have given to Bankim an important place in the pantheon of nationalist heroes. Hinduism was not the only religion practised in India and in Bankim's home province of Bengal more than half the population was Muslim. But for India as a whole, the majority of people could be said to have practised some form or other of Hinduism. However, now the very definition of a 'Hindu' religion had become enmeshed in the complex interplay between the thematic and problematic of nationalism. For the national–cultural project was not only to define a distinct cultural identity for the nation and to assert its claim to modernity, it was also to find a viable cultural basis for the convergence of the national and the popular. In the Indian case, unlike that of many countries in central and southern Europe, neither language nor racial distinctiveness was a suitable criterion for defining national solidarity. Rather, within this thematic and problematic, two elements combined to identify Hinduism as a likely candidate which could provide Indian nationalism with a viable cultural foundation of nationhood: first, the possibility of a large popular basis, and second, the very identification by modern Orientalist scholarship of the great spiritual qualities of classical Hinduism.

Bankim in fact identified both these elements quite clearly. In an unfinished manuscript entitled 'Letters on Hinduism', he attempted to state his definition of the 'modern Hindu religion'. He accepted straightaway that there were a great many differences in the religious beliefs and practices of groups of people who were generally called Hindu. 'It is no exaggeration to say that there is greater affinity between Mohamedanism and Christianity than between the Saktaism of the Tantras and the Vaisnavism of Chaitanya.'[59] In fact, the very designation of something called a 'Hindu religion' was the work of foreigners.

> Search through all the vast written literature of India, and you will not, except in modern writings where the Hindu has sought obsequiously to translate the phraseology of his conquerors, meet with any mention of such a thing as the *Hindu religion*. Search through all the vast records of pre-Mohamedan India, nowhere will you meet with even such a word as *Hindu*, let alone Hindu religion. Nay more. Search through the whole of that record, and nowhere will you meet with such a word as *religion*. The word *Dharma*, which is used in the modern vernaculars as its equivalent, was never used in pre-Mohamedan India in the same sense as *Religion*.
> . . . There is no Hindu conception answering to the term 'Hinduism', and the

question with which I began this letter, what is Hinduism, can only be answered by defining what it is that the foreigners who use the word mean by the term.[60]

The thematic now begins to take shape. The Hindu is defined by those who are *not* Hindu. He is also defined by a *difference*, as possessing in common with all other Hindus something that was essentially different from all other religions. What is this esential commonness? Two features stand out, says Bankim. First, the various religions which are designated as Hindu 'are all sprung from a common source, and therefore hold many doctrines in common'. Second, 'they are all supported by sacred scriptures in Sanskrita, or in some other language sprung from the Sanskrita'.[61] But these characteristics are not sufficient to define the religious beliefs held in common by all modern Hindus; there are more substantive features of commonness. And in identifying these substantive doctrinal and religious elements which make up modern Hinduism, European scholars are guilty of several errors.

First of all, by tracing their origins to a common source, the religions of India are often credited with a homogeneity which they do not possess. The error is the result of a lack of knowledge of the specific differences between the various faiths. It is like saying that Judaism and Christianity are the same religion because they are both derived from a common source. Second, the Hindu religion is often regarded as having had the same form since its inception. The fact that it has undergone considerable change through the ages is completely ignored. Third, a great deal that is not religious at all, but purely secular, is often treated as part and parcel of Hindu religion. Thus, principles of social ethics, politics, aesthetics, law, folklore, popular observances — 'everything Hindu is merged into that whirlpool of things — the Hindu religion'.[62] Finally, this compendious 'religion' is also made to include diverse beliefs and practices which have nothing to do with Hinduism — non-Aryan customs and observances, fetishism, popular superstitions, beliefs which are to be found in every country irrespective of its religion: 'a monstrous caricature of a national faith is thus manufactured and described in eloquent language, "as a tangled jungle of gods, ghosts, demons and saints" '.[63]

The result is a completely erroneous ethnology. Bankim clinches his argument with a brilliant reversal of the anthropological problem of cross-cultural understanding:

Suppose a Hindu, ignorant of European languages, travelled through Europe, and like most Europeans in his situation, set about writing an account of his travels. What would be his account of Christianity? Observing the worship of the Virgin and the Saints in Catholic countries, he would take Christianity to be a polytheism. The worship of images would lead him to believe, that Christianity was an idolatry also, and the reverence paid to the crucifix would induce him to think that there was also a leaven of fetishism in it. Protestant Christianity he would account to be a dualism, a religion of the good and evil principles — a religion of God and the Devil. And if he mixed well enough with the ignorant peasantry of Christendom, he too would meet with that tangled jungle of ghosts and demons which it has been Sir Alfred Lyall's lot to meet with in India. And who shall say that the Hindu's account of Christianity would be wider of the truth than many an account of Hinduism by European or native?[64]

But of course this reversal does not lead Bankim to a critique of the Orientalist thematic. What it does instead is strengthen his assertion about the superiority of a reformed Hindu religion as a complete 'system of culture', a 'theoretic body of doctrines' as well as a 'basis of practical life' which provides a far more adequate ethic for the modern Indian than the purely materialistic ideal of modern Europe. This ideal is that of a 'reformed, regenerated and purified' Hinduism, cleansed of 'the rubbish of the ages'. It is not a return to old and archaic types: 'that which was suited to people who lived three thousand years ago, may not be suited to the present and future generations ... The great principles of Hinduism are good for all ages and all mankind ... but its non-essential adjuncts have become effete and even pernicious in an altered state of society.'[65]

It is this ideal, the essential principles of a modern national religion for India, which Bankim described in his last works. It combined a rational theory of power with a non-possessive spirituality. It was an ideal which contained the potential for unifying within a single national culture the vast majority of the inhabitants of India. It was this ideal, once again, which produced in Bankim a barely concealed hostility towards Islam. He recognized in Islam a quest for power and glory, but he saw it as being completely devoid of spiritual or ethical qualities, a complete antithesis to his ideal religion, irrational, bigoted, devious, sensual and immoral. It is perfectly possible that apart from the prevalent cultural prejudices of the upper-caste Hindu Bengali elite of his time, Bankim's opinion was also shaped to a great extent by the stereotypes of post-Enlightenment European historiography. He shows little awareness of, let alone enthusiasm for, the rationalism of early medieval Islamic scholarship and its explorations in Greek philosophy, long before the European Renaissance of which Bankim was so appreciative.

The main task in establishing this national religion was a 'reformation' of Hinduism, 'not an unprecedented necessity for an ancient religion.'[66] The true *dharma* had to be extracted out of the impurities of folk religion and then disseminated among the people. The crucial medium here, according to Bankim, was education. At times, of course, he made the most exaggerated and hollow claims on its behalf, as for instance in the conclusion of his book *Sāmya* in which he called it 'the means to eliminate all social evils', including foreign economic exploitation, the poverty of the peasantry and the oppression of women.[67] But elsewhere, he is more specific. At one level, Bankim is concerned with elite education — the advancement of rational learning among those who would be the cultural and intellectual leaders of society, the new synthesizers of the best of the West and the best of the East. But he was not particularly impressed by the 'filtration' theory of education.

The argument is that it is only necessary for the upper classes to be educated; there is no need for a separate system of instruction for the lower classes ... The porousness of the newly educated class will guarantee that the ignorant masses will soon be soaked with knowledge! . . . We do not, however, have much faith that this will happen.[68]

It was necessary, Bankim thought, for the intellectual leadership to engage in a much more conscious programme of national education. A first step in this programme was to make available the results of modern learning in the Indian vernaculars. In his own case, it could certainly be said that his entire literary career was devoted to this single pursuit. Further, he was quite specific about the kinds of people to whom this popular literature in the vernaculars had to be addressed.

> The artizan and the shopkeeper who keep their own accounts, the village zemindar and the mofussil lawyer, the humbler official employé whose English carries him no further than the duties of his office, and the small proprietor who has as little to do with English as with office, all these classes read Bengali and Bengali only; all in fact between the ignorant peasant and the really well-educated classes. And if to these be added the vast numbers who are likely to benefit by a system of vernacular education, extended and developed so as to suit the requirements of the country, we may be in a position to appreciate fully the importance of a literature for the *people* of Bengal; for these classes constitute the *people*.[69]

But even more than this formal medium of the written word, Bankim was concerned with reviving the many cultural institutions of popular instruction which had long existed in India but which were rapidly dying out because of the exclusive concern of the upper classes with English education.

> It is not true that in our country there was always this lack of means of popular instruction. How else did Śākyasiṃha teach the Buddhist religion to all of India? Just think of it; even our modern philosophers find it excruciatingly difficult to unravel the complex arguments of Buddhist philosophy! Max Müller did not understand it at all . . . Yet Śākyasiṃha and his disciples taught this . . . immensely difficult doctrine to one and all . . . And then Śaṅkarācārya demolished this firmly established, world-conquering, egalitarian religion and taught all of India the Śaiva faith. How, if there were no means of popular instruction? Much more recently, Caitanya converted all of Orissa to the Vaiṣṇava religion. No means of popular instruction? But in our day, from Rammohun Roy to the latest hordes of college students, three and a half generations have been peddling Brahmoism, and yet the people do not accept their teachings. Before there used to be means of popular instruction; they do not exist any more.[70]

In the case of Bengal, Bankim was particularly impressed by the historical example of the Vaiṣṇava cultural efflorescence of the 14th and 15th centuries. In contrast to his consistently derisive reference to the efforts of the 19th century intelligentsia for religious and social reform, Bankim unhesitatingly located the 'renaissance' in Bengali culture in that earlier period of Bengal's history.

> How long has Europe been civilised? In the fifteenth century — only four hundred years ago — Europe was more uncivilised than we were. One event brought civilisation to Europe. Suddenly Europe rediscovered the long-forgotten

culture of the Greeks ... Petrarch, Luther, Galileo, Bacon: suddenly there seemed to be no end to Europe's good fortune. But there was a similar age in our history as well. The rise of Caitanya in Nabadwip, followed by Rūpa, Sanātana and countless other poets and theologians; Raghunātha Śiromaṇi, Gadādhara, Jagadīśa in philosophy; in law, Raghunandana and his followers. And then there was a new wave of Bengali poetry: Vidyāpati and Candīdāsa came before Caitanya, but the poetry which followed him is unparalleled in the whole world. Where did all this come from?

How did our Renaissance happen? Where did our nation get this sudden enlightenment? ... Why did this light go out? Perhaps it was because of the advent of Mughal rule — the land revenue settlement of the Hindu Raja Todar Mal. Gather the evidence and find out all of these things.[71]

This was, in fact, a major part of Bankim's project for a national history of Bengal. The hallmark of the 'renaissance' was its popular character. And this would have to be the character of the new national–cultural revival as well. It called for a very specific relationship between the intellectual leaders of society and the rest of the nation. The intellectual–moral leadership of the nation was based not on an elitism of birth or caste or privilege or wealth, but of excellence. The leaders were leaders because through *anuśīlan* they had attained an exemplary unity of knowledge and duty. Their relationship with the masses must, therefore, be one of sympathy on the one side and deference on the other: 'The English have a good name for it: Subordination ... Not fear, but respect.'[72]

VII

This is the characteristic form of nationalist thought at its moment of departure. It is born out of the encounter of a patriotic consciousness with the framework of knowledge imposed upon it by colonialism. It leads inevitably to an elitism of the intelligentsia, rooted in the vision of a radical regeneration of national culture. In Bankim's time, the heyday of colonial rule, this vision could not find any viable political means to actualize itself. Instead, it became a dream: a utopian political community in which the nation was the Mother, once resplendent in wealth and beauty, now in tatters. Relentlessly, she exhorts a small band of her sons, those of them who are brave and enlightened, to vanquish the enemy and win back her honour. Imprisoned within the rationalist framework of his theoretical discourse and powerless to reject its dominating implications, Bankim lived out his dreams of liberation in his later novels. In form, *Ānandamaṭh* (1882), *Devī Caudhurāṇī* (1884) and *Sītārām* (1887) are historical romances, but they are suffused with a utopianism which, by the power of the particular religious semiotic in which it was expressed, had a deep emotional influence on the new intelligentsia. It is not surprising that in the history of political movements in India, Bankim's direct disciples were the 'revolutionary terrorists', the small groups of armed activists drawn from the Hindu middle classes, wedded to secret underground organization and planned assassination.

Literary critics have often explained this overtly spiritualist and conservative turn in Bankim's last novels in terms of a tussle between a rationalism and an emotionalism, a conflict of the mind and the heart. His intellect, they have argued, was attracted by the rationality, historicity and scientific temper of the European Enlightenment. But his heart remained in the mysterious, dreamy world of the past. 'Irrational emotionalism on the one hand, dispassionate rationalism on the other: Bankim's mental world was lashed violently by these opposing currents.' His rationalism persuaded him that it was necessary to implant the scientific and historically progressive values of Western civilization in his own culture. But his heart refused to accept this solution; it kept pulling him back towards the imaginary authenticity of a glorious Hindu past. 'As a result, he mistook a relation between the present and the past for a relation of the present with the future.' This surrender to a backward-looking emotionalism was, according to these critics, an aberration in the onward march of rationalist and progressive thinking in modern India. It did sway some people for a time, particularly around the turn of the century, but the predominant trend was resumed soon after.[73]

This manner of interpreting the so-called 'conservative' trend in Indian nationalism misses the most crucial point of tension in *all* nationalist thought. It was not a question of a forward-looking rationality being swamped by a flood of archaic emotionalism. Much of this conservatism in fact rejected, as Bankim certainly did, any wishful dreams of a return to the past. To treat 'Hindu orthodoxy' of this kind as a backward-looking emotionalism would be to miss its very source of ideological strength, namely, its proclamation of a rational and modern religion suitable for the nation. Unlike the liberal reformers of the 19th century who could think of no way of 'modernizing' the antiquated institutions of their society except to rely on the legislative and administrative powers of the colonial state, it was the so-called 'conservative' or 'revivalist' trend which confronted for the first time the crucial question of power in the historical project of nationalism. Rather, the point of tension lay embedded in the contradictions of the thematic and the problematic of nationalism itself at its moment of departure. Both the so-called rationalism and the so-called emotionalism, progressive as well as conservative tendencies, proceeded from this point. Neither conservatives nor progressives were able to resolve the divergence between the *modern* and the *national* in any historically specific way, because the specificity of the modern and the specificity of the national remained distinct and opposed. But this was so because both conservatives and progressives were equally prisoners of the rationalism, historicism and scientism of the nationalist thematic. Theoretically, the modern and the national could be synthesised only in the ideal of the complete man, the true intellectual. But it was hardly possible to devise programmatic steps to achieve that ideal in the realm of politics. At its moment of departure, all nationalist thought remained trapped in this unresolved contradiction.

It was this contradiction which served as the basis for divergent political programmes within the national movement. An emphasis on the modern meant arguing for a period of tutelage until the leaders of the country and its material bases had been sufficiently 'modernized'. For a long time this meant a continuation of colonial rule, a sharing of power between colonial officials and a modernized elite, and an emphasis on state action to reform traditional institutions and bring into being modern ones. It also meant, and indeed still means, a continued period of 'collaboration' with the West. Usually a political programme of this sort has been associated with liberal, constitutionalist and pro-Western circles. On the other hand, a more uncompromising position on the question of colonial rule has meant an ideological emphasis on what is distinctly national, i.e. culturally distinct from the Western and the modern. This is seen to be characteristic of revivalist or fundamentalist cultural movements, usually of a religious–communal nature. Both possibilities are inherent in Bankim's unresolved problem.

The narrow elitism of the intelligentsia could hardly resolve the central problem of nationalist politics in a large agrarian country under colonial rule. To represent the nation as a political entity within a colonial state process which clearly possessed considerable resources to broaden its bases of legitimacy by intervening directly in the agrarian class struggle, it was necessary above all to take nationalist politics to the peasantry. Without this an emergent Indian bourgeoisie could never hope to pose an adequate challenge to colonial rule. Similarly, without devising suitable ways of establishing an intellectual–moral leadership over the vast masses of the peasantry, the organic functions of the new intelligentsia in building a national consensus for self-government were doomed to failure.

The problem, however, lay precisely in the insurmountable difficulty of reconciling the modes of thought characteristic of a peasant consciousness with the rationalist forms of an 'enlightened' nationalist politics. Either peasant consciousness would have to be transformed, or else it would have to be appropriated. The former would require a total transformation of the agrarian economy, the abolition of pre-capitalist forms of production and the virtual dissolution of the peasantry as a distinct form of the social existence of labour. Given the conditions of the colonial economy even in the early 20th century, this could hardly seem a viable political possibility. The other possibility then was an appropriation of peasant support for the historic cause of creating a nation-state in which the peasant masses would be represented, but of which they would not be a constituent part. In other words, passive revolution.

This is where the moment of manoeuvre occurs. To understand the significance of this moment in the historical constitution of a nationalist discourse, we must extricate the problem from questions of subjective motivations, influences, manipulations, who used whom to gain what, etc. Those are valid historical questions, but they lie at an entirely different analytical level. It is at this moment of manoeuvre — this critical moment in the task of constituting a historical bloc to achieve a 'passive revolution of capital' in India — that we examine the significance of the Gandhian intervention in Indian politics.

Notes

1. For biographical details, see Brajendranath Bandyopadhyay and Sajanikanta Das, *Sāhitya Sādhak Caritmālā*, vol.2 (Calcutta: Bangiya Sahitya Parishad, 1945), and most recently, Sisir Kumar Das, *The Artist in Chains: The Life of Bankimchandra Chatterji* (New Delhi: New Statesman, 1984).
2. 'Bhāratvarṣa parādhīn kena?' *Bankim Racanābalī*, ed. Jogesh Chandra Bagal, vol.2 (Calcutta: Sahitya Samsad, 1965) [hereafter BR], p.239. All translations from the Bengali are mine.
3. *BR*, pp.221-34.
4. 'Sāṅkhyadarśan', *BR*, p.222.
5. Letter to Sambhu Chandra Mookerjee, 28 December 1872, in 'The Secretary's Notes', *Bengal Past and Present*, 8, part 2, 16 (April-June 1914).
6. 'Buddhism and the Sánkhya Philosophy', *Calcutta Review*, 53 (1871), 106, pp.191-203.
7. 'Sāṅkhyadarśan', *BR*, p.226.
8. 'Baṅgālīr Vāhubal', *BR*, p.213.
9.

If the English go out to shoot birds, a history is written of the expedition. But Bengal has no history! . . . There is a specific reason why Indians have no history. Partly because of the environment, partly the fear of invaders, Indians are greatly devoted to their gods . . . As a result of this way of thinking, Indians are extremely modest: They do not think themselves the subjects of their own actions; it is always the gods who act through them . . . It is this modesty of attitude and devotion to the gods which are the reasons for our people not writing their own history. The Europeans are extremely proud. They think that even when they yawn, the achievement should be recorded as a memorable deed in the annals of world history. Proud nations have an abundance of historical writing; we have none.

'Bāṅgālār Itihās', *BR*, p.330.
10. *Kṛṣṇacaritra*, in *BR*, p.411.
11. Ibid., *BR*, p.413.
12. Letter to Sambhu Chandra Mookerjee, op.cit.
13. 'Kākātuyā', *BR*, p.110.
14. *Kṛṣṇacaritra*, in *BR*, p.413.
15. Ibid., *BR*, p.410.
16. 'Vedic Literature: An Address', *Bankim Racanabālī (English Works)*, ed. Jogesh Chandra Bagal (Calcutta: Sahitya Samsad, 1969), p.150.
17. 'European Versions of Hindoo Doctrine: An Exchange with Mr. Hastie', ibid., pp.204-5.
18. 'The Intellectual Superiority of Europe: An Exchange with Mr. Hastie', ibid., p.212.
19. Ibid., p.210.
20. *Kṛṣṇacaritra*, in *BR*, p.434.
21. 'Baṅgadeśer kṛṣak', *BR*, p.311.
22. Ibid., *BR*, p.289.
23. Ibid., *BR*, p.312.
24. Ibid.
25. When not bound down by the formal analytical requirements of a theoretical

discourse, Bankim was of course capable of considerable scepticism about the 'philanthropic' aspects of colonial rule. About his own work as a government official, he wrote to a friend:

> I have been doing right royal service to the State by trying to fill its coffers, so that it may rebuild the Jagur barracks and indulge in other magnificent pastimes, to the edification of the tax-paying public. What the devil do niggers want their money for? they had better pay in their all at the Government Treasuries, and Government will do them an immense deal of good by erecting uninhabitable barracks and abolishing slavery in Zanzibar. You see my work is genuine philanthrophy.

Letter to S.C. Mookerjee, op.cit.

26. Ibid., *BR*, p.310.
27. Ibid., *BR*, p.298.
28. Ibid., *BR*, p.301.
29. 'Rāmdhan Pod', *BR*, p.380.
30. 'Bhāratvarṣer svādhīnatā evaṃ parādhīnatā', *BR*, p.244.
31. Ibid., *BR*, p.245.
32. 'Anukaraṇ', *BR*, p.201.
33. Ibid., *BR*, p.203.
34. Ibid.
35. *Dharmatattva*, in *BR*, p.585.
36. Ibid., *BR*, p.630.
37. Ibid., *BR*, pp.628-9.
38. Ibid., *BR*, p.633.
39. Ibid., *BR*, p.647.
40. John Stuart Mill, *Nature, The Utility of Religion, and Theism* (London: Watts, 1904).
41. 'Tridev sambandhe vijñānśāstra ki bale', *BR*, p.280.
42. *Śrīmadbhagavadgītā*, in *BR*, pp.699-700.
43. Ibid., *BR*, p.701.
44. *Kṛṣṇacaritra*, in *BR*, pp.516-7.
45. Ibid., *BR*, p.529.
46. Ibid., *BR*, p.495.
47. Ibid., *BR*, p.533.
48. Ibid., *BR*, p.533.
49. Ibid., *BR*, p.534.
50. Ibid., *BR*, p.562.
51. Ibid., *BR*, p.563.
52. *Śrīmadbhagavadgītā*, in *BR*, p.744.
53. *Dharmatattva*, in *BR*, p.651.
54. 'Vahuvivāha', *BR*, p.315.
55. *Dharmatattva*, in *BR*, p.676.
56. Ibid., *BR*, p.668.
57. *Śrīmadbhagavadgītā*, in *BR*, p.695.
58. *Dharmatattva*, in *BR*, p.651.
59. 'Letters on Hinduism', *Baṅkim Racanābalī (English Works)*, p.230.
60. Ibid., pp.230-1.
61. Ibid., p.232.
62. Ibid., p.233.

63. Ibid.
64. Ibid., p.235.
65. Ibid., p.235-6.
66. Ibid., p.235.
67. *Sāmya*, in *BR*, pp.405-6.
68. 'Baṅgadarsaner patrasūcanā', *BR*, p.282.
69. 'A Popular Literature for Bengal', *Baṅkim Racanābalī (English Works)*, p.97.
70. 'Lokaśikṣā', *BR*, p.377.
71. 'Bāṅgālār itihās sambandhe kayekti kathā', *BR*, p.339.
72. *Dharmatattva*, in *BR*, p.619.
73. See in particular, Arabinda Poddar, *Baṅkim-mānas* (Calcutta: Indiana, 1960), especially pp.80, 111, 165-7.

4. The Moment of Manoeuvre: Gandhi and the Critique of Civil Society

My language is aphoristic, it lacks precision.
It is therefore open to several interpretations.
'Discussion with Dharmadev', *The Collected Works of
Mahatma Gandhi*, vol.53, Appendix III, p.485.

I

Although Gandhi's *Collected Works* will finally run into nearly ninety thick volumes, there exist few texts in which he can be seen attempting a systematic exposition of his ideas on state, society and nation. One of the first, and perhaps the fullest, is entitled *Hind Swaraj*, written in Gujarati in 1909 and published in an English translation in Johannesburg in 1910 after the original edition was proscribed by the Government of Bombay. It contains a statement of some of the fundamental elements of Gandhi's politics. Romain Rolland, one of his first sympathetic but critical commentators, saw in this book a reflection of the central features of Gandhi's thought: 'the negation of Progress and also of European science'.[1] A more recent commentator, Raghavan Iyer, sees it as 'a severe condemnation of modern civilzation' and 'the *point d'appui* of Gandhi's moral and political thought'.[2] I prefer to read it as a text in which Gandhi's relation to nationalism can be shown to rest on a fundamental critique of the idea of civil society.

On the surface, it is indeed a critique of modern civilization, 'a civilization only in name'.[3] And the argument proceeds, as it does in Bankim, from a consideration of the question: Why is India a subject nation? To start with, Gandhi's answer too seems to run along the same lines. He too is concerned more with locating the sources of Indian weakness than putting the blame on British avarice or deceit. But the emphasis is not so much on the elements of culture. Gandhi points much more forcefully to the moral failure.

> The English have not taken India; we have given it to them. They are not in India because of their strength, but because we keep them . . . Recall the Company Bahadur. Who made it Bahadur? They had not the slightest intention at the time of establishing a kingdom. Who assisted the Company's officers? Who was tempted at the sight of their silver? Who bought their goods? History testifies that we did all this . . . When our Princes fought among themselves, they sought the

assistance of Company Bahadur. That corporation was versed alike in commerce and war. It was unhampered by questions of morality . . . Is it not then useless to blame the English for what we did at the time? . . . it is truer to say that we gave India to the English than that India was lost.[4]

It was a moral failure on the part of Indians that led to the conquest of India. And in exploring the reasons behind this moral failure, Gandhi's answer becomes diametrically opposed to that of Bankim. It is not because Indian society lacked the necessary cultural attributes that it was unable to face up to the power of the English. It is not the backwardness or lack of modernity of India's culture that keeps it in continued subjection. And the task of achieving freedom would not be accomplished by creating a new modern culture for the nation. For Gandhi, it is precisely because Indians were seduced by the glitter of modern civilization that they became a subject people. And what keeps them in subjection is the acceptance by leading sections of Indians of the supposed benefits of civilization. Indeed, as long as Indians continue to harbour illusions about the 'progressive' qualities of modern civilization, they will remain a subject nation. Even if they succeed physically in driving out the English, they would still have 'English rule without the Englishman', because it is not the physical presence of the English which makes India a subject nation: it is civilization which subjects.

There then follows an indictment of modern civilization as it has emerged in the West and as it has been imported into India. Fundamentally, Gandhi attacks the very notions of modernity and progress and subverts the central claim made on behalf of those notions, viz. their correspondence with a new organization of society in which the productive capacities of human labour are multiplied several times, creating increased wealth and prosperity for all and hence increased leisure, comfort, health and happiness. Gandhi argues that far from achieving these objectives, what modern civilization does is make man a prisoner of his craving for luxury and self-indulgence, release the forces of unbridled competition and thereby bring upon society the evils of poverty, disease, war and suffering. It is precisely because modern civilization looks at man as a limitless consumer and thus sets out to open the floodgates of industrial production that it also becomes the source of inequality, oppression and violence on a scale hitherto unknown in human history.

Machinery, for instance, is intended to increase the productivity of labour and thus to satisfy the never-ending urge for consumption. But it only whets the appetite, it does not satisfy it. What it does instead is bring exploitation and disease to the industrial cities and unemployment and ruin to the countryside.

When I read Mr Dutt's *Economic History of India*, I wept; and as I think of it again my heart sickens. It is machinery that has impoverished India. It is difficult to measure the harm that Manchester has done to us. It is due to Manchester that Indian handicraft has all but disappeared.[5]

The driving social urge behind industrial production is the craving for excessive consumption. It is in this context that Gandhi interprets the modern spirit of scientific inquiry and technological advance; a tendency to let the mind wander uncontrolled and chase the objects of our passions.

> We notice that the mind is a restless bird; the more it gets the more it wants, and still remains unsatisfied. The more we indulge our passions, the more unbridled they become. Our ancestors, therefore, set a limit to our indulgences. They saw that happiness was largely a mental condition... Observing all this, our ancestors dissuaded us from luxuries and pleasures. We have managed with the same kind of plough as existed thousands of years ago. We have retained the same kind of cottages that we had in former times and our indigenous education remains the same as before. We have had no system of life-corroding competition... It was not that we did not know how to invent machinery, but our forefathers knew that if we set our hearts after such things, we would become slaves and lose our moral fibres. They, therefore, after due deliberation decided that we should only do what we could with our hands and feet.[6]

Hence, his solution to the social evils of industrialism is not just to remove its defects, because he thinks these so-called defects are germane to the very fundamentals of the modern system of production. His solution is to give up industrialism altogether: 'instead of welcoming machinery as a boon, we should look upon it as an evil'.[7] It is only a complete change in moral values that will change our perception of our social needs and thus enable us once again to set deliberate limits to social consumption. Nothing short of this will succeed.

> A certain degree of physical harmony and comfort is necessary, but above a certain level it becomes a hindrance instead of help. Therefore the ideal of creating an unlimited number of wants and satisfying them seems to be a delusion and a snare. The satisfaction of one's physical needs, even the intellectual needs of one's narrow self, must meet at a certain point a dead stop, before it degenerates into physical and intellectual voluptuousness.[8]

Clearly, then, Gandhi's critique of British rule in India attempted to situate it at a much more fundamental level than Bankim, or indeed any other nationalist writer of his time. Where they were criticizing merely the excesses of Western notions of patriotism and national glory which inevitably pushed those countries towards the pursuit of colonial conquests and victories in war, Gandhi has no doubt at all that the source of modern imperialism lies specifically in the system of social production which the countries of the Western world have adopted. It is the limitless desire for ever-increased production and ever-greater consumption, and the spirit of ruthless competitiveness which keeps the entire system going, that impel these countries to seek colonial possessions which can be exploited for economic purposes. Gandhi stated this position quite emphatically as early as in *Hind Swaraj* and held on to it all his life. It was, in fact, in many ways the most crucial theoretical foundation of his entire strategy of winning *svarāj* for India.

> Napoleon is said to have described the English as a nation of shop-keepers. It is a fitting description. They hold whatever dominions they have for the sake of their commerce. Their army and their navy are intended to protect it. When the Transvaal offered no such attractions, the late Mr Gladstone discovered that it was not right for the English to hold it. When it became a paying proposition,

resistance led to war. Mr Chamberlain soon discovered that England enjoyed a suzerainty over the Transvaal. It is related that someone asked the late President Kruger whether there was gold on the moon. He replied that it was highly unlikely because, if there were, the English would have annexed it. Many problems can be solved by remembering that money is their God . . . If you accept the above statements, it is proved that the English entered India for the purposes of trade. They remain in it for the same purpose . . . They wish to convert the whole world into a vast market for their goods. That they cannot do so is true, but the blame will not be theirs. They will leave no stone unturned to reach the goal.[9]

Thus, in the case of modern imperialism, morality and politics are both subordinated to the primary consideration of economics, and this consideration is directly related to a specific organization of social production characterized not so much by the nature of ownership of the means of production but fundamentally by the purposes and the processes of production. That is to say, whereas Gandhi is in this particular historical instance talking about the capitalist system of production in Britain, his characterization of the type of economy which leads to exploitation and colonial conquest is not necessarily restricted to capitalism alone, because as long as the purpose of social production is to continually expand it in order to satisfy an endless urge for consumption and as long as the process of production is based on ever-increased mechanization, those consequences would follow inevitably. And the purposes and processes of production take on this particular form whenever production is primarily directed not towards the creation of articles of immediate *use* but towards *exchange* — exchange between town and country and between metropolis and colony. Any kind of industrialization on a large scale would have to be based on certain determinate exchange relations between town and country, with the balance inevitably tipping against the latter whenever the pace of industrialization quickens. This would lead to unemployment and poverty in the villages or, which amounts to the same thing, to the exploitation of colonial possessions.

> Industrialization on a mass scale will necessarily lead to passive or active exploitation of the villagers as the problems of competition and marketing come in. Therefore we have to concentrate on the village being self-contained, manufacturing mainly for use.[10]

The mere socialization of industries would not alter this process in any way at all.

> Pandit Nehru wants industrialization because he thinks that, if it is socialized, it would be free from the evils of capitalism. My own view is that evils are inherent in industrialism, and no amount of socialization can eradicate them.[11]

In fact, Gandhi's argument was that there is no feasible way in which *any* process of industrialization can avoid the creation of exploitative and inhumane relations of exchange between town and country. He states this quite clearly when he argues that *khādī* is the only sound economic proposition for India.

'Khadi is the only true economic proposition in terms of the millions of villagers until such time, if ever, when a better system of supplying work and adequate wages for every able-bodied person above the age of sixteen, male or female, is found for his field, cottage or even factory in every one of the villages of India; or till sufficient cities are built up to displace the villages so as to give the villagers the necessary comforts and amenities that a well-regulated life demands and is entitled to.' I have only to state the proposition thus fully to show that khadi must hold the field for any length of time that we can think of.[12]

It is true, of course, that in the midst of continuing controversy about the economic policies of the Congress, and especially the programme of *khādī*, Gandhi increasingly tended to emphasize the strict economic argument against heavy industrialization in a large agrarian economy with an abundance of underemployed labour. During the 1920s and 1930s, the period of the growth of the national movement, he would often in fact prefer to suspend the debate about the larger moral issues of mechanization *per se* in order to win his point on the infeasibility of heavy industrialization in the particular context of India. 'I have no partiality,' he would say, 'for return to the primitive methods of grinding and husking for the sake of them. I suggest the return, because there is no other way of giving employment to the millions of villagers who are living in idleness.'[13] At times he even conceded that mechanization might have an economic logic in situations of labour scarcity.

Mechanization is good when the hands are too few for the work intended to be accomplished. It is an evil when there are more hands than required for the work, as is the case in India . . . The problem with us is not how to find leisure for the teeming millions inhabiting our villages. The problem is how to utilize their idle hours, which are equal to the working days of six months in the year . . . spinning and weaving mills have deprived the villagers of a substantial means of livelihood. It is no answer in reply to say that they turn out cheaper, better cloth, if they do so at all. For, if they have displaced thousands of workers, the cheapest mill cloth is dearer than the dearest khadi woven in the villages.[14]

But this was only a debating point, an attempt to bring round to the cause of his economic programme those who did not share his fundamental philosophical premises. Because ever so often, even as he argued about the practical economic necessity of *khādī*, he would remind his readers where exactly he stood with regard to the fundamental moral issues.

If I could do it, I would most assuredly destroy or radically change much that goes under the name of modern civilization. But that is an old story of life. The attempt is undoubtedly there. Its success depends upon God. But the attempt to revive and encourage the remunerative village industries is not part of such an attempt, except in so far as every one of my activities, including the propagation of non-violence, can be described as such an attempt.[15]

Even when it came to a question of the fundamental principles of organization of economic life, Gandhi would unhesitatingly state his opposition to the concept of the *homo oeconomicus*, to the supposed benefits of the social division of labour, and to the current faith in the laws of the marketplace transforming private vices into public virtues.

> I am always reminded of one thing which the well-known British economist Adam Smith has said in his famous treatise *The Wealth of Nations*. In it he has described some economic laws as universal and absolute. Then he has described certain situations which may be an obstacle to the operation of these laws. These disturbing factors are the human nature, the human temperament or altruism inherent in it. Now, the economics of khadi is just the opposite of it. Benevolence which is inherent in human nature is the very foundation of the economics of khadi. What Adam Smith has described as pure economic activity based merely on the calculations of profit and loss is a selfish attitude and it is an obstacle to the development of khadi; and it is the function of a champion of khadi to counteract this tendency.[16]

And thus one comes back to Gandhi's condemnation of what he calls 'modern civilization', which in fact is a fundamental critique of the entire edifice of bourgeois society: its continually expanding and prosperous economic life, based on individual property, the social division of labour and the impersonal laws of the market, described with clinical precision and complete moral approbation by Mandeville and Smith; its political institutions based on a dual notion of sovereignty in which the people in theory rule themselves, but are only allowed to do so through the medium of their representatives whose actions have to be ratified only once in so many years; its spirit of innovation, adventure and scientific progress; its rationalization of philosophy and ethics and secularization of art and education. As early as in *Hind Swaraj*, Gandhi launches a thoroughgoing critique against each of these constitutive features of civil society.

Parliament, for instance, he calls 'a sterile woman and a prostitute', the first because, despite being a sovereign institution, it cannot enact a law according to its own judgment but is constantly swayed by outside pressures, and the second because it continually shifts its allegiance from one set of ministers to another depending on which is more powerful. But basically, Gandhi objects to an entire structure of politics and government in which each individual is assumed to have his own individual interest, individuals are expected to come together into parties and alliances in terms of those self-interests, these combinations of interests are then supposed to exert pressure on each other by mobilizing public opinion and manipulating the levers of the governmental machinery, and legislative enactments are then expected to emerge as choices made on behalf of the whole society.

> It is generally acknowledged that the members [of Parliament] are hypocritical and selfish. Each thinks of his own little interest. It is fear that is the guiding motive ... Members vote for their party without a thought. Their so-called discipline binds them to it. If any member, by way of exception, gives an independent vote, he is considered a renegade ... The Prime Minister is more concerned about his power than about the welfare of Parliament. His energy is concentrated upon securing the success of his party. His care is not always that

Parliament should do right . . . If they are considered honest because they do not take what are generally known as bribes, let them be so considered, but they are open to subtler influences. In order to gain their ends, they certainly bribe people with honours. I do not hesitate to say that they have neither real honesty nor a living conscience.[17]

And the process by which support is mobilized on behalf of particular leaders or parties or interests is equally unworthy of moral approval.

To the English voters their newspaper is their Bible. They take their cue from their newspapers which are often dishonest. The same fact is differently interpreted by different newspapers, according to the party in whose interests they are edited . . . [The] people change their views frequently . . . These views swing like the pendulum of a clock and are never steadfast. The people would follow a powerful orator or a man who gives them parties, receptions, etc.[18]

Once again, Gandhi's criticism is aimed against the abrogation of moral responsibility involved in the duality of sovereignty and the mediation of complex legal–political institutions which distance the rulers of society from those they are supposed to represent. He does not accept the argument that if effective combinations are formed among individuals and groups sharing a set of common self-interests, then the institutions of representative democracy will ensure that the government will act in ways which are, on the whole, in the common interest of the entire collectivity. His argument is, in fact, that the dissociation of political values, based on self-interest, from social morality, based on certain universal ethical values shared by the whole community, leads to a structure and process of politics in which the wealthy and the powerful enjoy disproportionate opportunities to manipulate the machinery of government to their own sectional interests. Besides, the legal fiction of equality before the law and the supposed neutrality of state institutions only have the effect of perpetuating the inequalities and divisions which already exist in society: politics has no role in removing those inequalities or cementing the divisions. In fact, this very process of law and politics which thrives on conflict creates a vested interest among politicians, state officials and legal practitioners to perpetuate social divisions and indeed to create new ones.

[The lawyers'] duty is to side with their clients and to find out ways and arguments in favour of their clients, to which they (the clients) are often strangers . . . The lawyers, therefore, will, as a rule, advance quarrels instead of repressing them . . . It is within my knowledge that they are glad when men have disputes. Petty pleaders actually manufacture them.[19]

Similarly, the colonial state in India, by projecting an image of neutrality with regard to social divisions within Indian society, not only upholds the rigours of those divisions, such as the ones imposed by the caste system, but actually strengthens them.[20]

By contrast, it is only when politics is *directly* subordinated to a communal morality that the minority of exploiters in society can be resisted by the people and inequalities and divisions removed. As a political ideal, therefore, Gandhi counterposes against the system of representative government an undivided concept of popular sovereignty, where the community is self-regulating and political power is dissolved into the collective moral will.

> The power to control national life through national representatives is called political power. Representatives will become unnecessary if the national life becomes so perfect as to be self-controlled. It will then be a state of enlightened anarchy in which each person will become his own ruler. He will conduct himself in such a way that his behaviour will not hamper the well-being of his neighbours. In an ideal State there will be no political institution and therefore no political power.[21]

In its form, this political ideal is not meant to be a consensual democracy with complete and continual participation by every member of the polity. The utopia is *Rāmarājya*, a patriarchy in which the ruler, by his moral quality and habitual adherence to truth, always expresses the collective will.[22] It is also a utopia in which the economic organization of production, arranged according to a perfect four-fold *varṇa* scheme of specialization and a perfect system of reciprocity in the exchange of commodities and services, always ensures that there is no spirit of competition and no differences in status between different kinds of labour.[23] The ideal conception of *Rāmarājya*, in fact, encapsulates the critique of all that is morally reprehensible in the economic and political organization of civil society.

The argument is then extended to other aspects of civil society. The secularization of education, for instance, has made a 'fetish' of the knowledge of letters and has thereby both exaggerated and rationalized the inequalities in society. It ignores completely the ethical aspect of education and the need to integrate the individual within the collectively shared moral values of the community, and instead cultivates 'the pretension of learning many sciences'. The result is a pervasive feeling of dissatisfaction, of moral anarchy, and a license to individual self-seeking, to 'hypocrisy, tyranny, etc'.[24] It also rationalizes, by ascribing an economic logic to it, one of the fundamental aspects of the social division of labour in modern industrial society: the distinction between mental and manual work. It denies that intellectual labour is an aspect not of the creation of wealth but of human self-fulfilment and must, therefore, be made available to every human being, and this can only be done if all share equally in providing the needs of the body.

> May not men earn their bread by intellectual labour? No . . . Mere mental, that is, intellectual labour is for the soul and is its own satisfaction. It should never demand payment.[25]
>
> . . . Bodily sustenance should come from body labour, and intellectual labour is necessary for the culture of the mind. Division of labour there will necessarily be, but it will be a division into various species of body labour and not a division into intellectual labour to be confined to one class and body labour to be confined to another class.[26]

The spirit of scientific inquiry and technological innovation too is aimed more towards physical self-indulgence and luxury than towards the discovery of truth. The science of medicine, for instance, on whose behalf the tallest claims are made by the propagators of modernity, concerns itself more with enabling people to consume more than with the removal of disease.

> I overeat, I have indigestion, I go to the doctor, he gives me medicine, I am cured. I overeat again, I take his pills again. Had I not taken the pills in the first instance, I would have suffered the punishment deserved by me and I would not have overeaten again. The doctor intervened and helped me to indulge myself.[27]

And this, of course, only perpetuates the disease; it does not cure it. The modern science of medicine is satisfied by treating illnesses merely at the surface level of physical causality. The scientific spirit, divorced as it is from considerations of morality, does not feel obliged to look deeper into the true causes of diseases which must lie in the very mode of social living.

II

What appears on surface as a critique of Western civilization is, therefore, a total moral critique of the fundamental aspects of civil society. It is not, at this level, a critique of Western culture or religion,[28] nor is it an attempt to establish the superior spiritual claims of Hindu religion. In fact, the moral charge against the West is not that its religion is inferior, but that by whole-heartedly embracing the dubious virtues of modern civilization, it has forgotten the true teachings of the Christian faith. At this level of thought, therefore, Gandhi is not operating at all with the problematic of nationalism. His solution too is meant to be universal, applicable as much to the countries of the West as to nations such as India.

Not only that; what is even more striking, but equally clear, is that Gandhi does not even think within the thematic of nationalism. He seldom writes or speaks in terms of the conceptual frameworks or the modes of reasoning and inference adopted by the nationalists of his day, and quite emphatically rejects their rationalism, scientism and historicism. As early as in *Hind Swaraj*, Gandhi dismisses all historical objections to his project of freeing India, not by the strength of arms but by the force of the soul, by saying, 'To believe that what has not occurred in history will not occur at all is to argue disbelief in the dignity of man.'[29] He does not feel it necessary to even attempt a historical demonstration of the possibilities he is trying to point out. Indeed, he objects that the historical mode of reasoning is quite unsuitable, indeed irrelevant, for his purpose. History, he says, is built upon the records not of the working of the force of the soul but of its exact opposite. It is a record of the interruptions of peace.

> Two brothers quarrel; one of them repents and re-awakens the love that was lying dormant in him; the two again begin to leave in peace; nobody takes note of this. But if the two brothers, through the intervention of solicitors or some other reason take up arms or go to law — which is another form of the exhibition of brute force — their doings would be immediately noticed in the Press, they would be the talk

of their neighbours and would probably go down in history. And what is true of families and communities is true of nations.[30]

History therefore, does not record the Truth. Truth lies outside history; it is universal, unchanging. Truth has no history of its own.

It is instructive to compare the method Gandhi follows in his attempts to reinterpret the scriptures with those followed by practically every other nationalist reformer of the time — Bankim or Tilak or Dayanand, for example. Not only does he not attempt a historical examination of the authenticity of scriptural texts or of the historicity of the great characters of sacred history, he quite explicitly states that such exercises were quite irrelevant to the determination of truth. In *Anāsaktiyoga*, his commentaries on the *Gītā*, Gandhi does not bother at all about the history of the text itself or about the historicity of Krishna, although he was quite aware of the debates surrounding these questions. Mahadev Desai, in his introductory note to the English translation of *Anāsaktiyoga*, mentions the debate about the 'original' text of the *Gītā* and says,

> One may however say that, even when this original is discovered, it will not make much difference to souls like Gandhiji, every moment of whose life is a conscious effort to live the message of the Gita. This does not mean that Gandhiji is indifferent to the efforts of scholars in this direction. The smallest questions of historical detail interest him intensely as I can say from personal knowledge . . . But his attitude is that in the last analysis it is the message that abides, and he is sure that no textual discovery is going to affect by a jot the essence or universality of that message. The same thing may be said about questions of the historical Krishna and the genesis and history of the Krishna Vasudeva worship . . .[31]

Further, Gandhi did not regard the *Gītā*, or even the *Mahābhārata* of which it appears as a part, as a historical narrative. The historical underpinnings were merely a literary device; the message had nothing to do with history.

> Even in 1888-9, when I first became acquainted with the Gita, I felt that it was not a historical work, but that, under the guise of physical warfare, it described the duel that perpetually went on in the hearts of mankind, and that physical warfare was brought in merely to make the description of the internal duel more alluring. This preliminary intuition became more confirmed on a closer study of religion and the Gita. A study of the Mahabharata gave it added confirmation. I do not regard the Mahabharata as a historical work in the accepted sense. The *Adiparva* contains powerful evidence in support of my opinion. By ascribing to the chief actors superhuman or subhuman origins, the great Vyasa made short work of the history of kings and their peoples. The persons therein described may be historical, but the author of the Mahabharata has used them merely to drive home his religious theme.[32]

Indeed, whenever he was confronted with a historical argument about the great Indian epics, trying to point out, for instance, the reality of warfare and violence in human life and of the relevance of a text such as the *Gītā* as a practical consideration of the ethics of power politics, Gandhi would insist that the truth of the *Mahābhārata* or the *Rāmāyaṇa* was a 'poetic truth', not historical; the epics were allegories and not theoretical or historical treatises. 'That they most probably deal with historical figures does not affect my proposition. Each epic describes the eternal duel that goes on between the forces of darkness and light.'[33]

To discover the truth, one would, of course, have to interpret the text to the best of one's knowledge and belief.

> Who is the best interpreter? Not learned men surely. Learning there must be. But religion does not live by it. It lives in the experiences of its saints and seers, in their lives and sayings. When all the most learned commentators of the scriptures are utterly forgotten, the accumulated experience of the sages and saints will abide and be an inspiration for ages to come.[34]

There might, of course, be conflicting interpretations of the epics and the scriptures. But such a dispute could never be resolved theoretically. Only the living practice of one's faith could show whether or not one's interpretation was correct. Gandhi mentions, for instance, the difference between his interpretation of the *Gītā* and the one followed by those who believed in armed violence.

> The grim fact is that the terrorists have in absolute honesty, earnestness and with cogency used the *Gita*, which some of them know by heart, in defence of their doctrine and policy. Only they have no answer to my interpretation of the *Gita*, except to say that mine is wrong and theirs is right. Time alone will show whose is right. The *Gita* is not a theoretical treatise. It is a living but silent guide whose directions one has to understand by patient striving.[35]

Gandhi's argument was exactly the same when dealing with questions such as scriptural sanctions for all those social practices which he thought were unjust and immoral. He would not admit that the mere existence of scriptural texts was proof that they must be a constituent or consistent part of true religion. Nor would he agree to submit his case to a historical examination of the origins or evolution of particular social institutions. On the caste system, for instance, his position was as follows:

> Caste has nothing to do with religion. It is a custom whose origin I do not know and do not need to know for the satisfaction of my spiritual hunger. But I do know that it is harmful both to spiritual and national growth.[36]

When his critics argued that caste practices were quite explicitly sanctioned by the *śāstra*, his emphatic reply was: 'Nothing in the Shastras which is manifestly contrary to universal truths and morals can stand.'[37] So also on the question of the social status of women as described in the canonical *smṛiti* texts:

> it is sad to think that the *Smritis* contain texts which can command no respect from men who cherish the liberty of woman as their own and who regard her as the mother of the race ... The question arises as to what to do with the *Smritis* that contain texts ... that are repugnant to the moral sense. I have already

suggested . . . that all that is printed in the name of scriptures need not be taken as the word of God or the inspired word.[38]

Gandhi's position, then, is that the true principles of religion or morality are universal and unchanging. There do exist religious traditions which represent the attempts by various people through the ages to discover and interpret these principles. But those traditions were the products of history; they could not be taken to represent a corpus of truths.

The true dharma is unchanging, while tradition may change with time. If we were to follow some of the tenets of *Manusmriti*, there would be moral anarchy. We have quietly discarded them altogether.[39]

Not only did Gandhi not share the historicism of the nationalist writers, he did not share their confidence in rationality and the scientific mode of knowledge. He would repeatedly assert that the knowledge unearthed by the sciences was applicable only to very limited areas of human living. If one did not acknowledge this and pretended instead that rational inquiry and a scientific search for truth would provide the solution for every problem in life, one would be either led to insanity or reduced to impotence.

Nowadays, I am relying solely on my intellect. But mere intellect makes one insane or unmanly. That is its function. In such a situation Rama is the strength of the weak. My innermost urge is for pure non-violence. My weakness is that I do not know how to make it work. I use my intellect to overcome that weakness. If this intellectual cleverness loses the support of truth, it will blur my vision of non-violence, for is not non-violence the same as truth? Mere practical sense is but a covering for truth. 'The face of truth is hidden by a golden lid.' The reasoning faculty will raise a thousand issues. Only one thing will save us from these and that is faith.[40]

Perhaps the most celebrated public controversy over Gandhi's preference for instinctive faith over the claims of scientific reasoning was when he pronounced that the devastating earthquakes in Bihar in 1934 were a 'divine chastisement' for the sin of untouchability. Rabindranath Tagore reacted very strongly and criticized Gandhi not only for implying that God, in inflicting punishment upon sinners, was unable to distinguish between the guilty and the innocent, since an earthquake is indiscriminate in its destruction, but also for strengthening the forces of unreason which fostered the belief that cosmic phenomena had something to do with the fate of human beings on earth.[41] Gandhi stuck to his position with characteristic firmness, but there was a somewhat unusual touch of acerbity in his reply.[42] He refused to entertain questions about the rationality of divine action.

I am not affected by posers such as 'why punishment for an age-old sin' or 'why punishment to Bihar and not to the South' or 'why an earthquake and not some other form of punishment'. My answer is: I am not God. Therefore I have but a limited knowledge of His purpose.[43]

He reiterated his belief 'that physical phenomena produce results both physical and spiritual. The converse I hold to be equally true.'[44] He admitted that his belief was 'instinctive' and that he could not prove it. 'But I would be untruthful and cowardly if, for fear of ridicule, when those that are nearest and dearest to me are suffering, I did not proclaim my belief from the house-top.'[45] In any case, there were very few things which we understood well enough to be able to prove by the use of reason. And 'where reason cannot function, it is faith that works'. Some physical phenomena were intricately related to our ways of living, and since we had only an 'infinitesimal' knowledge of the rational working of physical laws, the proper attitude would be to not remain content with this partial knowledge but to take a unified moral view of those relations.

> Rain is a physical phenomenon; it is no doubt related to human happiness and unhappiness; if so, how could it fail to be related to his good and bad deeds? We know of no period in human history when countless people have not related events like earthquakes to sinful deeds of man. Even today, religious-minded people everywhere believe in such a relationship.[46]

Such faith was based on firm principles of morality. It was not, therefore, superstitious.

> I beseech you not to laugh within yourself and think I want to appeal to your instinct of superstition. I don't. I am not given to making any appeal to the superstitious fears of people. I may be called superstitious, but I cannot help telling you what I feel deep down in me . . . You are free to believe it or to reject it.[47]

But by believing it, one could turn a human catastrophe into a social good. It did not matter what the correct scientific explanation was for such phenomena; by taking a firm moral attitude towards it, one could strengthen one's resolution to fight all of those things which were evil in human life.

> If my belief turns out to be ill-founded, it will still have done good to me and those who believe with me. For we shall have been spurred to more vigorous efforts towards self-purification, assuming, of course, that untouchability is a deadly sin.[48]

To Gandhi, then, truth did not lie in history, nor did science have any privileged access to it. Truth was moral: unified, unchanging and transcendental. It was not an object of critical inquiry or philosophical speculation. It could only be found in the experience of one's life, by the unflinching practice of moral living. It could never be correctly expressed within the terms of rational theoretical discourse; its only true expression was lyrical and poetic.[49] The universalist religiosity of this conception is utterly inconsistent with the dominant thematic of post-Enlightenment thought.

III

From this evidence, it is tempting to characterize Gandhism as yet another example of that typical reaction of the intelligentsia in many parts of the world to the social and moral depredations of advancing capitalism: romanticism. For instance, Gandhi's descriptions of the ideal moral order and the standpoint of his moral critique of civil society suggest strong similarities with that aspect of Russian *narodnichestvo* which Lenin called 'economic romanticism'.[50] In Gandhi too, there seems to be the vision of a utopia — 'a backward-looking petty-bourgeois utopia' — and an idealization of pre-capitalist economic and social relations. One could, of course, concede to Gandhi, as indeed Lenin did to the Populists, that despite the backwardness of his solution to the fundamental problems of a society in the throes of capitalist penetration, he nevertheless took 'a big step forward' by posing, comprehensively and in all its economic, political and moral aspects, the democratic demand of the small producers, chiefly the peasants. But in the theoretical sense, Gandhian ideology would still be 'reactionary', since, as Lenin pointed out in the case of the Russian Populists, not only is there simply a romantic longing for a return to an idealized medieval world of security and contentment, there is also 'the attempt to measure the new society with the old patriarchal yardstick, the desire to find a model in the old order and traditions, which are totally unsuited to the changed economic institutions'.[51] In spite of conceding the 'democratic points' in Gandhi's thought, therefore, the Leninist would have to pronounce that it is based on a false, indeed reactionary, theory of the world-historical process, or else that it refuses to acknowledge a theory of history at all. In either case, it would be a variant of romanticism.

This characterization gains further weight when one considers the sources of literary influence, explicitly acknowledged by Gandhi himself, which went into the formulation of his ideas on state and society. There was, for instance, Edward Carpenter's *Civilisation: Its Cause and Cure* which greatly influenced Gandhi's ideas on the corrupting effects of science, especially modern medicine. On the social consequences of the processes of industrial production, perhaps the greatest influence was John Ruskin's *Unto This Last*, that intensely moralistic critique of 'the modern *soi-disant* science of political economy'. On the fundamentally repressive nature of the powers of the state, and on the moral duty of peaceful resistance, a strong formative influence came from the political works of Tolstoy. It is true, of course, that Gandhi was highly eclectic in his borrowings, a task made easier in his case by the fact that he was unhampered by the formal theoretical requirements of scientific disciplines and philosophical schools. But there is little doubt that he was inherently sympathetic to many of the strands of argument put forward by 19th century European romantics and critics of rationalism and industrial progress.

A detailed examination of this question of influences would take us a long way from the central argument of this chapter. But the point about Gandhi's selectiveness in picking ideas from his favourite authors can be illustrated a little more in order to lead on to my next proposition that the fundamental core of the Gandhian ideology does not lie in a romantic problematic. For instance, Gandhi liked Edward Carpenter's argument about how the limitless increase of man's powers of production, brought on by the advent of modern science and technology, draws him away '(1) from Nature, (2) from his true Self, (3) from his Fellows', and how it works 'in every way to disintegrate and corrupt man —

literally to corrupt — to *break up* the unity of his nature'.[52] But Carpenter's critique of modern-day civilization was also based on a somewhat idiosyncratic reading of the anthropological theories in Lewis Morgan's *Ancient Society* and Frederick Engels's *The Origin of the Family, Private Property and the State*. This, in fact, was the main theoretical foundation on which Carpenter built his argument about how civilization, by transforming the nature of 'property', destroys man's unity with nature. Yet Carpenter's theoretical efforts do not seem to have made any impression on his more illustrious reader.

So also with Ruskin: Gandhi accepted Ruskin's cricitism of that 'political economy founded on self-interest' which had made 'mammon service' the new religion of society. He particularly liked the idea that although there had to be different professions, such as those of the soldier, the physician, the pastor, the lawyer or the merchant, their incomes must only be a payment to them from society, a means of their livelihood, and 'not the objects of their life'. He approved of Ruskin's suggestion that 'that country is richest which nourishes the greatest number of noble and happy human beings; that man is richest who, having perfected the functions of his own life to the utmost, has also the widest helpful influence, both personal, and by means of his possessions, over the lives of others'.[53] But Ruskin was also a historicist, influenced in important ways by German idealism and particularly by Hegel. Despite the contradictoriness which he shared with all the other critics of industrial civilization in Victorian Britain, Ruskin was, in the fundamental elements of his thought, a 'modernist'. Collingwood points out, for instance, that 'he cared intensely for science and progress, for political reform, for the advancement of knowledge and for new movements in art and letters'.[54] His critique of political economy was meant to show the painful contradictions between the dictates of a supposedly rational science and those of altruistic morality, and to suggest that there was something fundamentally wrong with that 'so-called science'. It was never meant to be a call for the abandonment of Reason. He was aware of the limits of the intellect but never supposed 'that "conscience" or "faith" may guide us where "intellect" breaks down'.[55]

All of these concerns were quite far removed from Gandhi's theoretical world. The critique of civil society which appears on the pages of *Hind Swaraj* does not emerge out of a consideration of the historical contradictions of civil society *as perceived from within it*. Quite unlike any of the European romantics, Gandhi is not torn between the conflicting demands of Reason and Morality, Progress and Happiness, Historical Necessity and Human Will. His idealization of a peaceful, non-competitive just and happy Indian society of the past could not have been 'a romantic longing for the lost harmony of the archaic world', because unlike romanticism, Gandhi's problem is not conceived at all within the thematic bounds of post-Enlightenment thought. He was not, for instance, seriously troubled by the problems of reconciling individuality with universalism, of being oneself and at the same time feeling at one with the infinite variety of the world. Nor was his solution one in which the individual, without merging into the world, would want to embrace the rich diversity of the world in himself. Indeed, these were concerns which affected many Indian 'modernists' of Gandhi's time, perhaps the most illustrious of them being Rabindranath Tagore. Gandhi shared neither the spiritual anguish nor indeed the aestheticism of these literary romantics of his time. Instead, his moral beliefs never seemed to lose that almost obdurate certitude which men like Tagore, or even Jawaharlal Nehru, found so exasperating.

The critique of civil society which forms such a central element of Gandhi's moral and political thinking is one which arises from an epistemic standpoint situated *outside* the thematic of post-Enlightenment thought. As such, it is a standpoint which could have been adopted by any member of the traditional intelligentsia in India, sharing the modes and categories of thought of a large pre-capitalist agrarian society, and reacting to the alien economic, political and cultural institutions imposed on it by colonial rule. But if this is all there was to Gandhism, it could hardly have acquired the tremendous power that it undoubtedly did in the history of nationalism in India and in the formation of the contemporary Indian state. It would indeed be a gross error to regard Gandhi as merely another 'peasant intellectual'; despite the inherently 'peasant–communal' character of its critique of civil society, the correct perspective for understanding the Gandhian ideology *as a whole* would be to study it in relation to the historical development of elite-nationalist thought in India. For Gandhism, like Russian populism, was not a direct expression of peasant ideology. It was an ideology conceived as an intervention in the elite-nationalist discourse of the time and was formed and shaped by the experiences of a specifically national movement. It is only by looking at it in that historical context that it becomes possible to understand the unique achievement of Gandhism: its ability to open up the possibility for achieving perhaps the most important historical task for a successful national revolution in a country like India, viz., the political appropriation of the subaltern classes by a bourgeoisie aspiring for hegemony in the new nation-state. In the Indian case, the largest popular element of the nation was the peasantry. And it was the Gandhian ideology which opened up the historical possibility for its appropriation into the evolving political structures of the Indian state.

In its critique of civil society, Gandhism adopted a standpoint that lay entirely outside the thematic of post-Enlightenment thought, and hence of nationalist thought as well. In its formulation of the problem of town–country economic exchanges, of the cultural domination of the new urban educated classes, and above all, of the legitimacy of resistance to an oppressive state apparatus, it was able to encapsulate perfectly the specific political demands as well as the modalities of thought of a peasant–communal consciousness. If one wishes to pursue the point about European influences on the formation of Gandhi's thought, it is in fact Tolstoy who emerges as the most interesting comparison. For unlike the Russian Populists, and particularly unlike N.K. Mikhaĭlovskiĭ, against whom Lenin directed one of his first major polemical attacks,[56] Tolstoy was a consistent anarchist in his critique of the bourgeois political order, and this from a standpoint which, as Andrzej Walicki has pointed out, was 'genuinely archaic': unlike any of the Populists, Tolstoy was 'apparently more easily able to identify himself with the world outlook of the primitive, patriarchal villagers'.[57] Tolstoy, like Gandhi, believed that 'the cause of the miserable position of the workers' was not something specific to capitalism: 'The cause must lie in that which drives them from the villages'.[58] He, too, argued against the determinism inherent in the assumptions of economic science which was 'so sure that all the peasants have inevitably to become factory operatives in towns' that it continually affirmed 'that all the country people not only are not injured by the transition from the country to the town, but themselves desire it, and strive towards it'.[59] Even more significant was Tolstoy's characterization of the entire edifice of the state as the institutionalized expression of morally unjustifiable violence. His answer to state oppression was complete and implacable resistance. One must not, he said, 'neither willingly, nor under compulsion, take any part in Governmental activity . . . nor, in fact, hold any office connected with violence', nor should one 'voluntarily pay taxes to Governments' or 'appeal to Governmental violence for the protection of his possessions'.[60] This thoroughgoing anarchism in Tolstoy was not accompanied by any specific political programme. There was simply a belief that the exemplary action of a few individuals, resisting the state by the strength of their conscience, would sway the people towards a massive movement against the institutions of violence.

> Men who accept a new truth when it has reached a certain degree of dissemination always do so suddenly and in a mass . . . The same is true of the bulk of humanity which suddenly, not one by one but always in a mass, passes from one arrangement of life to another under the influence of a new public opinion . . . And therefore the transformation of human life . . . will not come about solely by all men consciously and separately assimilating a certain Christian conception of life, but will come when a Christian public opinion so definite and comprehensible as to reach everybody has arisen and subdued that whole inert mass which is not able to attain the truth by its own intuition and is therefore always swayed by public opinion.[61]

In one aspect of his thought, Gandhi shared the same standpoint; but his thought ranged far beyond this specific ideological aspect. And it is here that the comparison with Tolstoy breaks down, because Gandhism also concerned itself with the practical organizational questions of a political *movement*. And this was a *national* political movement, required to operate within the institutional processes set up and directed by a colonial state. In its latter aspect, therefore, Gandhism had perforce to reckon with the practical realities of a bourgeois legal and political structure as indeed of the organizational issues affecting a bourgeois political movement. It was the unique achievement of Gandhian thought to have attempted to reconcile these two contradictory aspects which were, at one and the same time, its integral parts: a nationalism which stood upon a critique of the very idea of civil society, a movement supported by the bourgeoisie which rejected the idea of progress, the ideology of a political organization fighting for the creation of a modern national state which accepted at the same time the ideal of an 'enlightened anarchy'. Clearly there are many ambiguities in Gandhism. And a proper understanding of its history must go into a detailed examination of how these ambiguities created the possibility for those two great movements that form part of the story of the formation of the new Indian state: on the one hand, the transformation, in its own distinctive way in each region and among each strata, of the demands of the people into 'the message of the Mahatma',[62] and on the other, the appropriation of this movement into the structural forms of a bourgeois organizational, and later constitutional, order. But that is the task of modern Indian historiography; for the present, we can only indicate the elements in Gandhian thought which made possible the coexistence of these contradictory aspects within a single ideological unity. Here, we must turn to the celebrated concepts of *ahiṃsā* and *satyāgraha* and their epistemic basis in a conception that can only be described, fully in accordance with Gandhian terminology, as 'experimental'.

IV

'Truth,' wrote Gandhi to Mirabehn in 1933, 'is what everyone for the moment feels it to be.'[63] It was a decidedly personal quest, but it did not for that reason imply a moral anarchy. A few days before, in another letter, he had explained to her:

> We know the fundamental truth we want to reach, we know also the way. The details we do not know, we shall never know them all, because we are but very humble instruments among millions of such, moving consciously or unconsciously towards the divine event. We shall reach the Absolute Truth, if we will faithfully and steadfastly work out the relative truth as each one of us knows it.[64]

More publicly, in the Introduction to the *Autobiography* in 1925, Gandhi had written:

> for me, truth is the sovereign principle, which includes numerous other principles. This truth is not only truthfulness in word, but truthfulness in thought also, and not only the relative truth of our conception, but the Absolute Truth, the Eternal Principle, that is God. There are innumerable definitions of God . . . But I worship God as Truth only. I have not yet found Him, but I am seeking after Him . . . But as long as I have not realized this Absolute Truth, so long must I hold by the relative truth as I have conceived it. That relative truth must, meanwhile, be my beacon, my shield and buckler.[65]

There did exist an Absolute Truth, absolute and transcendental; to discover it was the purpose of our lives. But one could only proceed to find it in the experience of living, through an unswerving moral and truthful practice. At every stage, one had to be firmly committed to the truth as one knew it. At the same time, one had to be prepared to learn from experience, to put one's belief to the test, to accept the consequences and revise those beliefs if they were found wanting. Only then would one have for one's moral practice an epistemic foundation that was both certain and flexible, determinate and yet adaptable, categorical as well as experiential.

So much has now been written about Gandhi's 'truths' — the Absolute Truth, which must be sought for, and the various relative truths of our conception — that it is difficult to talk about the subject without referring to various current interpretations of those concepts. But once again, this will take us away from the central line of my argument. I must, therefore, accept the risk of inviting charges of distortion and oversimplification, and without explaining its relation to the vast body of Gandhian literature, simply proceed to state my own understanding of the conception of 'truth' in the overall structure and effectivity of the Gandhian ideology. In *Hind Swaraj*, the critique of modern civilization, and the plea for a return to the simple self-sufficiency of 'traditional' village life were based on the idea that it was the very changelessness of Indian civilization, its timeless ahistoricity, which was proof of its truth. India was resistant to change because it was not necessary for it to change: its civilization had found the true principles of social organization.

> It is a charge against India that her people are so uncivilized, ignorant and stolid, that it is not possible to induce them to adopt any changes. It is a charge really against our merit. What we have tested and found true on the anvil of experience, we dare not change.[66]

All that was necessary now was to find a way of protecting that social organization from the destructive consequences of colonial rule and of eliminating the poverty that had been brought upon the people. The answer was a rejection of the entire institutional edifice of civil society, uncompromising resistance to its economic, cultural and political structures. There was no specific conception yet of a political process of struggle, of its organizational procedures, norms of practice, strategic and tactical principles. As Gandhi explained later in the *Autobiography*, 'In [*Hind Swaraj*] I took it as understood that anything that helped India to get rid of the grinding poverty of her masses would in the same process also establish swaraj.'[67] It was only in the context of the evolution of the political movement that the Gandhian ideology became something more than a utopian doctrine. It acquired a theory of the political process within which the movement was to function; it developed its own organizational principles of political practice. In course of the full working out of Gandhian thought, the sheer tactical malleability of the 'experimental' conception of truth became the principal means by which all the seemingly irreconcilable parts of that ideology were put together.

Consider *satyāgraha*, that celebrated Gandhian form of mass political action. In 1917 Gandhi explained that *satyāgraha* was not mere passive resistance. It meant 'intense activity' — political activity — by large masses of people. It was a legitimate, moral and truthful form of political action by the people against the injustices of the state, an active mass resistance to unjust rule. It was not aimed at the destruction of the state, nor was it — as yet — conceived as part of a political process intended to replace the functionaries of the state.

> We can . . . free ourselves of the unjust rule of the Government by defying the unjust rule and accepting the punishments that go with it. We do not bear malice towards the Government. When we set its fears at rest, when we do not desire

to make armed assaults on the administrators, nor to unseat them from power, but only to get rid of their injustice, they will at once be subdued to our will.[68]

Satyāgraha, at this stage, was intended to articulate only a 'negative consciousness'. It is, therefore, easy to recognise why it could express so effectively the characteristic modes of peasant–communal resistance to oppressive state authority.[69] It was true, of course, that peasant resistance to injustice was not always restricted to non-violent forms: there was much historical evidence to this effect. But at this stage, Gandhi was quite dismissive of these objections.

> It is said that it is a very difficult, if not an altogether impossible, task to educate ignorant peasants in satyagraha and that it is full of perils, for it is a very arduous business to transform unlettered ignorant people from one condition into another. Both the arguments are just silly. The people of India are perfectly fit to receive the training of satyagraha. India has knowledge of dharma, and where there is knowledge of dharma, satyagraha is a very simple matter . . . Some have a fear that once people get involved in satyagraha, they may at a later stage take arms. This fear is illusory. From the path of satyagraha, a transition to the path of *a-satyagraha* is impossible. It is possible of course that some people who believe in armed activity may mislead the satyagrahis by infiltrating into their ranks and later making them take to arms. This is possible in all enterprises. But as compared to other activities, it is less likely to happen in satyagraha, for their motives soon get exposed and when the people are not ready to take up arms, it becomes almost impossible to lead them on to that terrible path.[70]

Nor was the question of leadership, and of the relation between leaders and the masses, seen as being particularly problematical in the political sense:

> People in general always follow in the footsteps of the noble. There is no doubt that it is difficult to produce a satyagrahi leader. Our experience is that a satyagrahi needs many more virtues like self-control, fearlessness, etc., than are requisite for one who believes in armed action . . . The birth of such a man can bring about the salvation of India in no time. Not only India but the whole world awaits the advent of such a man. We may in the meantime prepare the ground as much as we can through satyagraha.[71]

It was this faith in the relatively spontaneous strength of popular resistance to injustice that lay behind the call to the nation to join in the agitations in 1919 against the Rowlatt Bill. There was little concern yet about the distinction between leader and *satyāgrahī* or the *satyāgrahī* and the masses, or about the precise degree of maturity before the masses could be asked to join a *satyāgraha*, or about the organizational and normative safeguards against the inherent unpredictability of a negative consciousness playing itself out in the political battleground. In March 1919, Gandhi was still able to say to the people:

> whether you are satyagrahis or not, so long as you disapprove of the Rowlatt legislation, all can join and I hope that there will be such a response throughout

the length and breadth of India as would convince the Government that we are
alive to what is going on in our midst.[72]

All this, of course, changed after the experience of the Rowlatt *satyāgraha*:
'a rapier run through my body could hardly have pained me more'.[73] He had
made a massive error of judgment and there was, he admitted, some truth in the
charge that he had ignored a few obvious lessons of political history.

> I think that I at least should have foreseen some of the consequences, specially in
> view of the gravest warnings that were given to me by friends whose advice I have
> always sought and valued. But I confess that I am dense. I am not joking. So
> many friends have told me that I am incapable of profiting by other people's
> experiences and that in every case I want to go through the fire myself and learn
> only after bitter experience. There is exaggeration in this charge, but there is also
> a substance of truth in it. This denseness in me is at once a weakness and a
> strength. I could not have remained a satyagrahi had I not cultivated the quality
> of stubborn resistance and such resistance can only come from experience and
> not from inference.[74]

But the experience of his first political agitation on a national scale brought in
Gandhi a 'new realization'. He now became aware of the fundamental
incompatibility of political action informed solely by a negative consciousness
with the procedural norms of a bourgeois legal order. The ethics of resistance, if
it was to be relevant to a bourgeois political movement, would have to be
reconciled with a theory of political obedience. 'Unfortunately,' he said,

> popular imagination has pictured satyagraha as purely and simply civil
> disobedience, if not in some cases even criminal disobedience . . . As satyagraha
> is being brought into play on a large scale on the political field for the first time, it
> is in an experimental stage. I am therefore ever making new discoveries. And my
> error in trying to let civil disobedience take the people by storm appears to me to
> be Himalayan because of the discovery I have made, namely, that he only is able
> and attains the right to offer civil disobedience who has known how to offer
> voluntary and deliberate obedience to the laws of the State in which he is
> living.[75]

And from this fundamental discovery flowed a new organizational principle; as
he later explained in the *Autobiography*:

> I wondered how I could have failed to perceive what was so obvious. I realized
> that before a people could be fit for offering civil disobedience, they should
> thoroughly understand its deeper implications. That being so, before restarting
> civil disobedience on a mass scale, it would be necessary to create a band of well-
> tried, pure-hearted volunteers who thoroughly understood the strict conditions of
> satyagraha.[76]

Thus was born the *political* concept of the *satyāgrahī* as leader. In the
course of his evidence before the Hunter Committee appointed to inquire into
the Rowlatt Bill agitations, Gandhi was asked about his conception of the
relation between leaders and followers.

C.H. Setalvad. I take it that your scheme, as you conceive it, involves the determination of what is the right path and the true path by people who are capable of high intellectual and moral equipment and a large number of other people following them without themselves being able to arrive at similar conclusions by reason of their lower moral and intellectual equipment?
Gandhi. I cannot subscribe to that, because I have not said that. I do not say that they are not to exercise their judgment, but I simply say that, in order that they may exercise their judgment, the same mental and moral equipment is not necessary.
C.H.S. Because they are to accept the judgment of people who are capable of exercising better judgment and equipped with better moral and intellectual standard?
G. Naturally, but I think that is in human nature, but I exact nothing more than I would exact from an ordinary human being.[77]

While mass resistance to unjust laws was the final and only certain guarantee against state oppression, the people would have to depend on their leaders for guidance.

Jagat Narayan. My point is, having regard to the circumstances, a sort of sanctity attaches to the laws of the Government of the time being?
Gandhi. Not in my estimation . . .
J.N. That is not the best check on the masses?
G. Not a blind adherence to laws, no check whatsoever. It is because either they blindly adhere or they blindly commit violence. Either event is undesirable.
J.N. So as every individual is not fit to judge for himself, he would have to follow somebody?
G. Certainly, he would have to follow somebody. The masses will have to choose their leaders most decidedly.[78]

The point was further clarified when Gandhi was asked about his understanding of the reasons why the agitations had become violent. Soon after the events in Ahmedabad, Gandhi had told a mass meeting: 'It seems that the deeds I have complained of have been done in an organized manner. There seems to be a definite design about them, and I am sure that there must be some educated and clever man or men behind them . . . You have been misled into doing these deeds by such people.'[79] Elaborating on what he meant by 'organized manner', Gandhi said to the Hunter Committee:

In my opinion, the thing was organised, but there it stands. There was no question whether it was a deep-laid conspiracy through the length and breadth of India or a deep-rooted organisation of which this was a part. The organisation was hastily constructed; the organisation was not in the sense in which we understand the word organisation . . . If I confined that word to Ahmedabad alone, to masses of absolutely unlettered men, who would be able to make no fine distinctions — then you have got the idea of what that organisation is . . . There were these poor deluded labourers whose one business was to see me released and see Anasuyabai released. That it was a wicked rumour deliberately started by somebody I have not the slightest doubt. As soon as these things happened the people thought there should be something behind it. Then there were the half-educated raw youths. This is the work of these, I am grieved to have to say. These youths possessed themselves with false ideas gathered from shows, such as the cinematograph shows that they have seen, gathered from silly novels and from the political literature of Europe . . . it was an organisation of this character.[80]

The direct physical form in which the masses appeared in the political arena was always that of a mob. It had no mind of its own.[81] Its behaviour was determined entirely by the way it was led: 'nothing is so easy as to train mobs, for the simple reason that they have no mind, no premeditation. They act in a frenzy. They repent quickly.'[82] For this reason, they were as susceptible to manipulation by mischief-makers as they were open to enlightened leadership. In order, therefore, to undertake mass political action, it was necessary first of all to create a selfless, dedicated and enlightened group of political workers who would lead the masses and protect them from being misguided.

> Before we can make real headway, we must train these masses of men who have a heart of gold, who feel for the country, who want to be taught and led. But a few intelligent, sincere, local workers are needed, and the whole nation can be organized to act intelligently, and democracy can be evolved out of mobocracy.[83]

This was the problematic which lay at the heart of what soon evolved into the other celebrated concept in the Gandhian ideology — the concept of *ahiṃsā*. In its application to politics, *ahiṃsā* was also about 'intense political activity' by large masses of people. But it was not so much about resistance as about the *modalities* of resistance, about organizational principles, rules of conduct, strategies and tactics. *Ahiṃsā* was the necessary complement to the concept of *satyāgraha* which both limited it and, at the same time, made it something more than 'purely and simply civil disobedience'. *Ahiṃsā* was the rule for concretizing the 'truth' of *satyāgraha*. 'Truth is a positive value, while non-violence is a negative value. Truth affirms. Non-violence forbids something which is real enough.'[84] *Ahiṃsā*, indeed, was the concept — both ethical and epistemological because it was defined within a moral and epistemic practice that was wholly 'experimental' — which supplied Gandhism with a theory of *politics*, enabling it to become the ideology of a national political movement. It was the organizing principle for a 'science' of politics — a science wholly different from all current conceptions of politics which had only succeeded in producing the 'sciences of violence', but a science nevertheless — the 'science of non-violence', the 'science of love'. It was the moral framework for solving every practical problem of the organized political movement.

The 'science of non-violence', consequently, dealt with questions such as the requirements for being a political *satyāgrahī*, his rules of conduct, his relations with the political leadership as well as with the masses, questions about the structure of decision-making, lines of command, political strategies and tactics, and about the practical issues of breaking as well as obeying the laws of the state. It was as much a 'science' of political struggle, indeed as much a military science, as the 'sciences of violence', only it was superior because it was a science not of arms but of the moral force of the soul. At this level, in fact, it was not a utopian conception at all. There was no assumption, for instance, of collective consensus in the making of decisions, for that would be wishing away the existence of a practical political problem. Decisions were to be taken by 'a few true satyagrahis'. This would provide a far more economic and efficient method of political action than that proposed by the 'sciences of violence': 'we would require a smaller army of satyagrahis than that of soldiers trained in modern warfare, and the cost will be insignificant compared to the fabulous sums devoted by nations to armaments'.[85] Second, the practice of this 'experimental science' of mass political action was not conditional upon the masses themselves understanding all its principles or their full implications.

> A soldier of an army does not know the whole of the military science; so also does a satyagrahi not know the whole science of satyagraha. It is enough if he trusts his commander and honestly follows his instructions and is ready to suffer unto death without bearing malice against the so-called enemy . . . [The satyagrahis] must render heart discipline to their commander. There should be no mental reservation.[86]

Third, the political employment of *ahiṃsā* did not depend upon everyone accepting it as a creed. It was possible for it to be regarded as a valid political theory even without its religious core. This, in fact, was the only way it could become a general guide for solving the practical problems of an organized political movement.

> Ahimsa with me is a creed, the breath of life. But it is never as a creed that I placed it before India or, for that matter, before anyone except in casual or informal talks. I placed it before the Congress as a political weapon, to be employed for the solution of practical problems.[87]

And thus we come to an explicit recognition, within the overall unity of the Gandhian ideology as it took shape in the course of the evolution of the national movement, of a *disjuncture* between morality and politics, between private conscience and public responsibility, indeed between Noble Folly and *Realpolitik*. It was a disjuncture which the 'experimental' conception of *ahiṃsā* was meant to bridge. And yet, it was a disjuncture the steadfast denial of whose very existence had been the foundation of the original conception of *Hind Swaraj*. Now, however, we see the spinning wheel, for instance, coming to acquire a dual significance, located on entirely different planes, and it is no longer considered politically necessary for the personal religion to be identified with a political programme.

> I have never tried to make anyone regard the spinning-wheel as his *kamadhenu* or universal provider . . . When in 1908 . . . I declared my faith in the spinning-wheel in the pages of *Hind Swaraj*, I stood absolutely alone . . . I do regard the spinning-wheel as a gateway to *my* spiritual salvation, but I recommend it to others only as a powerful weapon for the attainment of swaraj and the amelioration of the economic condition of the country.[88]

In 1930, on the eve of the Dandi March, we find Gandhi telling his colleagues that he did not know what form of democracy India should have. He was not particularly interested in the question: 'the method alone interests me, and by method I mean the agency through which the wishes of the people are reached. There are only two methods; one is that of fraud and force; the other is that of non-violence and truth.'[89] It did not matter even if the goal was beyond reach. The first responsibility of the political leader was to strictly adhere to his principles of morality.

> What I want to impress on everyone is that I do not want India to reach her goal through questionable means. Whether that is possible or not is another question. It is sufficient for my present purpose if the person who thinks out the plan and leads the people is absolutely above board and has non-violence and truth in him.[90]

And once there is a recognition of the disjuncture, the failure of politics to reach Utopia could be attributed to the loftiness of the ideal, noble, truthful and inherently unreachable, or else, equally credibly, to the imperfections of the human agency. The vision of a non-violent India could be 'a mere day-dream, a childish folly'.[91] Or else, one could argue with equal validity that the problem lay not with the ideal but with one's own deficiencies.

> I do not think it is right to say that the principles propounded in *Hind Swaraj* are not workable just because I cannot practise them perfectly . . . not only do I refuse to excuse myself, but positively confess my shortcoming.[92]

The result, of course, was that under the moral umbrella of the quest for utopia, the experimental conception of politics could accommodate a potentially limitless range of imperfections, adjustments, compromises and failures. For the authority of the political leader derived not from the inherent reasonableness of his programme or the feasibility of his project, not even from the accordance of that programme or project with a collective perception of common interests or goals. It derived entirely from a moral claim — of personal courage and sacrifice and a patent adherence to truth. So much so that the supreme test of political leadership was death itself. That was the final proof of the leader's claim to the allegiance of his people. At Anand, in the middle of the Dandi March, Gandhi said,

> This band of satyagrahis which has set out is not staging a play; its effect will not be merely temporary; even through death, it will prove true to its pledge — if death becomes necessary . . . Nothing will be better than if this band of satyagrahis perishes. If the satyagrahis meet with death, it will put a seal upon their claim.[93]

And when Jairamdas Doulatram was injured in a police firing in Karachi during the Civil Disobedience movement, Gandhi sent a telegram to the Congress office saying:

> CONSIDER JAIRAMDAS MOST FORTUNATE. BULLET WOUND THIGH BETTER THAN PRISON. WOUND HEART BETTER STILL. BAPU.[94]

Gandhism finally reconciled the contradictions between the utopian and the practical aspects of its political ideology by surrendering to the absolute truthfulness and supreme self-sacrifice of the *satyāgrahī*. It had gained its strength from an intensely powerful moral critique of the existing state of politics. In the end, it saved its Truth by escaping from politics.

V

And yet, as Gandhi himself put it, 'politics encircle us today like the coil of a snake'.[95] The historical impact of the Gandhian ideology on the evolution of Indian politics was of monumental significance.

The 'science of non-violence' was the form in which Gandhism addressed itself to the problematic of nationalism. That was the 'science' which was to provide answers to the problems of national politics, of concretizing the nation as an active historical subject rejecting the domination of a foreign power, of devising its political organization and the strategic and tactical principles of its struggle. In its specific historical effectivity, Gandhism provided for the first time in Indian politics an ideological basis for including the *whole people* within the political nation. In order to do this, it quite consciously sought to bridge even the most sanctified cultural barriers that divided the people in an immensely complex agrarian society. Thus, it was not simply a matter of bringing the peasantry into the national movement, but of consciously seeking the ideological means for bringing it in *as a whole*. This, for instance, is how one can interpret the strenuous efforts by Gandhi to obliterate the 'sin' of the existing *jāti* divisions in Indian society, and the 'deadly sin' of untouchability in particular, and to replace it by an idealized scheme based on the *varṇa* classification.[96] 'Do you not think', Gandhi was asked, 'that the improvement of the condition of starving peasants is more important than the service of Harijans? Will you not, therefore, form peasant organizations which will naturally include Harijans in so far as their economic condition is concerned?' 'Unfortunately,' Gandhi replied,

> the betterment of the economic condition of peasants will not necessarily include the betterment of that of the Harijans. The peasant who is not a Harijan can rise as high as he likes and opportunity permits him, but not so the poor suppressed Harijan. The latter cannot own and use land as freely as the *savarna* peasant . . . therefore, a special organization for the service of Harijans is a peremptory want in order to deal with the special and peculiar disabilities of Harijans. Substantial improvement of these, the lowest strata of society, must include the whole of society.[97]

Whether this idiom of solidarity necessarily referred to a cultural code that could be shown to be 'essentially Hindu', and whether that in turn alienated rather than united those sections of the people who were not 'Hindu', are of course important questions, but not strictly relevant in establishing the ideological intent behind Gandhi's efforts.

Thus, while the search was for an ideological means to unite the whole people, there was also a determinate political structure and process, specific and historically given, within which the task had to be accomplished. And here it was the 'experimental' conception of truth, combining the absolute moral legitimacy of *satyāgraha* with the tactical considerations of *ahiṃsā*, which made the Gandhian ideology into a powerful instrument in the historical task of constructing the new Indian state.

For now one could talk, within the overall unity of that ideology, of the constructive relation of the national movement to the evolving institutional structure of state power. Gandhi could say, on the one hand, 'I shall retain my disbelief in legislatures as an instrument for obtaining swaraj in terms of masses', and in the same breath go on to argue,

> But I see that I have failed to wean some of the Congressmen from their faith in council-entry. The question therefore is whether they should or should not enforce their desire to enter legislature as Congress representatives. I have no doubt that they must have the recognition they want. Not to give it will be to refuse to make use of the talents we possess.[98]

Indeed, the truth of the moral conception of utopia was for ever safe, no matter what compromises one had to make in the world of practical politics.

> The parliamentary work must be left to those who are so inclined. I hope that the majority will always remain untouched by the glamour of council work. In its own place, it will be useful. But . . . Swaraj can only come through an all-round conciousness of the masses.[99]

Similarly, the acceptance of ministerial office by Congressmen in 1937, an act apparently in complete contradiction with the spirit of non-cooperation enshrined in the Congress movement in 1920, now became 'not a repudiation but a fulfilment of the original, so long as the mentality behind all of them remains the same as in 1920'.[100] And if the disharmony between the act and the mentality became much too gross, the final moral act that would save the truth of the ideal was withdrawal. When the evidence became overwhelming that Congressmen as officers of the state were not exhibiting the selflessness, ability and incorruptibility that was the justification for their being in office, Gandhi's plea to Congressmen was to make a choice:

> either to apply the purge I have suggested, or, if that is not possible because of the Congress being already overmanned by those who have lost faith in its creed and its constructive programme on which depends its real strength, to secede from it for its own sake and proving his living faith in the creed and programme by practising the former and prosecuting the latter as if he had never seceded from the Congress of his ideal.[101]

Then again, the ideal of property as trust was 'true in theory only'. Like all other ideals, it would

> remain an unattainable ideal, so long as we are alive, but towards which we must ceaselessly strive. Those who own money now are asked to behave like trustees holding their riches on behalf of the poor. You may say that trusteeship is a legal fiction . . . Absolute trusteeship is an abstraction like Euclid's definition of a

point, and is equally unattainable. But if we strive for it, we shall be able to go further in realizing a state of equality on earth than by any other method.

Q. But if you say that private possession is incompatible with non-violence, why do you put up with it?

A. That is a concession one has to make to those who earn money but who would not voluntarily use their earnings for the benefit of mankind.[102]

Sometimes the justification for this concession was crassly empirical: 'I am quite clear that if a strictly honest and unchallengeable referendum of our millions were to be taken, they would not vote for wholesale expropriation of the propertied classes.'[103] At other times, it would seem to rest on a fairly sophisticated reading of the lessons of political history: the zamindars

must regard themselves, even as the Japanese nobles did, as trustees holding their wealth for the good of their wards, the ryots . . . I am convinced that the capitalist, if he follows the Samurai of Japan, has nothing really to lose and everything to gain. There is no other choice than between voluntary surrender on the part of the capitalist of superfluities and consequent acquisition of the real happiness of all on the one hand, and on the other the impending chaos into which, if the capitalist does not wake up betimes, awakened but ignorant, famishing millions will plunge the country and which not even the armed force that a powerful Government can bring into play can avert.[104]

But in considering questions of this sort, having to do with the practical organizational issues of a bourgeois political movement, Gandhism would inevitably slip into the familiar thematic of nationalist thought. It would argue in terms of categories such as capitalism, socialism, law, citizenship, private property, individual rights, and struggle to fit its formless utopia into the conceptual grid of post-Enlightenment social-scientific thought.

Let us not be obsessed with catchwords and seductive slogans imported from the West. Have we not our own distinct Eastern traditions? Are we not capable of finding our own solution to the question of capital and labour? . . . Let us study our Eastern institutions in that spirit of scientific inquiry and we shall evolve a truer socialism and a truer communism than the world has yet dreamed of. It is surely wrong to presume that Western socialism or communism is the last word on the question of mass poverty.[105]

. . . Class war is foreign to the essential genius of India which is capable of evolving a form of communism broad-based on the fundamental rights of all and equal justice to all.[106]

Sometimes, in trying to defend his political strategy of nationalist struggle, Gandhi would even feel forced to resort to some of the most naive cultural essentialisms of Orientalist thought:

By her very nature, India is a lover of peace . . . On the other hand, Mustafa Kamal Pasha succeeded with the sword because there is strength in every nerve of a Turk. The Turks have been fighters for centuries. The people of India have followed the path of peace for thousands of years . . . There is at the present time not a single country on the face of the earth which is weaker than India in point of physical strength. Even tiny Afghanistan can growl at her.[107]

These difficulties are symptomatic of the curious relationship between Gandhism and the thematic and problematic of nationalist thought. In its historical effectivity, we would be perfectly justified in characterizing the entire story of the Gandhian intervention in India's nationalist politics as the moment of manoeuvre in the 'passive revolution of capital' in India. But that is not something that can be read directly from the ideological intent expressed in Gandhian texts. Rather, we must identify the possibility of manoeuvre, the result of the struggle of social forces in the battlefield of politics, in the very tensions within Gandhism — in the fundamental ambiguity of its relation to nationalist thought, in the way in which it challenged the basic premises on which the latter was built and yet sought at the same time to insert itself into the process of a nationalist politics.

There was, as we have seen, a fundamental incompatibility between the utopianism which shaped the moral conception of Gandhian politics and the realities of power within a bourgeois constitutional order. It is not as though Gandhism was unaware of this disjunction; it did not dogmatically deny the existence of the gap nor did it insist that it could be bridged with ease. What it suggested was a certain method of political practice — imperfect but innately truthful, flexible and yet principled. But once the groundswell of popular upsurge had subsided and the nationalist state leadership knew that power was within its reach, it was not easy to determine what this truthful political practice was now going to be. What was the duty of the true servant of the Congress: take up the new responsibilities of running the state or stay outside it and continue the struggle towards what was known to be an unreachable goal?

Gandhi's belief was that the true *satyāgrahī* would always choose the latter. True non-violent *svarāj* would only come by pursuing the programme of rural construction; the parliamentary programme could at best bring 'political swaraj' which was not true *svarāj*.[108] As late as November 1945, Gandhi instructed members of the All India Spinners' Association, the central body of *khādī* workers, not to take part in elections or any other political activity of that sort.[109] But by 1945-6 many of his closest and most trusted associates in the constructive work programme were being asked by the Congress to enter government, and when they turned to him for advice his replies were curiously hesitant, sometimes even petulant: 'I do not want to dampen your interest. You have the aptitude for it. Nor would I consider your going into the Assembly a bad thing. After all someone has to go there. What I mean is that neither you nor anyone else can ride two horses at the same time.'[110] 'As regards the Provincial Assembly you may take it that I am not interested. But if you are inclined that way and have the ability for it, and if all others agree, please do go.'[111] In several cases he qualified his permission by a reminder about the importance of non-attachment in the life of a leader of the people:

Because all your friends want it, you may seek election to the Assembly if it can be done without any exertion on your part and on the clear understanding that it

113

will be a bed of thorns and not of velvet . . . Refrain from all arguments and discussions, observe silence, and if even then people elect you go to the Assembly. You should not make any effort on your part to get elected.[112]

. . . You can give your name for the Provincial election on the condition that you would neither beg for votes from the electorate nor spend any money. If you can get elected on this condition you may enter the Assembly.[113]

Later he issued a general message for all Congressmen:

I believe that some Congressmen ought to seek election in the legislatures or other elected bodies. In the past I did not hold this view. I had hoped that the boycott of legislatures would be complete. That was not to be. Moreover times have changed. Swaraj seems to be near. Under the circumstances it is necessary that Congress should contest every seat in the legislatures. The attraction should never be the honour that a seat in a legislature is said to give . . . Moreover those that are not selected by the Board should not feel hurt. On the contrary, they should feel happy that they are left there to render more useful service. But the painful fact is that those who are not selected by the Board do feel hurt.

The Congress should not have to spend money on the elections. Nominees of a popular organization should be elected without any effort on the latter's part . . .

Let us examine the utility value of legislatures . . . He who can tell the people why they become victims of the Government . . . and can teach them how to stand up against Government wrongs renders a real service. The members cannot do this essential service, for their business is to make people look to them for the redress of wrongs. [The Gujarati version of this article has a much stronger sentence: 'Councils are, have been and will be, an obstruction in this work.']

The other use of legislatures is to prevent undesirable legislation and bring in laws which are useful for the public, so that as much help as possible can be given to the constructive programme.[114]

Thus, even while conceding that many Congressmen must now enter the business of running the state machinery, Gandhi still appeared to see them in a largely oppositional role, pointing out the misdeeds of government and preventing the enactment of bad laws. The only positive role he could envisage for the national government was the support it might provide for the constructive programme. In mid-1946 he even made some specific suggestions in this regard:

The Government should notify the villagers that they will be expected to manufacture khaddar for the needs of their villages within a fixed date after which no cloth will be supplied to them. The Governments in their turn will supply the villagers with cotton seed or cotton wherever required, at cost price and the tools of manufacture also at cost, to be recovered in easy instalments . . .

The villages will be surveyed and a list prepared of things that can be manufactured locally with little or no help and which may be required for village use or for sale outside . . . If enough care is taken, the villages, most of them as good as dead or dying, will hum with life and exhibit the immense possibilities they have of supplying most of their wants themselves and of the cities and towns of India.[115]

In addition to these, Gandhi suggested two other areas in which the government could help: the preservation of cattle wealth and the spread of basic education. A few weeks later, he also proposed a modality of work: the ministers, he said, should pick out from the bureaucracy 'honest and incorruptible men' and put them under the guidance of organizations such as the All India Spinners' Association, the All India Village Industries Association and the Hindustani Talimi Sangh. The official notification regarding the stopping of mill cloth and the exclusive use of *khādī* in villages should include both villagers and mill-owners as parties to the scheme. 'The notification will show clearly that it is the people's measure, though bearing the Government stamp.' Visualizing himself in the role of minister in charge of the revival of villages, Gandhi posed the basic decision problem which he thought the new national government must face: 'The only question for me as minister is whether the AISA has the conviction and capacity to shoulder the burden of creating and guiding a khadi scheme to success. If it has, I would put my little barque to sea with all confidence.'[116]

Thus, even while identifying a specific role for the state in the programme of national construction, Gandhi was not abandoning his fundamental belief that the state could never be the appropriate machinery for carrying out this programme. What he was suggesting in fact was that the national state should formally use its legislative powers to *abdicate* its presumed responsibility of promoting 'development' and thus clear the ground for popular non-state agencies to take up the work of revitalizing the village economies.

Was he then advocating a sort of *laissez-faire* policy? If the state was to abandon its controlling role in the national economy, would it not leave the field open for exploiters and powerful vested interests to take an even firmer control over the means of economic exploitation? Now that the popular nationalist forces had come to power, was not a certain degree of intervention, even coercion, necessary and desirable in order to check those exploitative interests? This was the ideological argument which the increasingly dominant section of the nationalist state leadership offered against Gandhian 'visionaries'. For the national state to abandon its economic responsibilities, these leaders argued, would be a reactionary step.

Faced with this argument, Gandhi's response was to reassert the claims of his moral conception. The immediate political battle against colonial rule had been virtually won. Now the question of the relation between the nation and the state was posed more sharply than ever before. Having acceeded to the political compulsions of bourgeois politics for two and a half decades, Gandhi in the last years of his life resumed the struggle for Utopia.

Now he insisted with renewed conviction that mere 'political swaraj' could never be a substitute for 'true swaraj'. He reasserted the ideal of *Rāmarājya* and defined it concretely as 'independence — political, economic and moral':

'Political' necessarily means the removal of the control of the British army in every shape and form.

'Economic' means entire freedom from British capitalists and capital, as also their Indian counterparts . . . This can take place only by capital or capitalists sharing their skill and capital with the lowliest and the least.

'Moral' means freedom from armed defence forces. My conception of *Ramarajya* excludes replacement of the British army by a national army of occupation. A country that is governed by even its national army can never be morally free.[117]

While the existence of the state remained a practical reality, the true ideal of the stateless society needed to be posited with renewed emphasis, now that the immediate political battle had been won and yet the task of reconstructing the national society remained unaccomplished. The question was not whether statelessness could ever be actually achieved; the question was whether one's political practice should rest on a firm moral principle or whether the principle should be relinquished.

Would there be State power in an ideal society or would such a society be Stateless? I think the question is futile. If we continue to work towards the building of such a society, to some extent it is bound to be realized and to that extent people will benefit by it. Euclid has defined a straight line as having no breadth, but no one has yet succeeded in drawing such a line and no one ever will. Still we can progress in geometry only by postulating such a line. This is true of every ideal.

We might remember though that a Stateless society does not exist anywhere in the world. If such a society is possible it can be established first only in India. For attempts have been made in India towards bringing about such a society. We have not so far shown that supreme herosim. The only way is for those who believe in it to set the example.[118]

But no matter how relentlessly Gandhi insisted on a renewal of the moral battle, it had by then become patently obvious that the main body of the Congress leadership was now fully engaged in the task of running a modern state machinery on a national scale, using the full range of its coercive instruments. Gandhi saw this as a moral failure on the part of the political leadership, a surrender to the forces of violence. 'Congressmen think that now it is their government . . . Everywhere Congressmen are thus scrambling for power and favours . . . A government seems to have only military power behind it, but it cannot run on the strength of that power alone.'[119] Repeatedly in the last months of his life he spoke of his helplessness, a feeling that acquired greater poignancy in the midst of the mad violence of communal strife which marked the transfer of power.

Whatever the Congress decides will be done; nothing will be according to what I say. My writ runs no more. If it did the tragedies in the Punjab, Bihar and Noakhali would not have happened. No one listens to me any more. I am a small man. True, there was a time when mine was a big voice. Then everyone obeyed what I said; now neither the Congress nor the Hindus nor the Muslims listen to me. Where is the Congress today? It is disintegrating. I am crying in the wilderness.[120]

In sorrow not unmixed with anger Gandhi suggested that henceforth the Congress should stop talking about truth and non-violence and that it should remove the words 'peaceful and legitimate' from its constitution. 'I am convinced that so long as the army or the police continues to be used for conducting the administration we shall remain subservient to the British or some other foreign power, irrespective of whether the power is in the hands of the Congress or others.'[121] By not claiming to follow 'peaceful and legitimate' means, the Congress would at least not be hypocritical.[122]

Once again, therefore, Gandhism sought to explain the defeat of its utopian quest by putting the blame on the moral failings of those who claimed to be leaders of the people. But in truth Gandhism as a political ideology had now been brought face to face with its most irreconcilable contradiction. While it insisted on the need to stay firm in the adherence to its ideal, it was no longer able to specify concretely the modalities of implementing this as a viable *political* practice. Now that there were powerful and organized interests *within* the nation which clearly did not share the belief in the Gandhian ideal, there was no way in which the Gandhian ideology could identify a social force which would carry forward the struggle and overcome this opposition in the arena of politics.

VI

Nowhere was this basic ideological problem highlighted more clearly than in Gandhi's final battle for *khādī*. In 1944 Gandhi proposed a 'New Khadi Philosophy'. He had, he said, thought a great deal about *khādī* during his period of detention and was convinced that there was something fundamentally wrong about the way the work had been carried out for so long. 'The fault is not yours but mine' he told an assembly of *khādī* workers in September 1944. The main difficulty was that the programme so far had been guided exclusively by practical considerations; the principle had been lost sight of. 'I did not lay the necessary stress on the requisite outlook and the spirit which was to underlie it. I looked at it from its immediate practical aspect . . . But today I cannot continue to ask people to spin in that manner.'[123]

The new *khādī* 'philosophy' which Gandhi kept explaining over the next two years was based on the fundamental principle that rural production must be primarily for self-consumption and not for sale. This had not been followed in the *khādī* programme so far, because the emphasis was more on providing a little additional employment to the rural poor and most *khādī* was spun in return for wages. Besides, most of the *khādī* cloth produced from this yarn was sold in the cities. This was not in keeping with the fundamental objective of the *khādī* philosophy which was to create an economic order in which the direct producer would not have to depend on anyone else for his basic necessities. If villagers continued to spin only in order to sell the yarn to *khādī* organizations, then despite the popularity of *khādī* cloth in the cities the entire programme would be founded on wrong economic principles. 'An economics which runs counter to morality cannot be called true economics.'[124]

What was this morality? The moral significance of the *khādī* programme lay in its relation to the true conception of *svarāj*. It was a mistake to regard *khādī*

117

as any other industry and to work out its economics in terms of the principles of the marketplace.

If khadi is an industry it would have to be run purely on business lines. The difference between khadi and mill-cloth would then be that while a mill provides employment to a few thousand people in a city, khadi brings a crore of rupees to those scattered about in fifteen thousand villages. Both must be classified as industries, and we would hardly be justified in asking anybody to put on khadi and boycott mill-cloth. Nor can such khadi claim to be the herald of swaraj. On the other hand we have claimed that the real significance of khadi is that it is a means for uplifting the villages and thereby generating in the people the spontaneous strength for swaraj. Such a claim cannot then be sustained. It will not do to continue to help the villagers by appealing to the philanthropic sentiments of city-dwellers ... If we encouraged mills, the nation might get sufficient cloth. And if mills are nationalized cloth prices may also come down, people may not be exploited and may earn adequate wages. But our reason for putting forward khadi is that it is the only way to redeem the people from the disease of inertia and indifference, the only way to generate in them the strength of freedom.[125]

Thus Gandhi was now quite explicitly moving away from the 'practical' argument about the economic necessity of *khādī* with which for more than two decades he had sought to persuade those who did not share his moral presuppositions. Now he was reasserting the primacy of the moral objectives. In practical terms, the existing *khādī* programme had probably succeeded in providing some additional income to poor villagers. Many of his fellow workers were arguing that some 'decentralization' had also been achieved since cloth production was being carried out in village homes. But Gandhi was unwilling to accept this claim.

Even in Lancashire some cloth is made at home, not for the use of the home but for the use of the masters. It would be outrageous to call this decentralization. So also in Japan everything is made at home; but it is not for the use of the home; it is all for the Government which has centralized the whole business ... I would certainly not call this decentralization.[126]

What Gandhi suggested now was a complete change in the *modus operandi* of the *khādī* programme. An attempt should be made immediately to stop the spinning of yarn for sale. Instead *khādī* workers should persuade and educate people to spin for their own use. Villagers should not be encouraged to produce yarn on payment of wages and to use that income to buy mill-made cloth. It was this dependence of the small producer on the market which the *khādī* programme must attempt to break. The present terms of exchange between town and country must be reversed.[127] Now every village should produce the entire yarn needed to meet its cloth requirements and *khādī* should be put 'beyond commercial competition'.[128] Only in this way would it be possible to put an end to the growing inequality among the mass of the people, a process in which only the few who were lucky enough to find employment in industry had a chance to survive and the rest were doomed to starvation.[129] To make *khādī* the instrument for attaining *pūrṇa svarāj* [complete independence], it would have to be extricated from the cycle of money exchange; the only currency which could be permitted in the buying and selling of *khādī* was yarn.[130]

When Srikrishnadas Jaju, Secretary of the AISA, pointed out that this would mean that 300,000 spinners who were now in contact with the *khādī* organizations would lose their additional income and that probably not more than 30,000 could be persuaded to spin for self-sufficiency in cloth, Gandhi admitted that this might be the case at first, but 'these thirty thousand would later grow into three crores. Be it as it may, I at least will not be guilty of betraying the cause.'[131]

Even if Gandhi was able to convince his associates in *khādī* work that this was the right thing to do in principle, not many were sure that it was a practical or even a judicious step. The entire organizational structure of the *khādī* programme would be disrupted, and few believed that large numbers of rural people could be persuaded to spin all the yarn required for their own clothes. As a result, the *khādī* stores in the cities which were doing very well would have to close down. But Gandhi was insistent: 'Close them down,' he said, 'We cannot maintain khadi bhandars [stores] to sell khadi. You will say that if khadi bhandars in the city close down we shall have to sell khadi in the villages and that khadi cannot sell in the villages as it can in the cities. I agree that khadi cannot sell in the villages and it should not. Khadi is not to be sold in the villages, it is to be worn there. It is to be spun and worn.'[132] When his colleagues pointed out that there were not enough workers in the *khādī* programme who had the ability to do the new work being demanded of them, Gandhi replied: 'If that is our attitude there can be no swaraj through non-violence . . . I would then go my own way even if I have to work all alone . . . It is quite possible that people may not follow us . . . We should then renounce the tall claim we have made . . . Without hesitation, without flattering ourselves we must declare that we are weak like everybody else and that we are in no way better.'[133]

Why did Gandhi decide to demand so insistently that this drastic change be brought about in a programme built up with such care and hard work over so many years? The answer lay in the very nature of the historical conjuncture which the nationalist movement in India had reached, a conjuncture of which the predominant characteristic was a general anticipation of power. The Congress state leadership was clearly preparing to take up the reins of national power; its main concerns now were to formulate in concrete terms the economic and political details of a programme of 'national development'. The people too had anticipated a collapse of the established order and had set up during the revolt of 1942-3 a large number of localized centres of rebel authority, of varying sizes and duration, in forms characteristic of mass insurgency. Gandhi was also anticipating a transition of power, but he could not approve either the plans of development which his erstwhile Congress colleagues were chalking out in order to build a modern industrial nation or the forms of insurgent violence, disorderly and innately hateful, which was the basis of armed rebellion. In his determined, even frenetic, insistence on commencing a new programme of reconstruction aiming at an economy of self-sufficient small producers not having to enter into large-scale commodity exchange or sale of labour, Gandhi was emphasizing the historical urgency of resuming his original task, the task he had formulated in *Hind Swaraj*. The transition of power would create new possibilities. The national state leadership might decide, as Gandhi dearly wished but could not entirely believe, to abdicate its coercive authority in the field of social development and leave it to popular agencies consisting of trained and committed volunteers to carry out the work of economic reconstruction. In that case, the task of setting up those agencies and training the constructive workers would have to be taken up right away. On the other hand, the national state might decide to follow the path begun in the period of British rule, in which case the struggle would have to go on, in opposition to the state. In his discussions with *khādī* activists in 1944, Gandhi virtually put the problem in so many words:

> We may be expected to clothe the whole country with khadi after getting political power. Should we not therefore make such an arrangement from today so that we may be able to make the country self-sufficient in clothing in case the future government of free India were to provide the requisite facilities to the A.I.S.A. and ask it, as an expert body, to do this task? But if the government of the day were to close all its mills, and to charge us with this responsibility, we are apt to fail as things are today.[134]

On the other hand, if the state did not provide this opportunity, then the battle for *khādī*, a means for obtaining true *svarāj*, must be carried out in opposition to it.

> To be an instrument of swaraj, naturally [the spinning-wheel] must not flourish under Government or any other patronage. It must flourish, if need be, even in spite of the resistance from Government or the capitalist who is interested in his spinning and weaving mills. The spinning-wheel represents the millions in the villages as against the classes represented by the mill-owners and the like.[135]

Gandhi, in other words, now fully anticipated the possibility of manoeuvre. The historic battle for freedom had reached a stage where 'political swaraj' was within the reach of a nationalist leadership. It was possible that this could form a new basis for the struggle for 'real swaraj', if the political leadership was prepared to participate in the struggle. It was also possible that the state leadership would not cooperate with any degree of sincerity, in which case 'political swaraj' would itself become a major impediment in the way towards 'real swaraj' and the manoeuvre would have been accomplished. In either case, Gandhism was now called upon to resume its original quest and to clearly mark its differences with what it regarded as the narrow 'political' objectives of nationalism.

The new *khādī* programme was to be the spearhead of this struggle which would gradually bring within its fold a more extended plan of rural economic reconstruction encompassing the whole range of village artizanal production, animal husbandry and basic education.[136] The object was a 'decentralization' of power in society. The very nature of industrial production required a centralization of power in the hands of the state so that the overall conditions within which a national economy functioned could be controlled. Decentralization, on the other hand, would ideally mean that each individual producer would be entirely self-sufficient in the matter of providing his essential needs; with regard to non-essentials which too were a part of social life he would cooperate with others, not as an exchanger of commodities but in the way in which members of a family help one another.[137]

The crucial social unit in this scheme of decentralization was the village which would be self-sufficient not merely in economic matters but also in ruling and defending itself:

> Independence must begin at the bottom. Thus, every village will be a republic or *panchayat* having full powers. It follows, therefore, that every village has to be self-sustained and capable of managing its affairs even to the extent of defending itself against the whole world. It will be trained and prepared to perish in the attempt to defend itself against any onslaught from without.[138]

Within the village, each individual will try to be as self-sufficient as possible and will accept cooperation from others only to the extent that it is free and voluntary, not in the false sense in which commodity exchange is described as free but in the full moral sense of collective cooperation.

Beyond the unit of the self-sufficient village, society would be organized in the form of expanding circles — a group of villages, the taluka, the district, the province, and so on, each self-reliant in its own terms, no unit having to depend on a larger unit or dominate a smaller one.[139] Towns will not disappear completely, but only a small surplus, much smaller than at present, will go out of the villages[140] and the 700,000 villages of India will dominate 'the centre with its few towns'.[141]

> In this structure composed of innumerable villages, there will be ever-widening, never-ascending circles. Life will not be a pyramid with the apex sustained by the bottom. But it will be an oceanic circle . . . the outermost circumference will not wield power to crush the inner circle but will give strength to all within and derive its own strength from it.[142]

Of course, this was an ideal construction, a 'picture', but, as Gandhi put it using his favourite analogy, 'like Euclid's point . . . it had an imperishable value . . . We must have a proper picture of what we want, before we can have something approaching it.'[143] He acknowledged that in conceiving of this system of self-sufficient village republics, he was thinking of the ancient Indian village system as described by Henry Maine.[144] 'The towns were then subservient to the villages. They were emporia for the surplus village products and beautiful manufactures.' But this was only 'the skeleton of my picture'. The ancient village system had many grave defects, most notably that of caste and probably also of the despotism of the state, and these could have no place in the ideal structure of society.[145]

But how would the struggle be carried out in leading society to the path towards this ideal state? The period of colonial rule had resulted in the entrenchment on an unprecedented scale of the forces of corruption and violence deep within the foundations of Indian society. And now after the strength of popular resistance against colonialism had been aroused and mobilized, it was tending to give birth to a new political order which, far from seeking to eliminate those entrenched forces, was building itself on the same bases. How were these overpowering forces to be resisted? Who will resist?

Gandhism's answer, as we have seen, was a moral one. The ideal must be pursued, even if it was a quest that could never end, or end only in death. Those who were convinced of the truth of the ideal must pursue it, alone if necessary. The success of the struggle depended not just crucially but entirely on the selflessness, courage and moral will of the leaders of the people. Firm in its adherence to the principle of a truthful political practice, the Gandhian ideology asserted to the very end its faith in a moral theory of mediation. If the unswerving moral practice of a few did not appear to produce quick results in the broader arena of politics, that was no reason for giving up the quest. Echoing Tolstoy, Gandhi would say, 'History provides us with a whole series of miracles of masses of people being converted to a particular view in the twinkling of an eye.'[146]

But the theory of mediation remained an abstract theory. The success of mediation depended entirely on the morality of the mediator, not on the way his programme could be brought into conformity with a concrete set of collective ethical norms which an identifiable social force within the nation might be expected to hold. Explaining his idea of the *samagra grāmsevak*, the ideal constructive worker, Gandhi said:

> He will so win over the village that they will seek and follow his advice. Supposing I go and settle down in a village with a *ghani* (village oil-press), I won't be an ordinary *ghanchi* (oil-presser) earning 15-20 rupees a month. I will be a Mahatma *ghanchi*. I have used the word Mahatma in fun but what I mean to say is that as *ghanchi* I will become a model for the villagers to follow. I will be a *ghanchi* who knows the Gita and the Koran. I will be learned enough to teach their children . . . Real strength lies in knowledge. True knowledge gives a moral standing and moral strength. Everyone seeks the advice of such a man.[147]

The people, then, would *follow* the mediator because of his moral authority, which would be a consequence of his knowledge, which in turn would be obtained as a result of his unflinching moral practice. If the people were unwilling to listen to him, it would be because he had failed to attain the moral standing required of him. Seeking to launch its final battle for Utopia, the only concrete means of mediation which Gandhism could suggest was the *individual* moral will of the mediator.

> When the critics laugh at [the constructive programme], what they mean is that forty crores of people will never co-operate in the effort to fulfil the programme. No doubt, there is considerable truth in the scoff. My answer is, it is still worth the attempt. Given an indomitable will on the part of a band of earnest workers, the programme is as workable as any other and more so than most. Anyway, I have no substitute for it, if it is to be based on non-violence.[148]

The inadequacy of the theory as a *political* theory of mediation soon became obvious. For instance, in 1946 when T. Prakasam's government in Madras decided that in order to promote *khādī* it would not permit the setting up of any new cotton mills or the expansion of existing ones, industrial interests were not unexpectedly alarmed. Responding to their vociferous criticism of Prakasam, Gandhi wrote:

> It is hardly an honourable pastime to dismiss from consideration honest servants of the nation by dubbing them idealists, dreamers, fanatics and faddists.
>
> Let not capitalists and other entrenched personages range themselves against the poor villagers and prevent them from bettering their lot by dignified labour . . .
>
> Let it be remembered that the existing Madras mills will not be touched at present. That the whole mill industry will be affected if the scheme spreads like wildfire, as I expect some day such a thing must, goes without saying. Let not the largest capitalist rue the day when and if it comes.
>
> The only question then worth considering is whether the Madras Government are honest and competent. If they are not, everything will go wrong. If they are, the scheme must be blessed by all and must succeed.[149]

Yet mere honesty and competence could hardly ensure that such a scheme would be 'blessed by all'. There was decidedly a question of overcoming a serious political opposition. Here to attribute the likely failure of the scheme to the lack of honesty and competence of the government was to evade the fact that the scheme was not backed by a political programme which either anticipated the opposition or suggested the means of overcoming it.

In fact, whenever the contradiction between the political implications of modern industry and *khādī* was directly posed, as it now was with respect to the policies to be followed by the national state, the Gandhian ideology could not easily provide a political answer. It could not admit that capitalists must be coerced into surrendering their interests. Consequently, while asserting the urgency of the new *khādī* programme, Gandhi would immediately say: 'At the same time I believe that some key industries are necessary. I do not believe in armchair or armed socialism.'[150] On the other hand, asked how to explain how the competition between industrial manufactures and *khādī* was to be avoided, Gandhi's answer was that 'mill-cloth should not sell side by side with khadi. Our mills may export their manufactures.'[151] But this clearly violated a fundamental Gandhian premise about the need to eliminate competition and dependence between nations. Gandhism had no answer.

The same problem appeared when the question of suggesting a concrete structure of self-government for the village arose. Despite his fundamental disbelief in the institutions of representative government, Gandhi suggested that election by secret ballot was perhaps the only practicable step. Yet the dangers were obvious: 'While exercising centralized power over the country, the British Government has polluted the atmosphere in the villages. The petty village officials have become masters instead of being servants. So great care has to be taken to ensure that these gangster elements do not get into the panchayats.' But how was this to be ensured if they could by force or trickery elicit the required electoral support? 'They should be debarred.' How, except by a contrary coercive force? 'They should themselves keep out' was the final unconvincing reply.[152] If that was possible, the problem of power would not exist; to insist on this reply was to wish away the political problem.

Beginning its journey from the utopianism of *Hind Swaraj*, and yet picking up on the way the ideological baggage of a nationalist politics, Gandhism succeeded in opening up the historical possibility by which the largest popular element of the nation — the peasantry — could be appropriated within the evolving political forms of the new Indian state. While it was doubtless the close correspondence of the moral conception of Gandhi's *Rāmarājya* with the demands and forms of political justice in the contemporary peasant–communal consciousness which was one of the ideological conditions which made it possible for those demands to be transformed into 'the message of the Mahatma', the historical consequence of the Gandhian politics of non-violence was, in fact, to give to this process of appropriation its moral justification and its own distinctive ideological form. While it was the Gandhian intervention in elite-nationalist politics in India which established for the first time that an authentic national movement could only be built upon the organized support of the whole of the peasantry, the working out of the politics of non-violence also made it abundantly clear that the object of the political mobilization of the peasantry was not at all what Gandhi claimed on its behalf, 'to train the masses in self-consciousness and attainment of power'. Rather the peasantry were meant to become willing participants in a struggle wholly conceived and directed *by others*. Champaran, Kheda, Bardoli, Borsad — those were the model peasant movements, specific, local, conducted on issues that were well within 'their own personal and felt grievances'. This, for instance, was the specific ground on which Bardoli was commended as a model movement:

> The people of Bardoli could not secure justice so long as they were afraid of being punished by the Governr.ent . . . They freed themselves from its fear by surrendering their hearts to their Sardar.
>
> From this we find that the people require neither physical nor intellectual strength to secure their own freedom; moral courage is all that is needed. This latter is dependent on faith. In this case, they were required to have faith in their Sardar, and such faith cannot be artificially generated. They found in the Sardar a worthy object of such faith and like a magnet he drew the hearts of the people to himself . . . This is not to say that the people had accepted non-violence as a principle or that they did not harbour anger even in their minds. But they understood the practical advantage of non-violence, understood their own interest, controlled their anger and, instead of retaliating in a violent manner, suffered the hardships inflicted on them.[153]

While the national organization of the dominant classes could proceed to consolidate itself within the institutional structure of the new Indian state, '*kisans* and labour' were never to be organized 'on an all-India basis'.[154] Thus, forced to mark its differences with a nationalist state ideology, Gandhism could only assert the superiority of its moral claim; it could not find the ideological means to turn that morality into an instrument of the *political* organization of the largest popular elements of the nation against the coercive structures of the state.

And so we get, in the historical effectivity of Gandhism as a whole, the conception of a national framework of politics in which the peasants are mobilized but do not participate, of a nation of which they are a part, but a national state from which they are for ever distanced. How this possibility, which emerged from the very tensions within Gandhism, was identified by the nationalist analytic of a mature bourgeois ideology, and the Gandhian intervention in Indian politics turned into the moment of manoeuvre in the 'passive revolution of capital', are questions we will discuss in the next chapter. But it will remain a task of modern Indian historiography to explain the historical process, in its specific regional and organizational forms, by which these political possibilities inherent in the Gandhian ideology became the ideological weapons in the hands of the Indian bourgeoisie in its attempt to create a new state structure. The 'message of the Mahatma' meant different things to different people. As recent researches are beginning to show,[155] what it meant to peasants or tribals was completely different from the way it was interpreted by the literati. Operating in a process of class struggle in which the dominance of the bourgeoisie was constantly under challenge and its moral leadership for ever fragmented, the great historical achievement of the nationalist state leadership in India was to reconcile the ambiguities of the Gandhian ideology within a single differentiated political structure, to appropriate all its meanings in the body of the same discourse.

Yet the logic of Utopia could be irreconcilably ambiguous. Thomas More has been read as the author of a text that laid the moral foundations for the political demands of a rising, but still far from victorious, bourgeoisie. He has also been regarded as the progenitor of utopian socialism, that inchoate articulation of the spirit of resistance of the early proletariat in Europe.[156] It is not surprising, therefore, that in the unresolved class struggles within the social formation of contemporary India, oppositional movements can still claim their moral legitimacy from the message of Mahatma.

Notes

1. Romain Rolland, *Mahatma Gandhi: A Study in Indian Nationalism*, tr. L.V. Ramaswami Aiyar (Madras: S. Ganesan, 1923), p.30.
2. Raghavan N. Iyer, *The Moral and Political Thought of Mahatma Gandhi* (New York: Oxford University Press, 1973), p.24.
3. *Hind Swaraj* in *The Collected Works of Mahatma Gandhi* (New Delhi: Publications Division, 1958-   ) [hereafter *CW*], vol.10, p.18.
4. *Hind Swaraj*, *CW*, vol.10, pp.22-3.
5. Ibid., p.57.
6. Ibid., p.37.
7. Ibid., p.60.
8. Discussion with Maurice Frydman, 25 August 1936, *CW*, vol.63, p.241.

9. *Hind Swaraj, CW*, vol.10, p.23.

10. Discussion with Maurice Frydman, *CW*, vol.63, p.241.

11. Interview to Francis G. Hickman, 17 September 1940, *CW*, vol.73, pp.29-30.

12. 'Is Khadi Economically Sound?', *CW*, vol.63, pp.77-8.

13. 'Why Not Labour-Saving Devices', *CW*, vol.59, p.413.

14. 'Village Industries', *CW*, vol.59, p.356.

15. 'Its Meaning', *CW*, vol.60, pp.54-5.

16. 'New Life for Khadi', *CW*, vol.59, pp.205-6.

17. *Hind Swaraj, CW*, vol.10, pp:17-8.

18. Ibid., p.18.

19. Ibid., p.33.

20. Letter to David B. Hart, 21 September 1934, *CW*, vol.59, p.45.

21. 'Enlightened Anarchy: A Political Ideal', *CW*, vol.68, p.265.

22. For example, *CW*, vol.35, pp.489-90; *CW*, vol.45, pp.328-9.

23. For example, *CW*, vol.59, pp.61-7; *CW*, vol.50, pp.226-7.

24. *Hind Swaraj, CW*, vol.10, p.36.

25. 'Duty of Bread Labour', *CW*, vol.61, p.212.

26. Discussion with Gujarat Vidyapith Teachers, *CW*, vol.58, p.306.

27. *Hind Swaraj, CW*, vol.10, p.35.

28. 'It is only a critique of the "modern philosophy of life"; it is called "Western" only because it originated in the West'. *CW*, vol.57, p.498.

29. *Hind Swaraj, CW*, vol.10, p.40.

30. Ibid., p.48.

31. Mahadev Desai, *The Gospel of Selfless Action or the Gita According to Gandhi* (Ahmedabad: Navajivan, 1946), p.6.

32. Ibid., pp.123-4.

33. 'Teaching of Hinduism', *CW*, vol.63, p.339.

34. 'Dr. Ambedkar's Indictment-II', *CW*, vol.63, p.153.

35. 'The Law of Our Being', *CW*, vol.63, pp.319-20.

36. 'Dr. Ambedkar's Indictment-II', *CW*, vol.63, p.153.

37. 'Caste Has to Go', *CW*, vol.62, p.121.

38. 'Woman in the Smritis', *CW*, vol.64, p.85.

39. Letter to Ranchhodlal Patwari, 9 September 1918, *CW*, vol.15, p.45. Or, again,

> Khan Abdul Ghaffar Khan derives his belief in non-violence from the Koran, and the Bishop of London derives his belief in violence from the Bible. I derive my belief in non-violence in it. But if the worst came to the worst and if I came to the conclusion that the Koran teaches violence, I would still reject violence, but I would not therefore say that the Bible is superior to the Koran or that Mahomed is inferior to Jesus. It is not my function to judge Mahomed and Jesus. It is enough that my non-violence is independent of the sanction of scriptures.

Interview with Dr Crane, *CW*, vol.64, p.399.

40. Speech at Gandhi Seva Sangh Meeting, 28 March 1938, *CW*, vol.66, p.445.

41. For Tagore's statement, see Appendix I, *CW*, vol.57, pp.503-4.

42. To Vallabhbhai Patel he wrote: 'You must have read the Poet's attack. I am replying to it in *Harijan*. He of course made amends afterwards. He gets excited and writes, and then corrects himself. This is what he does every time.' Letter to

Vallabhbhai Patel, 13 February 1934, *CW*, vol.57, p.155.

43. 'Bihar and Untouchability', *CW*, vol.57, p.87.

44. 'Superstition v. Faith', *CW*, vol.57, pp.164-5.

45. Ibid., p.165.

46. 'Why Only Bihar?', *CW*, vol.57, p.392.

47. Speech at Reception by Merchants, Madura, 26 January 1934, *CW*, vol.57, p.51.

48. 'Superstition v. Faith', *CW*, vol.57, p.165.

49. 'Ramanama to me is all-sufficing . . . In the spiritual literature of the world, the *Ramayana* of Tulsidas takes a foremost place. It has charms that I miss in the *Mahabharata* and even in Valmiki's *Ramayana*.' *CW*, vol.58, p.291. Also, 'Power of "Ramanama" ', *CW*, vol.27, pp.107-12.

50. Thanks to the historical researches of Boris Pavlovich Koz'min and Andrzej Walicki, our present understanding of the complexities of Russian Populism has made us aware of many of the polemical excesses of Bolshevik criticism of the Narodniks. But this has sharpened, rather than obscured, the central theoretical opposition between Leninism and Populism.

51. V.I. Lenin, *A Characterisation of Economic Romanticism* in *Collected Works*, vol.2 (Moscow: Foreign Languages Publishing House, 1957), pp.129-265, esp. p.241.

52. Edward Carpenter, *Civilisation: Its Cause and Cure and Other Essays* (London: George Allen and Unwin, 1921; first edn. 1889), pp.46-9.

53. John Ruskin, *Unto This Last* (London: W.B. Clive, 1931; first edn. 1862), p.83.

54. R.G. Collingwood, *Ruskin's Philosophy* (Chichester, Sussex: Quentin Nelson, 1971; first edn. 1922), p.20.

55. Ibid., p.28.

56. V.I. Lenin, *What the 'Friends of the People' Are and How They Fight the Social-Democrats* in *Collected Works*, vol.1, pp.129-332.

57. Andrzej Walicki, *The Controversy over Capitalism: Studies in the Social Philosophy of the Russian Populists* (Oxford: Clarendon Press, 1969), p.66. Also, Walicki, *The Slavophile Controversy: History of a Conservative Utopia in Nineteenth Century Russian Thought*, tr. Hilda Andrews-Rusiecka (Oxford: Clarendon Press, 1975), p.280.

58. Leo Tolstoy, *The Slavery of Our Times*, tr. Aylmer Maude (London: John Lawrence, 1972; first edn. 1900), p.18.

59. Ibid., p.21.

60. Ibid., p.57.

61. Leo Tolstoy, 'The Kingdom of God is Within You' in *The Kingdom of God and Other Essays*, tr. Aylmer Maude (London: Oxford University Press, 1936; first edn. 1893), pp.301-2.

62. For a study of this process, see Shahid Amin, 'Gandhi as Mahatma: Gorakhpur District, Eastern U.P., 1921-1922' in Ranajit Guha, ed., *Subaltern Studies III* (Delhi: Oxford University Press, 1983), pp.1-61.

63. Letter to Mirabehn, 20 April 1933, *CW*, vol.54, p.456.

64. Letter to Mirabehn, 11 April 1933, *CW*, vol.54, p.372.

65. *An Autobiography* in *CW*, vol.39, p.4.

66. *Hind Swaraj*, *CW*, vol.10, p.36.

67. *Autobiography*, *CW*, vol.39, p.389.

68. 'Satyagraha — Not Passive Resistance', *CW*, vol.13, p.523.

69. For an explanation of the concept of negative consciousness, see Ranajit Guha, *Elementary Aspects of Peasant Insurgency in Colonial India* (Delhi: Oxford University Press, 1983), pp.18-76.

70. 'Satyagraha — Not Passive Resistance', *CW*, vol.13, p.524.

71. Ibid., pp.524-5.

72. Speech on Satyagraha Movement, Trichinopoly, 25 March 1919, *CW*, vol.15, p.155.

73. Speech at Mass Meeting, Ahmedabad, 14 April 1919, *CW*, vol.15, p.221.

74. Letter to Swami Shraddhanand, 17 April 1919, *CW*, vol.15, pp.238-9.

75. 'The Duty of Satyagrahis', *CW*, vol.15, p.436.

76. *Autobiography*, *CW*, vol.39, p.374.

77. Evidence before the Disorders Inquiry Committee, *CW*, vol.16, p.410.

78. Ibid., vol.16, p.441.

79. Speech at Mass Meeting, Ahmedabad, 14 April 1919, *CW*, vol.15, pp.221-2.

80. Evidence, *CW*, vol.16, pp.391-2.

81. Alexander Herzen, often regarded as one of the progenitors of Russian Populism, wrote about the crowd: 'I looked with horror mixed with disgust at the continually moving, swarming crowd, foreseeing how it would rob me of half of my seat at the theatre and in the diligence, how it would dash like a wild beast into the railway carriages, how it would heat and pervade the air.' Quoted in Walicki, *The Controversy over Capitalism*, p.11. Horror and disgust were the feelings which overwhelmed Gandhi too when he first encountered the Indian masses in a third-class railway carriage. See *Autobiography, CW*, vol.39, p.305.

82. 'Democracy v. Mobocracy', *CW*, vol.18, p.242.

83. 'Some Illustrations', *CW*, vol.18, p.275.

84. 'Meaning of the "Gita" ', *CW*, vol.28, p.317.

85. 'What Are Basic Assumptions?', *CW*, vol.67, p.436. It is quite remarkable how frequently Gandhi uses the military metaphor when talking about the 'science of non-violence'.

86. Ibid., pp.436-7.

87. Speech at AICC Meeting, Wardha, 15 January 1942, *CW*, vol.75, p.220.

88. 'Cobwebs of Ignorance', *CW*, vol.30, pp.450-1.

89. 'Answers to Questions', *CW*, vol.43, p.41.

90. Ibid.

91. 'A Complex Problem', *CW*, vol.40, p.364.

92. Letter to Labhshankar Mehta, 14 April 1926, *CW*, vol.30, p.283.

93. Speech at Anand, 17 March 1930, *CW*, vol.43, p.93.

94. Telegram to N.R. Malkani, 18 April 1930, *CW*, vol.43, p.282.

95. 'Neither a Saint nor a Politician', *CW*, vol.17, p.406.

96. Late in his life, Gandhi even seemed to suggest that the concept of *varṇāśrama* should also be dropped because it had acquired the connotation of differing privileges for different *varṇa*: '. . . in our present condition . . . our dharma lies in becoming Ati-Shudras voluntarily'. Foreword to 'Varnavyavastha', *CW*, vol.80, p.223.

97. 'Harijan v. Non-Harijan', *CW*, vol.58, pp.80-1.

98. Speech at AICC Meeting, Patna, 19 May 1934, *CW*, vol.58, pp.9-10.

99. Ibid., p.11.

100. 'My Meaning of Office-Acceptance', *CW*, vol.66, p.104.

101. 'Choice Before Congressmen', *CW*, vol.67, p.306.

102. Interview to Nirmal Kumar Bose, 9 November 1934, *CW*, vol.59, p.318.

103. 'Answers to Zamindars', *CW*, vol.58, p.247.

104. 'Zamindars and Talukdars', *CW*, vol.42, pp.239-40.

105. 'Discussion with Students', *CW*, vol.58, p.219.

106. 'Answers to Zamindars', *CW*, vol.58, p.248.

107. 'Divine Warning', *CW*, vol.22, pp.426-7.

108. Speech at AISA Meeting, Sevagram, 24 March 1945. *CW*, vol.79, p.297.

109. 'The Charkha Sangh and Politics', *CW*, vol.82, pp.17-9.

110. Letter to Purnima Bannerjee, 1 January 1946. *CW*, vol.82, pp.331-2. See also, Letter to Rameshwari Nehru, 15 January 1946, *CW*, vol.82, p.424; and to Sucheta Kripalani, 19 January 1946, *CW*, vol.82, p.440.

111. Letter to Shriman Narayan, 3 January 1946. *CW*, vol.82, p.341.

112. Letter to Dada Dharmadhikari, 28 December 1945. *CW*, vol.82, pp.290-1.

113. Letter to R.K. Patil, 1 January 1946. *CW*, vol.82, p.322. See also, Letter to Shankarrao Deo, 1 January 1946. *CW*, vol.82, p.323.

114. 'The Lure of Legislatures', *CW*, vol.83, pp.95-6.

115. 'Ministers' Duty', *CW*, vol.84, pp.44-5.

116. 'If I Were the Minister', *CW*, vol.85, pp.210-2.

117. 'Independence', *CW*, vol.84, pp.80-1.

118. 'Congress Ministries and Ahimsa', *CW*, vol.85, pp.266-7.

119. Speech at Prayer Meeting, Bikram, 21 May 1947. *CW*, vol.87, p.513.

120. Speech at Prayer Meeting, New Delhi, 1 April 1947. *CW*, vol.87, p.187.

121. 'Congress Ministries and Ahimsa', *CW*, vol.85, p.266.

122. Ibid. See also, 'Do Not Eliminate Truth and Nonviolence', *CW*, vol.85, pp.351-2; and 'Answers to Questions', *CW*, vol.85, p.364.

123. Speech at AISA Meeting, Sevagram, 1 September 1944. *CW,* vol.78, pp.62-7.

124. Discussion with Srikrishnadas Jaju, 11 October 1944. *CW*, vol.78, p.174.

125. Discussion with Srikrishnadas Jaju, 13 October 1944. *CW*, vol.78, pp.192-3.

126. Ibid., p.190.

127. 'Khadi in Towns', *CW*, vol.84, pp.438-9.

128. Speech at AISA Meeting, Sevagram, 24 March 1945. *CW*, vol.79, pp.299-300.

129. 'Why Khadi for Yarn and Not for Money?' *CW*, vol.81, pp.56-7.

130. 'Yarn Donation', *CW*, vol.81, p.137.

131. Discussion with Srikrishnadas Jaju, 13 October 1944. *CW*, vol.78, p.194.

132. 'Why the Insistence on the Yarn Clause', *CW*, vol.82, pp.122-3.

133. Discussion with Srikrishnadas Jaju, 13 October 1944. *CW*, vol.78, pp.194-5.

134. Ibid., p.190.

135. 'The Missing Link', *CW*, vol.81, p.89.

136. 'Ministers' Duty', *CW*, vol.84, p.45.

137. 'Answers to Questions', *CW*, vol.81, p.133, and Speech at Congress Workers' Conference, Sodepur, 6 January 1946, *CW*, vol.81, p.369.

138. 'Independence', *CW*, vol.85, p.32.

139. 'Decentralization', *CW*, vol.85, pp.459-60.

140. Discussion with Shriman Narayan, 2 June 1945. *CW*, vol.80, p.244.

141. Interview to P. Ramachandra Rao, before 19 June 1945. *CW*, vol.80, p.353.

142. 'Independence' *CW*, vol.85, p.33.

143. Ibid.

144. Henry Sumner Maine, *Ancient Law* (1861; New York: Dutton, 1931).

145. Speech at Meeting of Deccan Princes, Poona, 28 July 1946. *CW*, vol.85, p.79.

146. Discussion with Director of British Daily, before 28 October 1946. *CW*, vol.86, p.50.

147. Answers to Questions at Constructive Workers' Conference, Madras, 29 January 1946. *CW*, vol.83, p.46.

148. Foreword to 'Constructive Programme — Its Meaning and Place', *CW*, vol.82, p.67.

149. 'Handspun v. Mill Cloth', *CW*, vol.85, pp.472-4.

150. 'Alternative to Industrialism', *CW*, vol.85, p.206.

151. Discussion at Hindustani Talimi Sangh Meeting, Patna, 22 April 1947. *CW*, vol.87, p.330.

152. Talk with Village Representatives, Bir, 19 March 1947. *CW*, vol.87, pp.121-2.

153. 'Government's Power v. People's Power', *CW*, vol.37, pp.190-1.

154. 'Constructive Programme: Its Meaning and Place', *CW*, vol.75, pp.159-60.

155. See, for example, Shahid Amin, 'Gandhi as Mahatma'.

156. Martin Fleisher, *Radical Reform and Political Persuasion in the Life and Writings of Thomas More* (Geneva: Librairie Droz, 1973); Karl Kautsky, *Thomas More and his Utopia*, tr. H.J. Stenning (1890; London: Lawrence and Wishart, 1979).

5. The Moment of Arrival: Nehru and the Passive Revolution

There is something very wonderful about the high
achievements of science and modern technology . . .
The Discovery of India, p.415.

I

In September 1932, at a time when the Congress organization lay stunned and scattered after the massive repression unleashed by the Government on the Civil Disobedience movement, Gandhi announced from Yeravda prison in Poona that he would go on a 'fast unto death' to protest against Ramsay Macdonald's grant of a separate electorate to the 'Depressed Classes' in India. Jawaharlal Nehru was then in Dehra Dun jail, and the news came to him like a 'bombshell'. He was greatly annoyed with Gandhi

> for choosing a side-issue for his final sacrifice — just a question of electorate. What would be the result of our freedom movement? Would not the larger issues fade into the background, for the time being at least? . . . After so much sacrifice and brave endeavour, was our movement to tail off into something insignificant?
> I felt angry with him at his religious and sentimental approach to a political question, and his frequent references to God in connection with it. He even seemed to suggest that God had indicated the very date of his fast. What a terrible example to set![1]

Nehru was at this time much distressed by what he saw as the lack of clarity with regard to the political objectives of the national movement. It is a complaint that runs all the way through the *Autobiography* written in prison in 1934-5. It was not as though he did not approve of the association of social and economic questions with the demands of nationalism. In fact, he was one of the foremost leaders of the Congress Left which consistently demanded that nationalism be given a more definite 'economic and social content'. But the objective of all such campaigns had to be clear: it was the establishment of a sovereign national state. That was the political objective; the social and economic issues were necessary to mobilize the masses in the movement towards that goal. If the political objective was not kept firmly in mind, all attempts at social reform would flounder, energies would be wasted, and the movement would play into the hands of the foreign government now holding power. In fact, as far as the success of these social movements was concerned, the attempts at social reform could be successful only after power had been captured and a national state established.

> The real reason why the Congress and other non-official organisations cannot do much for social reform goes deeper . . .
>
> Past experience shows us that we can make little social progress under present conditions . . . for generations past the British Government has crushed initiative and ruled despotically, or paternally, as it has itself called it. It does not approve of any big organised effort by non-officials, and suspects ulterior motives. The Harijan movement, in spite of every precaution taken by its organisers, has occasionally come in conflict with officials. I am sure that if Congress started a nation-wide propaganda for the greater use of soap it would come in conflict with Government in many places.
>
> I do not think it is very difficult to convert the masses to social reform if the State takes the matter in hand. But alien rulers are always suspect, and they cannot go far in the process of conversion. If the alien element was removed and economic changes were given precedence, an energetic administration could easily introduce far-reaching social reforms.[2]

Nehru's reaction to Gandhi's Harijan movement stemmed from an entirely novel ideological reconstruction of the elements of nationalist thought that was then being undertaken in the final, fully mature, stage of the development of nationalism in India — its moment of arrival. It was a reconstruction whose specific form was to situate nationalism within the domain of a *state ideology*. Given the historical constraints imposed on the Indian bourgeoisie within the colonial social formation, its intellectual–moral leadership could never be firmly established in the domain of civil society. Of historical necessity, its revolution had to be passive. The specific ideological form of the passive revolution in India was an *étatisme*, explicitly recognizing a central, autonomous and directing role of the state and legitimizing it by a specifically nationalist marriage between the ideas of progress and social justice.

This mature ideological form of nationalist thought can be clearly demonstrated in the writings of Jawaharlal Nehru. Nehru was a far less systematic writer than Bankimchandra, and his writings do not have the same kind of logical strength born out of solid moral convictions which one finds in Gandhi. His two major books, the *Autobiography* and *The Discovery of India*, both written during long periods of imprisonment, are rambling, bristling with the most obvious contradictions, and grossly overwritten, the latter, by his own admission, coming to an end only because his supply of paper ran out.[3] But it is in the writings of this principal political architect of the new Indian state that one can find, more clearly than anywhere else, the key ideological elements and relations of nationalist thought at its moment of arrival.

To make my presentation easier, let me first summarize what I think is the crucial line of reasoning that holds together this final ideological reconstruction of nationalism. It is an ideology of which the central organizing principle is the autonomy of the state; the legitimizing principle is a conception of social justice.

132

The argument then runs as follows: social justice for all cannot be provided within the old framework because it is antiquated, decadent and incapable of dynamism. What is necessary is to create a new framework of institutions which can embody the spirit of progress or, a synonym, modernity. Progress or modernity, according to the terms of the 20th century, means giving primacy to the sphere of the economic, because it is only by a thorough reorganization of the systems of economic production and distribution that enough wealth can be created to ensure social justice for all. But the latest knowledge built up by the modern social sciences shows clearly that it is not possible to undertake an effective reorganization of the economic structures of society if the state does not assume a central coordinating and directing role. And the colonial state, in accordance with its imperial interests, will never take up this role; in fact, it has consistently acted as the chief impediment to all attempts at such a restructuring. Hence the principal political task before the nation is to establish a sovereign national state. Once established, this state will stand above the narrow interests of groups and classes in society, take an overall view of the matter and, in accordance with the best scientific procedures, plan and direct the economic processes in order to create enough social wealth to ensure welfare and justice for all.

Let us now see how Nehru attempts to establish this argument as the main constitutive principle of the mature ideological form of nationalist thought in India.

II

'The East bow'd low before the blast
In patient, deep disdain;
She let the legions thunder past,
And plunged in thought again.'

In *The Discovery of India*, Nehru quotes Matthew Arnold, and immediately proceeds to contradict him:

But it is not true that India has ever bowed patiently before the blast or been indifferent to the passage of foreign legions. Always she has resisted them, often successfully, sometimes unsuccessfully, and even when she failed for the time being, she has remembered and prepared herself for the next attempt. Her method has been twofold: to fight them and drive them out, and to absorb those who could not be driven away . . . The urge to freedom, to independence, has always been there, and the refusal to submit to alien domination.[4]

A few pages later, he offers a more direct rebuttal of the essentialist dichotomy between Eastern and Western cultures.

Ancient Greece is supposed to be the fountainhead of European civilisation, and much has been written about the fundamental difference between the Orient and the Occident. I do not understand this; a great deal of it seems to be vague and unscientific without much basis in fact. Till recently many European thinkers imagined that everything that was worth while had its origin in Greece or Rome . . . Even when some knowledge of what peoples of Asia had done in the past soaked into the European mind, it was not willingly accepted. There was an unconscious resistance to it . . . If scholars thought so, much more so did the unread crowd believe in some essential difference between the East and the West. The industrialization of Europe and the consequent material progress impressed this difference still further on the popular mind, and by an odd process of rationalization ancient Greece became the father or mother of modern Europe and America.[5]

But this difference was only about industrialization and lack of industrialization; it had nothing to do with ancient cultural traditions.

I do not understand the use of the words Orient and Occident, except in the sense that Europe and America are highly industrialized and Asia is backward in this respect. This industrialization is something new in the world's history . . . There is no organic connection between Hellenic civilization and modern European and American civilization.[6]

In fact, the spirit and outlook of ancient Greece were much closer to those of ancient India and ancient China than of the nations of modern Europe.

They all had the same broad, tolerant, pagan outlook, joy in life and in the surprising beauty and infinite variety of nature, love of art, and the wisdom that comes from the accumulated experience of an old race.[7]

The real reason why we do not see these similarities and instead fall into the trap of confused thinking is that those who teach us are interested in having us think that way.

India, it is said, is religious, philosophical, speculative, metaphysical, uncon-cerned with this world, and lost in dreams of the beyond and the hereafter. So we are told, and perhaps those who tell us so would like India to remain plunged in thought and entangled in speculation, so that they might possess this world and the fullness thereof, unhindered by these thinkers, and take their joy of it.[8]

At last, it would seem, nationalist thought has come to grips with the Orientalist thematic; it is now able to criticize it. It has got rid of those cultural essentialisms that had confined it since its birth and, at last, it is able to look at the histories of the nation and of the world in their true specificities. But wait! What does it make of its own past, now that it has shed the old thematic? What is the new framework of historical understanding which it adopts?

From Nehru's recounting of India's past, it would appear that there are two great movements in the nation's history, consisting of a long cycle and a short cycle. The long cycle begins with the earliest known historical period, that of the Indus Valley civilization, and ends with the first Turko–Afghan invasions of the 11th century. It is a period which saw the flowering of a great civilization, rich and vigorous, marked by some astonishing achievements in the fields of philosophy, literature, drama, art, science and mathematics. The economy expanded and prospered, and there were widespread trade and cultural contacts with many other parts of the world. And yet, well before the close of the millennium,

> an inner weakness seems to seize India which affects not only her political status but her creative activities. There is no date for this, for the process was a slow and creeping one, and it affected North India earlier than the South.[9]

The evidence is clear enough: there is no great work in philosophy after Śaṅkara, or in literature after Bhavabhūti, both in the 8th century; the great era of foreign trade ends in the same period; emigrations for colonial settlement in south-east Asia continue from the South until the 9th century; the Cholas are finished as a great maritime power in the 11th century.

> We thus see that India was drying up and losing her creative genius and vitality . . . What were the causes of this political decline and cultural stagnation? Was this due to age alone . . . ? Or were external causes and invasions responsible for it? . . . But why should political freedom be lost unless some kind of decay has preceded it? . . . That internal decay is clearly evident in India at the close of those thousand years.[10]

The most significant evidence of this decay was in 'the growing rigidity and exclusiveness of the Indian social structure as represented chiefly by the caste system'.[11]

> Life became all cut up into set frames where each man's job was fixed and permanent and he had little concern with others . . . Thus particular types of activity became hereditary, and there was a tendency to avoid new types of work and activity and to confine oneself to the old groove, to restrict initiative and the spirit of innovation . . . So long as that structure afforded avenues for growth and expansion, it was progressive; when it reached the limits of expansion open to it, it became stationary, unprogressive, and, later, inevitably regressive.
>   Because of this there was decline all along the line — intellectual, philosophical, political, in technique and methods of warfare, in knowledge of and contacts with the outside world, in shrinking economy, and there was a growth of local sentiments and feudal and small-group feeling at the expanse of the larger conceptions of India as a whole.[12]

And thus the long cycle came to an end because India shrank within its shell, became rigid and lost its earlier creativity and innovativeness. But it did not mean the death of Indian civilization. Some vitality remained, and even as it succumbed to a whole series of invasions, there was a historical continuity as India moved into its second, this time a somewhat shorter, cycle of efflorescence.

> Yet, as later ages were to show, there was yet vitality in the old structure and an amazing tenacity, as well as some flexibility and capacity for adaptation. Because of this it managed to survive and to profit by new contacts and waves of thought, and even progress in some ways. But that progress was always tied down to and hampered by far too many relics of the past.[13]

The second cycle occurs in the period of the Islamic empires, reaching its peak during the reign of the Mughal Emperor Akbar. It takes the form of a new cultural synthesis between indigenous and Turkish, Afghan, Iranian and Arabic elements, and attains great brilliance in art, architecture, literature, music, and even some synthetic religious cults and philosophies. But to Nehru, the movement is very much a state-sponsored effort, the personality of the Emperor in particular playing a crucial role. Akbar was by far the most remarkable figure in this movement, 'an idealist and a dreamer but also a man of action and a leader of men who roused the passionate loyalty of his followers'.[14] With wise statesmanship and imaginative patronage, he sought to unite the country politically and culturally. 'In him, the old dream of a united India again took shape, united not only politically in one state but organically fused into one people.'[15]

Yet the overall effects of this cultural synthesis were not deep enough to change in any fundamental way the structure of society or the ways of life of the people. The effects 'were more or less superficial, and the social culture remained much the same as it used to be. In some respects, indeed, it became more rigid.'[16] Despite the courage and imagination of imperial efforts to change society, the outlook was inherently limited and the methods far too unsubtle and unappreciative of the complexities of the task.

> Akbar might have laid the foundations of social change if his eager, inquisitive mind had turned in that direction and sought to find out what was happening in other parts of the world. But he was too busy consolidating his empire, and the big problem that faced him was how to reconcile a proselytizing religion like Islam with the national religion and customs of the people, and thus to build up the national unity. He tried to interpret religion in a rational spirit, and for the moment he appeared to have brought about a remarkable transformation of the Indian scene. But this direct approach did not succeed as it has seldom succeeded elsewhere.
>
> So not even Akbar made any basic difference to that social context of India, and after him that air of change and mental adventure which he had introduced subsided, and India resumed her static and unchanging life.[17]

Thus, despite a short period of state-sponsored cultural dynamism, 'life' itself did not change. The same historical period was seeing the most far-reaching and revolutionary changes in Europe, but 'Asia, static and dormant, still carried on in the old traditional way relying on man's toil and labor.'[18] On the eve of the European conquest of the East, therefore, there did exist a quite fundamental difference between the attitudes and outlook on life of the European nations, searching out in new directions, breaking the fetters of tradition and dogma and subjugating the whole world to their will and domination, and those of the peoples of Asia, bound by the customs and institutions of a bygone era, paralysed in body and spirit. That explains why the Asian nations succumbed to the European onslaught. They could not resist because they had lost their inner vigour and vitality.

And so we come back again to the Orientalist thematic. Only now the difference between East and West is reduced from the essential to the conjunctural. There is nothing organic or essential in European civilization which has made it dynamic and powerful: it is just that at a certain point in history it suddenly found a new spirit, new sources of energy and creativity. And similarly, there is nothing organic or essential in Asian civilizations which has made them static and powerless: after a long period of magnificent growth, the old springs of vitality and innovation had gradually dried up. It was at this historical conjuncture that the clash had occurred between West and East: the West conquered, the East submitted.

In this new nationalist reinterpretation of the colonial impact, therefore, historical time itself becomes episodic. Every civilization, it is now argued, has its periods of growth and periods of decay. There are no essential or organic, or insuperable, connections between them. Each is explained by a set of conjunctural factors: economic, political, intellectual, whatever. Further, the cultural values, or the 'spirit', which go with a particular sort of growth are capable of being extracted from their particular civilizational context and made universal historical values. Then they are no longer the 'property' of any particular culture, nor are they essentially or organically tied with that culture.

Thus, past and present can be separated out of the histories of particular nations and represented as the progression of a universal 'spirit of the age'. That determined the norm of world-historical development in relation to which particular nations could be shown to be advanced or backward, and the particular stage of that cycle explained in terms of specific conjunctural factors. Thus, the lack of modernity in colonial India had nothing to do with any essential cultural failings of Indian civilization. The particular historical conjuncture at which India had come under foreign subjugation was one where the European nations were forward-looking and dynamic while Indian society was in a stage of stultification. The subsequent failure of Indian society to match up to the universal historical norm of development was explicable entirely by the circumstances of colonial rule: it was because the dominant foreign power consistently impeded the growth of the forces of modernity that Indian society was finding it impossible to develop.

> When the British came to India, though technologically somewhat backward she was still among the advanced commercial nations of the world. Technical changes would undoubtedly have come and changed India as they had changed some Western countries. But her normal development was arrested by the British power. Industrial growth was checked, and as a consequence social growth was also arrested. The normal power relationships of society could not adjust themselves and find an equilibrium, as all power was concentrated in the alien authority, which based itself on force and encouraged groups and classes which had ceased to have any real significance . . . They had long ago finished their role in history and would have been pushed aside by new forces if they had not been given foreign protection . . . Normally they would have been weeded out or diverted to some more appropriate function by revolution or democratic process. But so long as foreign authoritarian rule continued, no such development could take place.[19]

The fact, then, that India's Present seemed to be so dominated by the Past had nothing to do with anything inherent in its culture. It was the consequence of a particular political circumstance, whose removal constituted the principal political task before the nation. By accomplishing that task, the Indian nation would take the first significant step towards coming in tune with the 'spirit of the age'. That is why the political convulsions in India represented 'the anonymous and unthinking will of an awakening people, who seem to be outgrowing their past'.[20]

It also followed that by looking for its Present not in its own past, but Elsewhere, in the universal representation of the 'spirit of the age', the Indian nation was only attempting to work back into the trajectory of its 'normal' development. This did not necessarily represent any threat to its distinctive cultural identity.

> We in India do not have to go abroad in search of the Past and the Distant. We have them here in abundance. If we go to foreign countries it is in search of the Present. That search is necessary, for isolation from it means backwardness and decay.[21]

III

But what is it that is so distinctive about this 'spirit of the age', this Present which exists Elsewhere and therefore has to be found Elsewhere? Nehru attempts to define it:

> The modern mind, that is to say the better type of the modern mind, is practical and pragmatic, ethical and social, altruistic and humanitarian. It is governed by a practical idealism for social betterment. The ideals which move it represent the spirit of the age, the Zeitgeist, the *Yugadharma*. It has discarded to a large extent the philosophical approach of the ancients, their search for ultimate reality, as well as the devotionalism and mysticism of the medieval period. Humanity is its god and social service its religion . . .
> We have therefore to function in line with the highest ideals of the age we live in . . . Those ideals may be classed under two heads: humanism and the scientific spirit.[22]

Is this, then, a return to Bankim's problematic? For does not this definition of the spirit of the age depend on the same sort of distinction between the material and the spiritual? And is not Nehru saying that in order to become a modern nation we must learn the material skills from the West without losing our spiritual heritage? At times, Nehru does indeed say exactly this:

> India, as well as China, must learn from the West, for the modern West has much to teach, and the spirit of the age is represented by the West. But the West is also obviously in need of learning much, and its advances in technology will bring it little comfort if it does not learn some of the deeper lessons of life, which have absorbed the minds of thinkers in all ages and in all countries.[23]

More generally, the distinctions between the scientific and the unscientific, the rational and the irrational, the practical and the metaphysical, are exactly those which, in their most general terms, had come to dominate post-Enlightenment rationalist, and more specifically positivist, thought in Europe. It accepted the 'givenness' of science, as a body of knowledge with its distinctive methodological principles and techniques of practical application that had demonstrated its usefulness, and hence its validity. The 'spirit of science' or the 'scientific temper' meant, therefore, not just a rationalism, but a rationalism solidly based on 'empirical facts', on 'empirically verifiable truths'. It meant a concern with 'practical' questions and a refusal to engage in 'excessive' and 'fruitless' speculation. For speculative philosophy

> has usually lived in its ivory tower cut off from life and its day-to-day problems, concentrating on ultimate purposes and failing to link them with the life of man. Logic and reason were its guides, and they took it far in many directions, but that logic was too much the product of the mind and unconcerned with fact.[24]

Science, on the other hand, looks 'at fact alone'.[25] Whatever its limits, therefore, it is science alone which offers us a reliable body of knowledge for practical living.

> It is better to understand a part of the truth, and apply it to our lives, than to understand nothing at all and flounder helplessly in a vain attempt to pierce the mystery of existence . . . It is the scientific approach, the adventurous and yet critical temper of science, the search for truth and new knowledge, the refusal to accept anything without testing and trial, the capacity to change previous conclusions in the face of new evidence, the reliance on observed fact and not on preconceived theory, the hard discipline of the mind — all this is necessary, not merely for the application of science but for life itself and the solution of its many problems.[26]

But apart from these general implications of post-Enlightenment rationalism, the 'scientific method' and the 'scientific approach to life' also meant something much more specific to Nehru than it did to someone like Bankim. At its most general level, in fact, Nehru could even assert, like Bankim, that ancient Indian thought was much closer in spirit to the scientific attitude than the overall cultural values of the modern West.

> Science has dominated the Western world and everyone there pays tribute to it, and yet the West is still far from having developed the real temper of science. It has still to bring the spirit and the flesh into creative harmony . . . the essential basis of Indian thought for ages past, though not its later manifestations, fits in with the scientific temper and approach, as well as with internationalism. It is based on a fearless search for truth, on the solidarity of man, even on the divinity of everything living, and on the free and co-operative development of the individual and the species, ever to greater freedom and higher stages of human growth.[27]

But this is not what is most distinctive about the mature reconstruction of nationalist ideology. To Nehru, the 'scientific method' also meant quite specifically the primacy of the sphere of the economic in all social questions. This in particular was what men like Nehru believed to be the distinctively modern, or 20th century, way of looking at history and society. Whether it was a question of political programmes, or economic policy, or social and cultural issues, a 'scientific' analysis must always proceed by relating it to the basic economic structure of society. The correct solutions to such problems must also be searched for in terms of a restructuring of those economic arrangements of society. 'If there is one thing that history shows,' declared Nehru, 'it is this: that economic interests shape the political views of groups and classes. Neither reason nor moral considerations override those interests.'[28]

This now becomes the new theoretical framework for a reconstructed nationalism. It supplies to it the key to a whole new series of rationalist positions on the vital political questions facing it: its assessment of colonial rule, defining the boundaries of the nation, the role of traditional social institutions, of religion, the scale and the pace of industrialization, and above all, the role of the state. From these positions, it is even able to appropriate for purely nationalist purposes 'the scientific method of Marxism' as the most advanced expression yet of the rationalism of the European Enlightenment.

> The theory and philosophy of Marxism lightened up many a dark corner of my mind. History came to have a new meaning for me. The Marxist interpretation threw a flood of light on it, and it became an unfolding drama with some order and purpose, however unconscious, behind it . . .
>
> The great world crisis and slump seemed to justify the Marxist analysis. While other systems and theories were groping about in the dark, Marxism alone explained it more or less satisfactorily and offered a real solution.
>
> As this conviction grew upon me, I was filled with a new excitement and my depression at the non-success of civil disobedience grew much less. Was not the world marching rapidly towards the desired consummation? . . . Our national struggle became a stage in the longer journey . . . Time was in our favour.[29]

This appropriation of Marxism was, of course, deliberately selective, as we will see in a moment. But it provided a new scientific legitimation to a whole set of rationalist distinctions between the modern and the traditional, the secular and the religious, the progressive and the obscurantist, the advanced and the backward. In every case, the argument was as follows: in the present day and age, there is but one general historically given direction in which the economy must move: the direction of rapid industrialization. The position of each social group or class *vis-à-vis* the requirements for such a rapid industrialization of the economy determined the 'real economic interests' of that group or class. Those whose real economic interests are in accordance with those requirements are 'progressive' classes; those whose interests are opposed to those requirements are 'reactionary classes'. However, quite apart from the real economic interests, there also existed subjective beliefs and ideologies in society which prevented particular groups and classes from perceiving their real economic interests and acting in accordance with them. These were the backward ideologies — primordial loyalties, sectarian sentiments, religious obscurantisms, etc. — and those reactionary classes which were opposed to progressive changes often perpetuated their otherwise obsolete domination by playing upon these subjective social beliefs.

the beliefs/consciousness of the 'subaltern'

Thus, for example, that ubiquitous problem of 'communalism' which has consistently dogged Indian nationalism in the 20th century. In theory, the problem as Nehru saw it was simple enough: the fundamental political requirement was the legal guarantee of full and equal rights of citizenship, irrespective of religious, linguistic or other cultural differences. That was the basic liberal premise on which individual civil rights would be established. In addition, there had to be a consideration of welfare or social justice:

> every effort should be made by the state as well as by private agencies to remove all invidious social and customary barriers which came in the way of the full development of the individual as well as any group, and that educationally and economically backward classes should be helped to get rid of their disabilities as rapidly as possible. This applied especially to the depressed classes. It was further laid down that women should share in every way with men in the privileges of citizenship.[30]

It was true, of course, that the colonial state was hardly interested in providing these conditions for the full growth of citizenship. It was an external political force, intervening in the political conflicts in India in order to further its own particular interests, and therefore 'playing off' one side against the other by distributing special privileges on a sectarian basis. But that was all the more reason to conclude that a solution of the 'communal' problem required, as a first step, the elimination of the colonial state and the creation of a true national state.

But once these premises of the national state were granted there could not exist a 'communal' problem any more. The only problems which would then be real were economic problems.

> Having assured the protection of religion and culture, etc., the major problems that were bound to come up were economic ones which had nothing to do with a person's religion. Class conflicts there might well be, but not religious conflicts, except in so far as religion itself represented some vested interest.[31]

And once again, it was clear enough that a solution of these 'real economic problems' would require a fundamental restructuring of the economic processes of society, so that a massive increase in the social product could yield sufficient resources to satisfy the urge for equitable distribution and welfare of all groups. No true solution to the 'communal' problem could be found by attempting to tinker with the existing structure.

> Only by thinking in terms of a different political framework — and even more so a different social framework — can we build up a stable foundation for joint action. The whole idea underlying the demand for independence was this: to make people realise that we were struggling for an entirely different political structure . . .
>
> But almost all our leaders continued to think within the narrow steel frame of the existing political, and of course the social, structure. They faced every problem — communal or constitutional — with this background, and inevitably, they played into the hands of the British Government, which controlled completely

that structure . . . the time had gone by when any political or economic or communal problem in India could be satisfactorily solved by reformist methods. Revolutionary outlook and planning and revolutionary solutions were demanded by the situation . . .

The want of clear ideals and objectives in our struggle for freedom undoubtedly helped the spread of communalism. The masses saw no clear connection between their day-to-day sufferings and the fight for swaraj.[32]

Yet, while all this might be clear enough from a 'scientific' analysis of the problem, the subjective beliefs held by the people did not necessarily allow them to see the solution in such a clear light. 'They fought well enough at times by instinct, but that was a feeble weapon which could be easily blunted or even turned aside for other purposes. There was no reason behind it.'[33] And then there was fear:

Fear that bigger numbers might politically overwhelm a minority . . . people had grown so accustomed to think along lines of religious cleavage, and were continually being encouraged to do so by communal religious organizations and government action, that the fear of the major religious community, that is the Hindus, swamping others continued to exercise the minds of many Moslems . . . fear is not unreasonable.[34]

The masses did not act according to 'reason' because they had not been taught to do so. They acted by 'instinct' and were therefore susceptible to 'religious passions'. Thus, although the demands of 'communalism' were quite clearly those of a very small reactionary upper class within each community, the political support those demands received from the community at large were, by any standards of rational explanation, quite 'extraordinary'.

It is nevertheless extraordinary how the bourgeois classes, both among the Hindus and the Muslims, succeeded, in the sacred name of religion, in getting a measure of mass sympathy and support for programmes and demands which had absolutely nothing to do with the masses, or even the lower middle class. Every one of the communal demands put forward by any communal group is, in the final analysis, a demand for jobs, and these jobs could only go to a handful of the upper middle class. There is also, of course, the demand for special and additional seats in the legislature, as symbolising political power, but this too is looked upon chiefly as the power to exercise patronage. These narrow political demands, benefiting at the most a small number of the upper middle classes, and often creating barriers in the way of national unity and progress, were cleverly made to appear the demands of the masses of that particular religious group. Religious passion was hitched on to them in order to hide their barrenness.

In this way political reactionaries came back to the political field in the guise of communal leaders, and the real explanation of the various steps they took was not so much their communal bias as their desire to obstruct political advance.[35]

Within the new 'scientific' construction of society and politics the problem of the subjective beliefs of the masses, as distinct from their 'objective economic interests', was not one which could be rationally comprehended, for these beliefs were located in the realm of 'unreason', of 'passions', of 'spontaneity'. All that could be comprehended were the motivations and interests of political leaders and organizations which sought to manipulate the masses by playing upon their religious passions. And so, understanding the politics of 'communalism' becomes a problem of identifying which group of politicians used which particular isses to mislead which sections of the people. Sir Syed Ahmed Khan, who launched a movement in the late 19th century to popularize Western education among Indian Muslims, was not a 'reactionary' because without this education, Muslims would have remained backward. 'The Muslims were not historically or ideologically ready then for the *bourgeois* nationalist movement as they had developed no *bourgeoisie*, as the Hindus had done. Sir Syed's activities, therefore, although seemingly very moderate, were in the right revolutionary direction.'[36] (Incidentally, the unstated assumption here is that the Muslims needed a 'Muslim bourgeoisie' in order to become historically ready for the national movement; an 'Indian bourgeoisie' would not have served the purpose.) However, in the early 20th century, when the Aga Khan emerged as a leader of the Muslims, it meant 'the lining up of the Muslim landed classes as well as the growing *bourgeoisie* with the British Government' by using the religious issue to forestall any potential threat to the stability of British rule or to the vested interests of the upper classes.[37] Still 'the inevitable drift of the Muslim *bourgeoisie* towards nationalism' could not be stopped.

Following World War I, the Ali brothers, M.A. Ansari, Abul Kalam Azad, 'and a number of other *bourgeois* leaders . . . began to play an important part in the political affairs of the Muslims'. Soon most of them were 'swept' by Gandhi into the Non-cooperation movement.[38] But the 'communal and backward elements, both among the Hindus and the Muslims' came back into the picture. There was 'a struggle for jobs for the middle-class intelligentsia'. There was also the special problem in Punjab, Sind and Bengal where the Hindus were 'the richer, creditor, urban class' and the Muslims 'the poorer, debtor, rural class'. 'The conflict between the two was therefore often economic, but it was always given a communal colouring.' There was communalism on the part of Hindu politicians as well, masquerading 'under a nationalist cloak' but really seeking to protect upper-class Hindu interests.[39] But in each of these cases, there was a particular political leadership or organization which played upon the religious sentiments of the masses in order to gather support for particular policies or interests affecting only the upper classes. When those policies were in favour of the broad goals of a united national movement, they were 'progressive'; when not, they represented the activities of 'a small upper class reactionary group' which had set out to 'exploit and take advantage of the religious passions of the masses for their own ends'.[40]

Take another vital question of the Indian national movement: the question of industrialization. Here again, Nehru's argument is similar: the spirit of the age demanded industrialization; without it, not only would the basic economic problems of poverty remain unsolved, but even the political foundations of independent nationhood would be threatened. It was not, therefore, a matter of moral or aesthetic choice. It was a simple fact of modern life, determined globally by the conditions of modern-day economic production.

> It can hardly be challenged that, in the context of the modern world, no country can be politically and economically independent, even within the framework of international interdependence, unless it is highly industrialized and has developed its power resources to the utmost. Nor can it achieve or maintain high standards of living and liquidate poverty without the aid of modern technology in almost every sphere of life. An industrially backward country will continually upset the world's equilibrium and encourage the aggressive tendencies of more developed countries.[41]

Thus, the question of a choice between two alternative paths of economic development, one based on large-scale heavy industry and the other on decentralized small-scale industry, simply did not arise. A political choice of this sort must proceed by granting a primacy to the economic determinants. And in that area, the choice had already been made — Elsewhere, by History, by 'the spirit of the age'.

> Any argument as to the relative merits of small-scale and large-scale industry seems strangely irrelevant today, when the world and the dominating facts of the situation that confront it have decided in favor of the latter.[42]

On the question of industrialization, therefore, there was, on the one hand, a consideration of national power, of the economy, i.e. an industrialized economy, providing the key to the economic and political independence of the nation. An economy based on cottage and small-scale industries was 'doomed to failure' because it could only 'fit in with the world framework' as a 'colonial appendage'.[43] But by the same logic, there was also the implication that the requisite level of industrialization for the nation would always have to be set by global standards. For science set its own technological standards, its own standards of efficiency and obsolescence; and science, of course, was a universal value. Thus the progression of Time in the domain of science was also something which took place Elsewhere. The question of small-scale and large-scale industry was not, therefore,

> a mere question of adjustment of the two forms of production and economy. One must be dominating and paramount, with the other complementary to it, fitting in where it can. The economy based on the latest technical achievements of the day must necessarily be the dominating one. If technology demands the big machine, as it does today in a large measure, then the big machine with all its implications and consequences must be accepted . . . the latest technique has to be followed, and to adhere to outworn and out-of-date methods of production, except as a temporary and stop-gap measure, is to arrest growth and development.[44]

Within the ideological framework of mature nationalism, therefore, the path of economic development was clearly set out in terms of the 'scientific' understanding of society and history. There were three fundamental requirements: 'a heavy engineering and machine-making sector, scientific research institutes, and electric power'.[45] It is also worth pointing out that when this nationalist understanding appealed to 'the scientific outlook of Marxism', it found ready theoretical support in the Bolshevik understanding of the problem of economic development, popularized in particular in the phase of Soviet industrialization. Nationalists like Nehru found in 'the primacy of the economic' a particularly useful theoretical foothold from which they could reach out and embrace the rationalist and egalitarian side of Marxism, leaving its political core well alone. Whether the Bolshevik understanding itself provided the theoretical conditions for such a selective appropriation is, of course, another matter.[46]

The historically determined and scientifically demonstrated need for national industrialization having been established, all that remained was to identify the political forces, and the policies, which were either in favour of or against such industrialization. The fundamental obstacle was, of course, the colonial state. It was true that the values of modernity and industrialization were historically established in India in the period of colonial rule and in the process of the colonial impact. But that was only a reflection of the fact that in the given historical era it was Britain, or more generally the West, which represented the universal spirit of the age. The specific consequences of colonial rule, however, were wholly injurious to Indian nationhood. In fact, at the time when Britain conquered India, there were, according to Nehru, 'two Englands'. One was 'the England of Shakespeare and Milton, of noble speech and writing and brave deeds, of political revolution and the struggle for freedom, of science and technical progress'. The other was 'the England of the savage penal code and brutal behaviour, of entrenched feudalism and reaction'. 'Which of these two Englands came to India?' he asks. The two were, of course, fused into a single entity, and one could hardly be separated from the other. 'Yet in every major action one plays the leading role, dominating the other, and it was inevitable that the wrong England should play that role in India and should come in contact with and encourage the wrong India in the process.'[47]

With respect to the industrial economy, the 'wrong' England represented the narrow and regressive interests of British capital. Having first destroyed the traditional industrial base of the country in the early phase of conquest, not only was the colonial state in its later phase not interested in Indian industrial development, it actively impeded such growth in order to protect the dominant interests of British industrial and commercial capital. Whatever facilities were conceded to Indian capital were because of special circumstances, such as wartime compulsions. Consequently, Indian industry had grown as far as it had 'in spite of the strenuous opposition of the British government in India and of vested interests in Britain'.[48] Secondly, the colonial state in India had consistently propped up an obsolete feudal order in the countryside and was thus preventing a solution of the massive agrarian problem without which no country can industrialize on a stable basis.

Hence, the most desirable national policy of industrialization would be, first of all, to replace the colonial state with a truly national state; second, to eradicate feudalism in the countryside and undertake fundamental land reforms; and third, to carefully plan the industrial development of the country, under the central coordinating aegis of the state, using the best available scientific and technical expertise and taking the broadest possible view of the range of interrelated social consequences. The performance of Indian industry in the years of World War II had shown 'the enormous capacity of India to advance with rapidity on all fronts. If this striking effort can be made under discouraging conditions,' Nehru wrote in 1944, 'and under a foreign government which disapproved of industrial growth in India, it is obvious that planned development under a free national government would completely change the face of India within a few years'.[49]

IV

The ideological reconstruction undertaken by nationalist thought at its moment of arrival placed the idea of the national state at its very heart. It is a state which must embrace the whole people, give everyone an equal right of citizenship, irrespective of sex, language, religion, caste, wealth or education. In particular, it must be based on a consciousness of national solidarity which includes, in an active political process, the vast mass of the peasantry. This was the central political objective of the Indian national movement in its mature phase.

> Often as I wandered from meeting to meeting I spoke to my audience of this India of ours, of Hindustan and of Bharata, the old Sanskrit name derived from the mythical founder of the race. I seldom did so in the cities, for there the audiences were more sophisticated and wanted stronger fare. But to the peasant, with his limited outlook, I spoke of this great country for whose freedom we were struggling, of how each part differed from the other and yet was India, of common problems of the peasants from north to south and east to west, of the *Swaraj*, the self-rule that could only be for all and every part and not for some . . .
>
> Sometimes as I reached a gathering, a great roar of welcome would greet me: *Bharat Mata ki Jai* — Victory to Mother India! I would ask them unexpectedly what they meant by that cry, who was this *Bharat Mata*, Mother India, whose victory they wanted? My question would amuse them and surprise them, and then, not knowing exactly what to answer, they would look at each other and at me. I persisted in my questioning. At last a vigorous Jat, wedded to the soil from immemorial generations, would say that it was the *dharti*, the good earth of India, that they meant. What earth? Their particular village patch, or all the patches in the district or province, or in the whole of India? And so question and answer went on, till they would ask me impatiently to tell them all about it. I would endeavour to do so and explain that India was all this that they had thought, but it was so much more. The mountains and the rivers of India, and the forests and the broad fields, which gave us food, were all dear to us, but what counted ultimately were the people of India, people like them and me, who were spread out all over this vast land. *Bharat Mata*, Mother India, was essentially these millions of people, and victory to her meant victory to these people. You are parts of this *Bharat Mata*, I told them, you are in a manner yourselves *Bharat Mata*, and as this idea slowly soaked into their brains, their eyes would light up as if they had made a great discovery.[50]

We do not have at hand any corresponding texts that record the peasants' perception of this explication by Jawaharlal Nehru of the idea of *Bharat Mata*; we must, therefore, reserve our judgement on how far the idea 'soaked into their brains'. But this remarkable passage tells us a great deal more about the ideological presuppositions of the new nationalist state leadership. To this leadership, the representation of the nation as Mother carried little of the utopian meaning, dream-like and yet passionately real, charged with a deeply religious semiotic, with which the nationalist intelligentsia had endowed it in its late 19th century phase of Hindu revivalism. It conveyed none of that sense of anguish of a small alienated middle class, daily insulted by the realities of political subjection and yet powerless to hit back, summoning up from the depths of its soul the will and the courage to deliver the ultimate sacrifice that would save the honour of the nation. We do not have here a Bankim of *Ānandamaṭh*[51] or a Rabindranath Tagore in his Swadeshi phase.[52] We have instead a state-builder, pragmatic and self-conscious. The nation as Mother comes to him as part of a political language he has taught himself to use; it is just another political slogan which had gained currency and established itself in the meeting-grounds of the Congress. It does not figure in his own 'scientific' vocabulary of politics. But he can use it, because it has become part of the language which the masses speak when they come to political meetings. So he interprets the word, giving it his own rationalist construction: the nation was the whole people, the victory of the nation meant the victory of the whole people, 'people like them and me'.

Men like Jawaharlal Nehru were acutely conscious of the immense cultural gap which separated the 'them' from the 'me'; in *The Discovery of India*, Nehru had written:

India was in my blood and there was much in her that instinctively thrilled me. And yet, I approached her almost as an alien critic, full of dislike for the present as well as for many of the relics of the past that I saw. To some extent I came to her via the West and looked at her as a friendly Westerner might have done. I was eager and anxious to change her outlook and appearance and give her the garb of modernity. And yet doubts rose within me. Did I know India, I who presumed to scrap much of her past heritage?[53]

The process of 'knowing' India too began quite accidentally, 'almost without any will of my own'[54] when in 1920, Ramachandra, the peasant leader of Uttar Pradesh, came with two hundred peasants to Allahabad to 'beg' the great Congress leaders to come with them to Partabgarh district.[55]

They showered their affection on us and looked on us with loving and hopeful eyes, as if we were the bearers of good tidings, the guides who were to lead them to the promised land. Looking at them and their misery and overflowing gratitude, I was filled with shame and sorrow, shame at my own easy-going and comfortable life and our petty politics of the city which ignored this vast multitude of semi-naked sons and daughters of India, sorrow at the degradation and overwhelming poverty of India. A new picture of India seemed to rise before me, naked, starving, crushed, and utterly miserable. And their faith in us, casual visitors from the distant city, embarrassed me and filled me with a new responsibility that frightened me.[56]

It was 'responsibility' that was the feeling which determined the attitude of the new nationalist state leadership towards the peasantry. This feeling of responsibility was not self-consciously paternalistic, for that was the attitude, condescending and inherently insulting, of the hated British administrator. Rather it was mediated by a whole series of concepts, scientific and theoretical, about politics and the state, about the principles of political organization, about relations between leaders and the masses in political movements, about strategies and tactics. The masses had to be 'represented'; the leaders must therefore learn to 'act on their behalf' and 'in their true interests'.

It was this concept of 'responsibility' as mature and self-conscious *political representation* which shaped Nehru's ideas on the place of the peasantry in the national movement and, by extension, in the new national state. Left to their own devices, peasants often rebelled. These upheavals were 'symptoms of a deep-seated unrest'.[57] While they lasted, the countryside would be 'afire with enthusiasm'[58] and the peasants would seem 'to expect strange happenings which would, as if by a miracle, put an end to their long misery'.[59] But the uprisings were always spontaneous and localized. 'The Indian *kisans* have little staying power, little energy to resist for long.'[60] And that is why leaders such as Ramachandra, who rise up on the crest of 'spontaneous' upheavals of this kind, turn out to be 'irresponsible'.

> Having organised the peasantry to some extent he made all manner of promises to them, vague and nebulous but full of hope for them. He had no programme of any kind and when he had brought them to a pitch of excitement he tried to shift the responsibility to others . . . he turned out later to be a very irresponsible and unreliable person.[61]

Peasants were 'ignorant' and subject to 'passions'. They were 'dull certainly, uninteresting individually, but in the mass they produced a feeling of overwhelming pity and a sense of ever-impending tragedy'.[62] They needed to be led properly, controlled, not by force or fear, but by 'gaining their trust', by teaching them their true interests. Thus when peasants caused 'trouble' in Rae Bareli in 1921 by demanding that some of the villagers who had been arrested recently by the police be released, and the local authorities refused permission to Nehru to address them and instead resorted to shooting, Nehru was 'quite sure that if I or someone [the peasants] trusted had been there and had asked them to do so they would have dispersed. They refused to take their orders from men they did not trust.'[63]

But even for a leadership which had gained the trust of the peasantry, the problem of control was not necessarily a simple one. The very domain of this kind of politics lay in a zone where a great deal was unknown and unpredictable. Often the sense of responsibility towards the peasantry would compel this leadership even to cooperate with an alien state power in order to prevent or control the sudden outbursts of peasant violence. At other times, in periods of widespread agrarian unrest, it became necessary to coordinate and control a series of localized and sporadic agitations in order to put maximum pressure on the colonial government. But the irrationality of the emotions which drove these movements and the unpredictability of their course made it very difficult for even a sympatic leadership to keep a tight grip over its peasant followers. The chapter on 'Agrarian Troubles in the United Provinces'[64] in Nehru's *Autobiography* is, for instance, interspersed with a series of questions such as 'What could they do? What could we do? What advice could we give? What was to be done to them? What would happen then?' many of the questions in fact repeated several times. At one point, when the peasants came to the Congress leaders 'complaining bitterly', Nehru confesses that he 'felt like running away and hiding somewhere, anywhere, to escape this dreadful predicament'.[65]

The problems of incomprehension and unpredictability were compounded by the fact that at moments of agrarian unrest, the peasants were often in such a state of excitement that they could easily be misled into acting in ways totally contrary to their best interests. In Fyzabad in 1921, for instance, the peasants had looted the property of a landlord at the instigation of the servants of a rival landlord.

> The poor ignorant peasants were actually told that it was the wish of Mahatma Gandhi that they should loot and they willingly agreed to carry out this behest, shouting 'Mahatma Gandhi ki jai' in the process.
>
> I was very angry when I heard of this and within a day or two of the occurrence I was on the spot . . . within a few hours five or six thousand persons had collected from numerous villages within a radius of ten miles. I spoke harshly to them for the shame they had brought on themselves and our cause and said that the guilty persons must confess publicly. (I was full in those days of what I conceived to be the spirit of Gandhiji's Satyagraha). I called upon those who had participated in the looting to raise their hands, and strange to say, there, in the presence of numerous police officials, about two dozen hands went up. That meant certain trouble for them.
>
> When I spoke to many of them privately later and heard their artless story of how they had been misled I felt very sorry for them and I began to regret having exposed these foolish and simple folk to long terms of imprisonment . . . full advantage was taken of this occasion to crush the agrarian movement in that district. Over a thousand arrests were made . . . Many died in prison during the trial. Many others received long sentences and in later years, when I went to prison, I came across some of them, boys and young men, spending their youth in prison.[66]

Faced with a situation like this, perhaps not all nationalist leaders would have exhibited quite the same amount of self-righteousness in the presence of police officials, or later regretted the consequences with the same degree of equanimity. But the underlying conception about peasants and politics would have been the same. Peasants are poor and ignorant, unthinking and subject to unreasonable excitements. They must be controlled and led by responsible leaders who would show them how they could fit, entirely in accordance with their true and rational interests, into the national movement. To do this, the nationalist political programme must highlight the main agrarian issues and show how the creation of a truly national state would mean a convincing and rational solution of the agrarian problem.

But no matter how comprehensive and scientific this understanding of the social and economic bases of a united national movement, the practical experience of agrarian upheavals repeatedly demonstrated the incomprehensibility of peasant consciousness within the conceptual domain of bourgeois rationality. When Nehru first came in touch with the widespread peasant agitation in Awadh in 1920, he found it amazing that 'this should have developed quite spontaneously without any city help or intervention of politicians and the like'.[67] Left to themselves, such upheavals were 'notoriously violent, leading to *jacqueries*', because at times like these the peasants were 'desperate and at white heat'.[68] To turn the springs of localized and spontaneous resistance by the peasantry into the broad stream of the national struggle for political freedom was the task of the organized national movement. Yet the task could never be accomplished by acting according to the rational principles of political organization. This, according to Nehru, was the principal reason for the failure of the Communist Party in India to mobilize the peasantry. They were in the habit of judging the Indian situation from 'European Labour standards'.[69] They did not realize that socialism in a country in which the peasants formed the overwhelming part of the population was 'more than mere logic'.[70] To control and direct the peasantry within an organized nation-wide movement, it was of course necessary to constantly keep in the foreground of one's rational political understanding the importance of agrarian issues for a comprehensive programme of mobilization. But this mobilization could never be achieved by a rational programme alone. It required the intervention of a political genius: it required the 'spellbinding' of a Gandhi.[71]

Indeed, on reading the many pages Nehru has written by way of explaining the phenomenon of Gandhi, what comes through most strongly is a feeling of total incomprehension. Here was a political leader who acted 'on instinct', for surely that is what it was and not what Gandhi called it, an 'inner voice' or an 'answer to prayer'.[72] Yet he had 'repeatedly shown what a wonderful knack he has of sensing the mass mind and of acting at the psychological moment'.[73] His economic and social ideas were obsolete, often idiosyncratic, and in general 'reactionary'. 'But the fact remains that this "reactionary" knows India, understands India, almost *is* peasant India, and has shaken up India as no so-called revolutionary has done.'[74] He effected, Nehru says, an almost miraculous 'psychological change, almost as if some expert in psychoanalytical method had probed deep into the patient's past, found out the origins of his complexes, exposed them to his view, and thus rid him of that burden'.[75] But this is only a very tentative image, and immediately it turns out to be an inappropriate one, because Gandhi's 'knack' was not derived from any clinical expertise in a science of mass psychotherapy. It was more in the nature of magic: 'how can I presume to advise a magician?' Nehru had once written to Gandhi at a point of extreme ideological disagreement.[76] In fact, Gandhi's appeal was not primarily to the faculty of reason; on the contrary, the appeal was essentially hypnotic, calling for a suspension of reason.

His calm, deep eyes would hold one and gently probe into the depths; his voice, clear and limpid, would purr its way into the heart and evoke an emotional response. Whether his audience consisted of one person or a thousand, the charm and magnetism of the man passed on to it, and each one had a feeling of communion with the speaker. This feeling had little to do with the mind, though the appeal to the mind was not wholly ignored. But mind and reason definitely had second place. The process of 'spell-binding' was not brought about by oratory or the hypnotism of silken phrases . . . It was the utter sincerity of the man and his personality that gripped; he gave the impression of tremendous inner reserves of power. Perhaps also it was a tradition that had grown up about him which helped in creating a suitable atmosphere. A stranger, ignorant of this tradition and not in harmony with the surroundings, would probably not have been touched by that spell, or, at any rate, not to the same extent.[77]

And so the explanation proceeds, bending and weaving its way over an unfamiliar terrain, seeking a rational answer in some supreme expertise in the science of mass psychology, giving it up for a description in terms of magical powers, but skipping back at the very next moment to an account of the 'tradition' that had been built up around the person. But how was this 'tradition' built up? Was it the appeal to religion, the fact that the masses regarded him as a supremely religious man and therefore endowed him with an unassailable spiritual authority? To be sure, there was a lot of this in Gandhi. His politics was based on 'a definitely religious outlook on life'. But in that case it could only have been a reactionary politics; the whole movement was, in fact, 'strongly influenced' by his religious outlook and 'took on a revivalist character so far as the masses were concerned'.[78] And yet Gandhi's politics was highly revolutionary in its consequences. Was it the case, then, that there was a difference between the politics and the language, between the action and the theory that it was overtly based on? Could the metaphysical assumptions be separated from the political consequences, and the latter supported while ignoring the former?

I used to be troubled sometimes at the growth of this religious element in our politics . . . I did not like it at all . . . [The] history and sociology and economics appeared to me all wrong, and the religious twist that was given to everything prevented all clear thinking. Even some of Gandhiji's phrases sometimes jarred upon me — thus his frequent reference to *Rama Raj* as a golden age which was to return. But I was powerless to intervene, and I consoled myself with the thought that Gandhiji used the words because they were well known and understood by the masses. He had an amazing knack of reaching the heart of the people . . .

He was a very difficult person to understand, sometimes his language was almost incomprehensible to an average modern. But we felt that we knew him well enough to realise he was a great and unique man and a glorious leader, and having put our faith in him we gave him an almost blank cheque, for the time being at least. Often we discussed his fads and peculiarities among ourselves and said, half-humorously, that when Swaraj came these fads must not be encouraged.[79]

Once again, this remarkable passage tells us much less in terms of explaining the phenomenon of Gandhi than it does about the politics of the nationalist state leadership. For it lays down in the space of a few sentences the entire strategy of the passive revolution in India. To start with, it sets out the contrast between 'we', on the one hand, and 'Gandhi' on the other. Thus, on the one hand, it states that

1) we *know* the correct history, sociology and economics, but
2) we are *powerless* to intervene. On the other hand,
3) Gandhi operates with a religious element, i.e. he has a wrong history, sociology and economics. He has fads and peculiarities. His language is almost *incomprehensible*. But
4) Gandhi uses words that are well known and understood by the masses. He has an amazing *knack* of reaching the heart of the people. Therefore,
5) Gandhi is a great and *unique* man and a glorious leader. It follows as an unstated deduction that
6) Gandhi has the power to mobilize the masses towards Swaraj. The strategy then follows:
7) We *know* him well enough.
8) We give him an almost blank cheque *for the time being*.
9) *After* Swaraj, his fads and peculiarities must not be encouraged.

The argument, in other words, is that whereas our very knowledge of society tells us that 'we' are powerless, Gandhi's unique and incomprehensible knack of reaching the people makes him powerful; however, for that very reason, our knowledge of the consequences of Gandhi's power enables us to let him act on our behalf for the time being but to resume our own control afterwards.

The strategy is set down here in astonishingly stark terms. Yet it is the product of a complex, even if contradictory, understanding of history and society, continually seeking a rational legitimation of its single-minded pursuit of political power. From its own understanding of Indian society, this emerging state leadership recognized the historical limits of its powers of direct intervention. It was a 'progressive' leadership, with its own conception of the sort of changes that were necessary if Indian society was to progress. It identified the chief obstacle to these changes in the existence of a colonial state power, and looked towards its replacement by a national state power as the central agency of change. But it also knew that a successful movement to create a new national state would require the incorporation of the vast mass of the peasantry into the political nation. And here its own understanding of society had made it conscious of the great inconsistencies that existed between the real objective interests of the peasants and their unreasonable subjective beliefs. It also knew, and this is what distinguished them as an emerging *state* leadership, that given its historical circumstances, it could not realistically hope for a transformation of the social and cultural conditions of Indian agrarian society before the political objective was reached. The colonial state was an insurmountable impediment to all such attempts at a transformation. Hence, rather than wasting one's energies in futile projects like 'constructive work in the villages', it was necessary first of all to concentrate on the immediate political task of winning self-government. The task of transforming the countryside could be taken up *afterwards*.

And yet the colonial state itself could not be overthrown unless the peasantry was mobilized into the national movement. How could this be done if the peasantry did not see that it was in its objective interest to join in the struggle for an independent and united national state? To accomplish this historical task, it was necessary, first of all, to be 'sympathetic' towards the conditions of the peasantry, to 'gain their trust'. If the political leadership was prepared to adopt this sympathetic attitude, it would immediately become apparent that the peasants were capable of heroic resistance 'in their own way'. There were, of course, major limitations to these forms of resistance: they were guided by irrational emotions, they were localized and sporadic and prone to violence, they could easily be misdirected by unscrupulous and irresponsible leaders. But that precisely was the task of a responsible national leadership: to organize, coordinate and keep under control a whole series of local movements of this kind.

But this would still leave unresolved the problem of releasing in the first place these more or less spontaneous forces of resistance within the peasantry. How were they to be moved into political action? This could be done by 'reaching into their hearts', by speaking a language which they understood. One must have a 'knack' for this, because it was not a language that would emerge out of a rational understanding of objective interests. It would have to be a very special 'knack', and only a great and unique man like Gandhi would have it.

And so the split between two domains of politics — one, a politics of the elite, and the other, a politics of the subaltern classes — was replicated in the sphere of mature nationalist thought by an explicit recognition of the split between a domain of rationality and a domain of unreason, a domain of science and a domain of faith, a domain of organization and a domain of spontaneity. But it was a rational understanding which, by the very act of its recognition of the Other, also effaced the Other.

If the consciousness of the peasantry lay in the domain of unreason, it could never be understood in rational terms. Thus by the very recognition of its Otherness, the possibility was denied that it could be rationally comprehended in its specific subjectivity. It could only be reached by a political 'genius', a 'unique' man with a 'knack' for 'spellbinding' the masses. And thus, once again, by the very recognition of his power as unique, and therefore not subject to normal criteria of judgment, the specific historical subjectivity of the 'genius' was consigned to the zone of incomprehensibility.

But the *consequences* of his intervention were capable of being appropriated. They could become part of the rational progression of history, because they were capable of being understood rationally. In fact, these excursions into the other domain had to be judged by a criterion of functionality — whether or not they fitted in with the rational (the scientific/the desired) progression of history, defined, of course, in the rational domain — and approved or disapproved of accordingly. Thus, the Gandhian intervention, though its fundamental nature was incomprehensible, was worthy of approval because it was functional in its consequences. 'Communalist' interventions, equally incomprehensible in their powers of mobilization, were to be disapproved of because they were divisive, and hence dysfunctional in their consequences. It was with this notion of functionality, then, that the recognition of the split between the two domains of politics, and of the interventions from one domain into the other, could be reconstituted into the monistic unity of a linear progression of *real* history, both rational and progressive.

The notion of functionality also served to break up this linear progression into distinct, tactically manageable, historical *stages*. There is first a stage where conditions are created in the 'real' domain of politics for a sympathetic approach into the other domain. Then comes the second stage when a 'blank cheque' is given to the great and 'unique' leader to reach out into that other domain: the result is a mobilization of the peasantry. The third stage is when the consequences of the mobilization are appropriated within the 'real' domain of politics and direct control over the now reconstituted political process is resumed.

We have seen in the previous chapter how the thought of Gandhi, beginning as it did from a critique of the very idea of civil society, proceeded to make itself relevant as an effective intervention in the domain of elite-nationalist politics by coming to terms with the problematic and thematic of nationalism. It was, to be sure, a profoundly ambiguous agreement. But by agreeing to recognize the practicality of the problematic, and by implication the validity of the thematic, it connived in the transference of its fundamental moral critique from the domain of the political to that of the utopian. Now Nehru could say, without desecrating the moral sanctity of Gandhi's 'utter sincerity', that he was merely 'a peasant', albeit a great one, 'with a peasant's blindness to some aspects of life'. He could say that Gandhi's project was 'impossible of achievement'. Once Gandhism had acknowledged that the sinfulness of political life might finally force it to save its morality by withdrawing from politics, the path was opened for a new state leadership to appropriate the political consequences of the Gandhian intervention at the same time as it rejected its Truth. The critical point of Gandhism's ideological intervention was now pushed back into the zone of the 'purely religious' or the metaphysical; only its political consequences were 'real'. Thus, it now became possible for Jawaharlal Nehru, Prime Minister of India, to inaugurate on Gandhi's birthday a new factory for making railway coaches and say, 'I am quite sure that if it had been our good fortune to have Gandhiji with us today he would have been glad at the opening of this factory.'[80] For now, Gandhi's Truth had surrendered the specificity of its moral critique: it had been cleansed of its religious idiom and subsumed under the rational monism of historical progress. Was it not true, after all, that Gandhi's 'real' objective was the welfare of the masses? Was it not possible, then, to interpret Gandhi's opposition to machinery in its proper rational context? 'People think that he was against machinery. I don't think he was against it. He did not want machinery except in the context of the well-being of the mass of our people.'[81] Indeed, once the Truth of Gandhism had been retrieved from the irrational trappings of its 'language', the possibilities were endless: it could justify everything that was 'progressive'. Thus the Congress 'formulated a policy of land reform and social justice, and took some steps towards the formulation of a public sector. The whole philosophy of Gandhiji, although he did not talk perhaps in a modern language, was not only one of social justice, but of social reform and land reform. All these concepts were his.'[82]

It is possible, of course, to argue that this is what his political successors had made of Gandhi; it had nothing to do with the Gandhian ideology itself. To take this position would, I think, involve the danger of overlooking the very real effectivity of the new nationalist state ideology. It would imply our having to characterize that ideology as a massive and cynical fraud perpetrated on the Indian people. That in turn would confound the very problem of isolating the justificatory structures of the ideology. If instead we look at the specific unity of the process of development of a mature nationalist ideology constructed around the contemporary Indian state, we would see that the Gandhian intervention was a *necessary* stage in that process, the stage in the passive revolution where the possibility emerged for 'the thesis to incorporate a part of the antithesis'. Paradoxical as it is, the fact still remains that Gandhism, originally the product of an anarchist philosophy of resistance to state oppression, itself becomes a participant in its imbrication with a nationalist state ideology.

Let us briefly glance through Nehru's own representation of the history of the Gandhian intervention in the politics of the nation, and the nature of this imbrication will emerge more clearly. The Gandhian intervention 'forced India to think of the poor peasant in human terms', it bridged the gap between 'the English-educated class' and the 'mass of the population' and 'forced [the former] to turn their heads and look towards their own people'.[83] At this stage, the 'India' which was forced to think of the poor peasant is identical with the 'English-educated class' which was forced to look towards their own people, for that indeed was the political nation. 'And then Gandhi came . . . suddenly, as it were, that black pall of fear was lifted from the people's shoulders.'[84] As Gandhi began to perform his 'spellbinding' on the masses, the whole character of the organized national movement changed completely. 'Now the peasants rolled in, and in its new garb it began to assume the look of a vast agrarian organization with a strong sprinkling of the middle classes.'[85] Gandhi transformed 'the Indian habit of mind' which was 'essentially one of quietism'.[86] He, indeed, 'effected a vast psychological revolution'.[87] He came to 'represent the peasant masses of India'. In fact, he was more than a mere representative:

> he is the quintessence of the conscious and subconscious will of those millions . . . he is the idealised personification of those vast millions . . . withal he is the great peasant, with a peasant's outlook on affairs, and with a peasant's blindness to some aspects of life. But India is peasant India, and so he knows his India well and reacts to her slightest tremors, and gauges a situation accurately and almost instinctively, and has a knack of acting at the psychological moment.

What a problem and a puzzle he has been not only to the British Government, but to his own people and his closest associates![88]

His ideas on history and society were, of course, all wrong. They were guided by 'metaphysical and mystical reasons'.[89] He had a 'pure religious attitude to life and its problems'.[90] The ideas of *Hind Swaraj* represented an 'utterly wrong and harmful doctrine, and impossible of achievement'.[91] He was always 'thinking in terms of personal salvation and of sin, while most of us have society's welfare uppermost in our minds'.[92]

But despite all this, 'with all his greatness and his contradictions and power of moving masses, he is above the usual standards. One cannot measure him or judge him as we would others.'[93] He was a genius, a man with unique and incomprehensible powers. 'He was obviously not of the world's ordinary coinage; he was minted of a different and rare variety, and often the unknown stared at us through his eyes.'[94]

His power to move people was incomprehensible, but the consequences were not. Many who joined him

> did not agree with his philosophy of life, or even with many of his ideals. Often they did not understand him. But the action that he proposed was something tangible which could be understood and appreciated intellectually ... Step by step he convinced us of the rightness of the action, and we went with him, although we did not accept his philosophy. To divorce action from the thought underlying it was not perhaps a proper procedure and was bound to lead to mental conflict and trouble later ... [But] the road he was following was the right one thus far, and if the future meant a parting it would be folly to anticipate it ...
>
> Always we had the feeling that while we might be more logical, Gandhi knew India far better than we did, and a man who could command such tremendous devotion and loyalty must have something in him that corresponded to the needs and aspirations of the masses.[95]

But in the final analysis, it was the logical, the rational, the scientific, which had to be the basis for one's understanding of the *real* progression of history. The resort to an incomprehensible power which could rouse the masses was only a functional loop, a necessary detour into the domain of the irrational and the unknown. Soon the rational path of real history would have to be resumed in order to move on to the next historical stage. The detour had meant 'solid gain for the country'. But 'the real thing is the attainment of the goal and every step that we take must be taken from the viewpoint of the very early attainment of this goal'. It had to be consciously borne in mind that the detour was indeed a detour. Or else, one would 'relapse into a dreary round of activity, good in itself, but feeble and ineffective and wholly uninspiring from the larger viewpoint. There are some people who perhaps imagine that the goal is really a distant one and that immediately we must aim at something else. This cannot be the Congress viewpoint and can be ignored.'[96] The goal now was definitely set before the emerging state leadership: 'What then are we aiming at? We have definitely put before us the attainment of a revolutionary, that is root and branch, change in our national political structure.'[97] The perspective was that of the creation of a new national *state*. And this could only be undertaken in the domain of rational politics. And it was obvious, therefore, that Gandhi could no longer be the appropriate guide at this stage of the journey. The disjuncture between the philosophy and the politics could be successfully handled only as long as the detour was recognised as a detour, a move into a 'special field'. When the time came to resume the real course of history, that philosophy could only act as a source of confusion and had to be firmly rejected.

> I came to the conclusion that Gandhiji's difficulties had been caused because he was moving in an unfamiliar medium. He was superb in his special field of Satyagrahic direct action, and his instinct unerringly led him to take the right steps. He was also very good in working himself and making others work quietly for social reform among the masses. He could understand absolute war or absolute peace. Anything in between he did not appreciate.[98]

Gandhian politics was not guided by 'clearly conceived ends', by a conception of historical objectives. 'In spite of the closest association with him for many years I am not clear in my own mind about his objective. I doubt if he is clear himself. One step enough for me, he says, and he does not try to peep into the future or to have a clearly conceived end before him.'[99] He was 'more or less of a philosophical anarchist'[100] and however functional such a philosophy might be in the stage of rousing the masses to political resistance, it could hardly be a reliable guide when the immediate task was to create a new state.

And so the final stage of the nationalist project was defined. No matter how imperfect the preparation, how difficult the circumstances, or even how incomplete and fragmented the final result, the struggle was now one of building the new national state.

> It is a race between the forces of peaceful progress and construction and those of disruption and disaster . . . We can view this prospect as optimists or as pessimists, according to our predilections and mental make-up. Those who have faith in a moral ordering of the universe and in the ultimate triumph of virtue can, fortunately for them, function as lookers on or as helpers, and cast the burden on God. Others will have to carry that burden on their own weak shoulders, hoping for the best and preparing for the worst.[101]

This was the epitaph, wondrous and yet condescending, put up on the grave of Gandhian politics by the new nationalist state leadership. The relentless thrust of its rationalist thematic turned the Gandhian intervention into a mere interlude in the unfolding of the real history of the nation. And thus it was that the political consequences of that intervention were fully appropriated within the monistic progression of real history.

V

'Socialism is more than mere logic', Nehru had said when criticizing Communists for being overly dogmatic and theoretical and not paying enough attention to the cultural peculiarities of India. But talking about the socialism which he envisaged for a free India, he was equally forthright: 'The emotional appeal to socialism is not enough. This must be supplemented by an intellectual and reasoned appeal based on facts and arguments and detailed criticism . . . We want experts in the job who study and prepare detailed plans.'[102]

The emphasis on expertise was a distinctive, and central, element in the reconstitution of nationalism as a state ideology. The principal architect in the construction of a modern nation would be a scientific consciousness, knowledgeable and wise, with a broad and subtle understanding of the course of world history, marshalling the latest knowledge made available by science and technology, collecting the widest possible range of information on the precise empirical state of the economy, registering the particular interests and demands of each separate group in society, and then taking a finely balanced view to propose the most efficient as well as the most widely acceptable course for the progress of the economy. The necessary political focus would, of course, be provided by the state. For the state would represent the balanced aggregate interest of the people as a whole. It would not be dominated by any particular group or class; it would not even be the site for the struggle, always potentially violent, between classes. It would stand above these conflicts and provide an autonomous political will to control and direct the economy in the interest of the people as a whole.

A primary object of this scientifically planned development would, of course, be the rapid industrialization of the economy. This was an object which had been globally determined by the inexorable logic of universal history, and there were no grounds left for a moral choice on its desirability or otherwise. Indeed, this objective had now attained a historical status that was quite independent of social ideologies and political programmes.

> We are trying to catch up, as far as we can, with the Industrial Revolution that occurred long ago in Western countries . . . The Revolution ultimately branched off in two directions which are, at present, represented by the high degree of technological development in the United States of America on the one hand and by the Soviet Union on the other. These two types of development, even though they might be in conflict, are branches of the same tree.[103]

It was now a demonstrated truth of history that only an industrialized economy could provide sufficient resources for the balanced satisfaction of wants of all sections of society. The alternative was simply a balanced distribution of poverty. Unless the productive processes of society were revitalized by industrialization, there would be nothing to distribute. It was also a demonstrated truth that an advanced industrial society required a considerable degree of state control and coordination. Things could not be left to the mythical balancing mechanism of the 'hidden hand'. That was yet another economic dogma that had been falsified by history. *Laissez faire*

> is a bullock-cart variety of economic talk, which has no relation with the present. If one wants to live in this modern age of technology, one must also think in terms of modern thought.[104]
>
> . . . practically nobody now believes in *laissez faire* . . . Everywhere, even in the most highly developed countries of the capitalist economy, the State functions in a way which possibly a socialist fifty years ago did not dream of.[105]

158

The question of state control, too, had nothing to do with socialism *per se*; its validity derived simply from its being a constituent part of modernity.

Where socialism did come in was on the question of equality. 'Scientific planning enables us to increase our production, and socialism comes in when we plan to distribute production evenly.'[106] But what justified the adoption of equality as a goal of planned development? Was it simply a recognition of the empirical fact that a lot of people wanted equality? That would be a very uncertain justification, for it was not at all clear that everyone meant the same thing by equality or that everyone wanted the same degree of equality. The principle of equality could not be left to be determined on such a contentious field. No, equality was justified by a much more universal logic:

> The spirit of the age is in favour of equality, though practice denies it almost everywhere . . . Yet the spirit of the age will triumph. In India, at any rate, we must aim at equality. That does not and cannot mean that everybody is physically or intellectually or spiritually equal or can be made so. But it does mean equal opportunities for all and no political, economic, or social barrier in the way of any individual or group. It means a faith in humanity and a belief that there is no race or group that cannot advance and make good in its own way, given the chance to do so. It means a realization of the fact that the backwardness or degradation of any group is not due to inherent failings in it but principally to lack of opportunities and long suppression by other groups . . . Any such attempt to open the doors of opportunity to all in India will release enormous energy and ability and transform the country with amazing speed.[107]

Thus, the need for equality was entailed in the very logic of progress: progress meant industrialization, industrialization required the removal of barriers which prevented particular groups from fully participating in the entire range of new economic activities, hence industrialization required equality of opportunity. It did not necessarily mean a fundamental reallocation of rights in society, or a revolution in the nature of property. It did not mean an equalization of incomes either. Only a 'progressive tendency' towards equalization of incomes would result from the fact that every person had the freedom to choose his occupation. 'In any event, the vast differences that exist today will disappear completely, and class distinctions, which are essentially based on differences in income, will begin to fade out.'[108]

Thus, neither industrialization nor equality were innately political questions to be resolved in the battlefield of politics. The universal principle and the world standards had been already set by history; there was no room for choice on those matters. Only the specific national path remained to be determined. But this was now a *technical* problem, a problem of balancing and optimisation. It was a job for experts. 'Planning,' Nehru would later say in 1957, 'essentially consists in balancing: the balancing between industry and agriculture, the balancing between heavy industry and light industry, the balancing between cottage industry and other industry. If one of them goes wrong then the whole economy is upset.'[109] The question was one of collecting detailed information on as many aspects of the economy as possible, of working out the complex interdependence of each of those aspects. There was no merit in imposing one's preconceived theoretical ideas on what was essentially a technical problem. Already in 1938-9, when the National Planning Committee set up by the Congress began its work, Nehru realized that the fact that the need to achieve a broad-based consensus meant the abandonment of abstract theories and definite guidelines was not necessarily a drawback; on the contrary, there were distinct advantages in the situation. 'We decided to consider the general problem of planning as well as each individual problem concretely and not in the abstract, and allow principles to develop out of such considerations.'[110] Help was also taken of a very large number of experts, from universities, chambers of commerce, trade unions, research institutes and public bodies. In the end, Nehru

> was greatly surprised at the large measure of unanimity achieved by us in spite of the incongruous elements in our committee. The big-business element was the biggest single group, and its outlook on many matters, especially financial and commercial, was definitely conservative. Yet the urge for rapid progress, and the conviction that only thus could we solve our problems of poverty and unemployment, were so great that all of us were forced out of our grooves and compelled to think on new lines. We had avoided a theoretical approach, and as each practical problem was viewed in its larger context, it led us inevitably in a particular direction. To me the spirit of co-operation of the members of the Planning Committee was particularly soothing and gratifying, for I found it a pleasant contrast to the squabbles and conflicts of politics.[111]

This now became the new utopia, a realist's utopia, a utopia here and now. It was a utopia supremely statist, where the function of government was wholly abstracted out of the messy business of politics and established in its pristine purity as rational decision-making conducted through the most advanced operational techniques provided by the sciences of economic management. Indeed it was a systems-theorist's utopia, where government was the perfect black box, receiving inputs from all parts of society, processing them, and finally allocating the optimal values for the common satisfaction and preservation of society as a whole. No squabbles, no struggles for power, no politics. Place all your prayers at the feet of the *sarkar*, the omnipotent and supremely enlightened state, and they will be duly passed on to the body of experts who are planning for the overall progress of the country. If your requests are consistent with the requirements of progress, they will be granted.

Socialism, Nehru would now repeatedly warn, should not be looked at in purely political terms. A constant emphasis on politics and class struggle 'distorts' the vision of socialism. 'Socialism should . . . be considered apart from these political elements or the inevitability of violence.' All that socialism taught us was that 'the general character of social, political and intellectual life in a society is governed by its productive resources'.[112] Socialism, therefore, was a business of rational management of productive resources. It should also not be defined in *a priori* theoretical terms. 'I do not see why I should be asked to define socialism in precise, rigid terms.'[113] It was something that must evolve from the concrete, the particular: 'We cannot bind the future. We can only deal with facts as they are.'[114] And it is not surprising that an attempt now to morally unify such an infinitely regressive technicism would lead to that most metaphysical of all conceptions, which a younger Jawaharlal would have regarded as wholly imprecise and vague, where everything is related to everything else. Now he would appeal to 'the old Vedantic conception that everything, whether sentient or insentient, finds a place in the organic whole: that everything has a spark of what might be called the divine impulse or the basic energy or life force which pervades the Universe'.[115]

The world of the concrete, the world of differences, of conflict, of the struggle between classes, of history and politics, now finds its unity in the life of the state. The aim was ultimately to achieve equality, a classless society, indeed a lot more:

> Our final aim can only be a classless society with equal economic justice and opportunity for all, a society organised on a planned basis for the raising of mankind to higher material and cultured levels, to a cultivation of spiritual values, of cooperation, unselfishness, the spirit of service, the desire to do right, goodwill and love — ultimately a world order.[116]

This might seem 'fanciful and Utopian', but it was not. It could be realized here and now, in the rational life of the state. The mistaken path, fruitless and destructive, was in fact to try to achieve that final aim by means of politics, through the violent struggle between classes. Nothing would be achieved by the clash of particular interests.

> India is not only a big country but a country with a good deal of variety; and if any one takes to the sword, he will inevitably be faced with the sword of someone else. This clash between swords will degenerate into fruitless violence and, in the process, the limited energies of the nation will be dissipated or, at any rate, greatly undermined.[117]

So was there no violence in the life of the state? Was it not in itself an institution which exercised power over the various parts of society? What if there were impediments in the path of progress? Would not the state, acting on behalf of society as a whole, be required to exercise power to remove those impediments?

> Everything that comes in the way will have to be removed, gently if possible, forcibly if necessary. And there seems to be little doubt that coercion will often be necessary. But [and this is a significant 'but'] . . . if force is used it should not be in the spirit of hatred or cruelty, but with the dispassionate desire to remove an obstruction.[118]

The coercion of the state was itself a rational instrument for the achievement of progress by the nation. It was to be used by the state with surgical dispassion, and would be justified by the rationality of its own ends.

Nationalism has arrived; it has now constituted itself into a state ideology; it has appropriated the life of the nation into the life of the state. It is rational and progressive, a particular manifestation of the universal march of Reason; it has accepted the global realities of power, accepted the fact that World History

161

resides Elsewhere. Only it has now found its place within that universal scheme of things.

Has the history of nationalism then exhausted itself? Such a conclusion will be unwarranted. For hardly anywhere in the post-colonial world has it been possible for the nation-state to fully appropriate the life of the nation into its own. Everywhere the intellectual-moral leadership of the ruling classes is based on a spurious ideological unity. The fissures are clearly marked on its surface.

Where then will the critique emerge of nationalism? How will nationalism supersede itself? A historical discourse, unfortunately, can only struggle with its own terms. Its evolution will be determined by history itself.

Notes

1. Jawaharlal Nehru, *An Autobiography* (London: Bodley Head, 1936) [hereafter *A*], p.370.
2. *A*, pp.383-4.
3. Jawaharlal Nehru, *The Discovery of India* (New York: John Day, 1946) [hereafter *DI*].
4. *DI*, pp.133-4.
5. *DI*, pp.141-2.
6. *DI*, p.142.
7. *DI*, p.143.
8. *DI*, p.143.
9. *DI*, p.217.
10. *DI*, p.220.
11. *DI*, p.221.
12. *DI*, pp.221-2.
13. *DI*, p.222.
14. *DI*, p.256.
15. *DI*, p.256.
16. *DI*, p.261.
17. *DI*, pp.261-2.
18. *DI*, p.261.
19. *DI*, p.518.
20. *DI*, p.516.
21. *DI*, p.578.
22. *DI*, pp.570-1.
23. *DI*, pp.517-8.
24. *DI*, p.522.
25. *DI*, p.522.
26. *DI*, p.523.
27. *DI*, p.526. It is also interesting to note that the most conclusive evidence of the greatness of Indian civilization is found when 'the better type of the modern mind', can be shown to be appreciative of its intrinsic worth. The sections of *The Discovery of India* dealing with the achievements of the classical Indian civilization are replete with dozens of quotations from Schopenhauer, von Humboldt, Max Müller, Sylvain Lévi, Romain Rolland, even H.G. Wells, and one from 'M.

Foucher, the French savant' on the charms of Kashmir. *DI*, p.568.

28. *A*, p.544. In 1934, criticizing communalist politicians for their ignorance of economic matters, Nehru said

> It is notorious that the era of politics has passed away and we live in an age when economics dominate national and international affairs. What have the communal organizations to say in regard to these economic matters? . . . whether socialism or communism is the right answer or some other, one thing is certain — that the answer must be in terms of economics and not merely politics. For India and the world are oppressed by economic problems and there is no escaping them.

Statement to the press, Allahabad, 5 January 1934. *Selected Works of Jawaharlal Nehru* (New Delhi: Orient Longman, 1972-82) [hereafter *SW*], vol.6, pp.184-5.

29. *A*, pp.362-3.

30. *DI*, p.387.

31. *DI*, p.387. There are innumerable places in Nehru's works where he says quite categorically that communalism has nothing to do with religion, that its causes are partly economic and partly political, and that if the economic problems are solved and the foreign power removed, there would be no communalism any more. For example:

> The communal problem is not a religious problem, it has nothing to do with religion. It is partly an economic problem, and partly a middle class problem in a largely political sense . . . I do not think it is a very difficult problem to solve. If social and economic issues come to the front the communal problem falls into the background.

Interview to the press in London, 27 January 1936. *SW*, vol.7, p.82.

> Fundamentally this communal problem is a problem of the conflict between the members of the upper middle-class Hindus and Moslems for jobs and power under the new constitution. It does not affect the masses at all. Not a single communal demand has the least reference to any economic issues in India or has the least reference to the masses.

Discussion with the India Conciliation Group in London, 4 February 1936. *SW*, vol.7, pp.96-7.

> Communalism is essentially a hunt for favours from a third party — the ruling power. The communalist can only think in terms of a continuation of foreign domination and he tries to make the best of it for his own particular group. Delete the foreign power and the communal arguments and demands fall to the ground.

Statement to the press, Allahabad, 5 January 1934. *SW*, vol.6, p.182.

32. *A*, p.137.

33. *A*, pp.137-8.

34. *DI*, p.387.

35. *A*, p.138.

36. *A*, p.462.

37. *A*, p.465.

38. *A*, p.466.

39. *A*, pp.466-7.

40. *A*, pp.467-8.
41. *DI*, p.413.
42. *DI*, p.414.
43. *DI*, p.413.
44. *DI*, p.414.
45. *DI*, p.416.
46. For an interesting argument on this point, see Carmen Claudin-Urondo, *Lenin and the Cultural Revolution*, tr. Brian Pearce (Brighton: Harvester Press, 1977). Returning from his first visit to the Soviet Union in 1928, Nehru made the intriguing comment: 'The Soviet system has become so much identified with Bolshevism and Russia that it is difficult to think of it apart from them. Yet it is conceivable that it may exist, or rather that its outward structure may exist, without communism.' 'The Soviet System', *SW*, vol.2, p.390.
47. *DI*, pp.286-7.
48. *DI*, p.300.
49. *DI*, p.515.
50. *DI*, pp.48-9.
51. In 1908, a young Jawaharlal had written to his mother from Trinity College, Cambridge: 'You have written to me that you are going to read *Anand Math*. Do read it. Although I have not read the book myself, I think it is a good book.' *SW*, vol.1, p.63.
52. For a discussion of the symbolisms of this phase of middle-class nationalism, see in particular Sumit Sarkar, *The Swadeshi Movement in Bengal 1903-08* (New Delhi: People's Publishing House, 1973), esp. pp.252-335.
53. *DI*, p.38.
54. *A*, p.49.
55. For the historical details, see Gyan Pandey, 'Peasant Revolt and Indian Nationalism: The Peasant Movement in Awadh, 1919-1922' in Ranajit Guha, ed., *Subaltern Studies I: Writings on South Asian History and Society* (Delhi: Oxford University Press, 1982), pp.143-97; and Majid Hayat Siddiqi, *Agrarian Unrest in North India: The United Provinces, 1918-22* (New Delhi: Vikas, 1978).
56. *A*, p.52.
57. *A*, p.63.
58. *A*, p.51.
59. *A*, p.52.
60. *A*, p.62.
61. *A*, p.53.
62. *A*, p.78.
63. *A*, p.60.
64. *A*, pp.297-312.
65. *A*, p.305.
66. *A*, pp.61-2.
67. *A*, p.54.
68. *A*, p.59.
69. *A*, p.366.
70. *A*, p.368.
71. It is instructive to note for the sake of comparison what Nehru wrote on Lenin after a visit to the Soviet Union in 1927:

It is difficult for most of us to think of our ideals and our theories in terms of reality . . . In Russia also the revolutionaries of an older generation lived in a

world of theory, and hardly believed in the realisation of their ideals. But Lenin
came with his directness and realism and shook the fabric of old time orthodox
socialism and revolution. He taught people to think that the ideal they had
dreamed of and worked for was not mere theory but something to be realised then
and there. By amazing force of will he hypnotised a nation and filled a disunited
and demoralised people with energy and determination and the strength to
endure and suffer for a cause.

'Lenin', *SW*, vol.2, p.408.
   72. *A*, p.505.
   73. *A*, p.506.
   74. *A*, p.406.
   75. *DI*, p.362.
   76. *A*, p.372.
   77. *A*, pp.129-30.
   78. *A*, p.72.
   79. *A*, pp.72-3.
   80. Speech at the inauguration of production at the Integral Coach Factory, Perambur, Madras, 2 October 1955. *Jawaharlal Nehru's Speeches* (New Delhi: Publications Division, 1954-1968) [hereafter *S*], vol.3, p.23.
   81. Speech at a Seminar on Social Welfare in a Developing Economy, New Delhi, 22 September 1963. *S*, vol.5, p.104.
   82. Speech on the No-Confidence Motion in Parliament, 22 August 1963. *S*, vol.5, p.80.
   83. *DI*, pp.412-3.
   84. *DI*, p.361.
   85. *DI*, pp.363.
   86. *DI*, p.364.
   87. *DI*, p.367.
   88. *A*, p.253.
   89. *A*, p.506.
   90. *A*, p.536.
   91. *A*, p.510.
   92. *A*, p.511.
   93. *A*, p.548.
   94. *A*, p.254.
   95. *A*, pp.254-5.
   96. Note written in Naini Central Jail, *SW*, vol.4, pp.444-51.
   97. Ibid.
   98. *A*, pp.127-8.
   99. *A*, p.509.
   100. *A*, p.515.
   101. *DI*, p.520.
   102. *A*, pp.588-9.
   103. Speech in Parliament, 15 December 1952. *S*, vol.2, p.93.
   104. Address to the Associated Chambers of Commerce, Calcutta, 14 December 1953. *S*, vol.3, p.59.
   105. Speech in Parliament, 21 December 1953. *S*, vol.3, p.13.
   106. Speech at a public meeting, Bangalore, 6 February 1962. *S*, vol.4, p.151.
   107. *DI*, pp.532-3.

108. *DI*, p.534.

109. Speech to All-India Congress Committee, Indore, 4 January 1957. *S*, vol.3, p.51.

110. *DI*, p.401.

111. *DI*, p.405.

112. 'The Basic Approach', *S*, vol.4, p.121.

113. Speech to All-India Congress Committee, Indore, 4 January 1957. *S*, vol.3, p.52.

114. Speech in Parliament, 15 December 1952. *S*, vol.2, p.96.

115. 'The Basic Approach', *S*, vol.4, p.119.

116. *A*, p.552.

117. Speech in Parliament, 15 December 1952. *S*, vol.2, p.95.

118. *A*, p.552. In 1935, he wrote:

State violence is preferable to private violence in many ways, for one major violence is far better than numerous petty private violences. State violence is also likely to be a more or less ordered violence and thus preferable to the disorderly violence of private groups and individuals, for even in violence order is better than disorder ... But when a state goes off the rails completely and begins to indulge in disorderly violence, then indeed it is a terrible thing.

'The Mind of a Judge', *SW*, vol.6, pp.487-8.

6. The Cunning of Reason

> Thus God knows the world, because He conceived it in
> His mind, as if from the outside, before it was created,
> and we do not know its rule, because we live inside it,
> having found it already made.
>
> Umberto Eco, *The Name of the Rose*

There is a scene in Dinabandhu Mitra's play *Sadhabār Ekādaśī* (1866) in which the leading character, Nimchand Datta, a product of the 19th century 'renaissance' in Bengal and, quite typically, alienated from the rest of his society by his own enlightenment, roams drunkenly at night through the streets of Calcutta giving vent to his feelings of irreverent, anarchic anguish, at which point an English police sergeant, dutifully performing his task of preserving the public order, appears.

	[Enter Sergeant with two native sentries]
Nimchand.	[looking at the lamp in the Sergeant's hand] Hail, holy light, offspring of Heaven first-born, Or of th' Eternal co-eternal beam, May I express thee unblamed?
Sergeant.	What is this?
Sentry 1.	A drunkard, sir.
Sergeant.	What is the matter with you?
Nimchand.	Thou canst not say I did it: never shake Thy gory locks at me.
Sergeant.	Ah, you're scared? You know what'll happen to you, don't you?
Nimchand.	Dear aunt, hold out your arms, save me! I am Ahalyā, turned into stone!
Sergeant.	You'll have to come to the police station. Get up!
Nimchand.	Man but a rush against Othello's breast, And he retires.
Sergeant.	Who are you?
Nimchand.	I am Maināka, son of the mountain, now cooling my wings in the bosom of the ocean.
Sergeant.	I will drown you in the Hooghly.
Nimchand.	. . . drown cats and blind puppies.

167

Sergeant.	Pick him up, quick!
Sentry 2.	Get up, you bastard! [ties his hands and drags him]
Sergeant.	Every drunkard should be treated thus.
Nimchand.	And made a son-in-law . . . Yes, let us go to the nuptial chamber. [Exit][1]

That is the story of Enlightenment in the colonies; it comes in the hands of the policeman, and the marriage is consummated in the station-house. And when those who have seen the light try to assert the sovereignty of the admittedly 'particular' ethical values of their nation, including its 'vices, deceptions, and the like', can we then conclude that the Cunning of Reason has met its match? Unfortunately not. Reason is, indeed, far more cunning than the liberal conscience will care to acknowledge. It sets 'the passions to work in its service'; it keeps Itself 'in the background, untouched and unharmed', while it 'sends forth the particular interests of passion to fight and wear themselves out in its stead'.[2] No, the universality — the sovereign, tyrannical universality — of Reason remains unscathed.

Nationalist thought has not emerged as the antagonist of universal Reason in the arena of world history. To attain this position, it will need to supersede itself. For ever since the Age of Enlightenment, Reason in its universalizing mission has been parasitic upon a much less lofty, much more mundane, palpably material and singularly invidious force, namely the universalist urge of capital. From at least the middle of the 18th century, for two hundred years, Reason has travelled the world piggyback, carried across oceans and continents by colonial powers eager to find new grounds for trade, extraction and the productive expansion of capital. To the extent that nationalism opposed colonial rule, it administered a check on a specific political form of metropolitan capitalist dominance. In the process, it dealt a death blow (or so at least one hopes) to such blatantly ethnic slogans of dominance as the civilizing mission of the West, the white man's burden, etc. That must be counted as one of the major achievements in world history of nationalist movements in colonial countries.

But this was achieved in the very name of Reason. Nowhere in the world has nationalism qua nationalism challenged the legitimacy of the marriage between Reason and capital. Nationalist thought, as we have tried to show above, does not possess the ideological means to make this challenge. The conflict between metropolitan capital and the people–nation it resolves by absorbing the political life of the nation into the body of the state. Conservatory of the passive revolution, the national state now proceeds to find for 'the nation' a place in the global order of capital, while striving to keep the contradictions between capital and the people in perpetual suspension. All politics is now sought to be subsumed under the overwhelming requirements of the state-representing-the-nation. The state now acts as the rational allocator and arbitrator for the nation. Any movement which questions this presumed identity between the people–nation and the state-representing-the-nation is denied the status of legitimate politics. Protected by the cultural–ideological sway of this identity between the nation and the state, capital continues its passive revolution by assiduously exploring the possibilities of marginal development, using the state as the principal mobiliser, planner, guarantor and legitimator of productive invest-ment.

By now, of course, the historical identity between Reason and capital has taken on the form of an epistemic privilege, namely, 'development' as dictated by the advances of modern science and technology. Notwithstanding the occasional recognition of problems of 'appropriateness' or 'absorption' of modern technology, the sovereignty of science itself in its given, historically evolved form is presumed to lie outside the pale of national or other particularities of cultural formations. This sovereignty nationalist thought can hardly question. It can only submit to it and adapt its own path of development to those requirements. But like all relations of subordination, this one too remains fraught with tension, for even in submitting to the dominance of a world order it is powerless to change, nationalism remains reluctant, complaining, demanding, sometimes angry, at other times just shamefaced. The political success of nationalism in ending colonial rule does not signify a true resolution of the contradictions between the problematic and thematic of nationalist thought. Rather, there is a forced closure of possibilities, a 'blocked dialectic'; in other words, a false resolution which carries the marks of its own fragility.

The incompleteness of the ideological resolution accomplished by nationalist thought in its fully developed form can be identified in the very process by which it reaches its moment of arrival. It is a characteristic of the passive revolution that it 'incorporates in the thesis a part of the antithesis'. We have shown above how in its journey nationalist thought necessarily passes through its moment of manoeuvre. The political appropriation of the Gandhian intervention in nationalist politics in India is only a particular and rather intricate example of this process. There could be other ways in which the conflict between capital and the people–nation can be posed and the political consequences appro-priated by the passive revolution of capital: Mexico and Algeria readily appear as two dramatic examples. What is historically decisive in this process is precisely the asymmetry between the contending 'subjective forces'. The victorious side enjoys the crucial advantage of affiliation with a 'world consciousness', thus having access to vastly superior ideological resources for running the machineries of a 'modern' state. In this it can, as we have seen, even mobilize for purely nationalist purposes the 'economic' slogans of a socialist ideology.

But no matter how skilfully employed, modern statecraft and the application of technology cannot effectively suppress the very real tensions which remain unresolved. They are apparent in the political life of every post-colonial nationalist regime in the world. In numerous cases they appear as separatist movements based on ethnic identities, proofs of the incomplete resolution of 'the national question'. More significantly, they often appear as fervently anti-modern, anti-Western strands of politics, rejecting capitalism too for its association with modernism and the West and preaching either a fundamentalist cultural revival or a utopian millennialism. There too the fragility of the forced resolution by nationalism of the contradiction between capital and the people–nation is shown up.

But to the extent that these antagonisms remain bound by ideological forms such as ethnic separatism or peasant populism, they are in principle capable of being appropriated by the passive revolution by means of yet another manoeuvre. The asymmetry between the 'subjective forces' can be removed only when the antithesis acquires the political–ideological resources to match the 'universal' consciousness of capital. This is no simple task. For a large part of this century it was believed that the association of national liberation movements with the ideology of socialism could achieve not only the completion of the democratic tasks of the national revolution but also the world-wide consolidation of the struggle against capital and the establishment of a socialist internationalism. The experience of the last three decades has shown that the task is far more difficult than what the founding fathers of socialism had visualized. In fact, many of the problems faced by socialist countries today show to what extent the identity between Reason and capital, in its contemporary form of the unchallenged prerogative of 'modern' technology, still remains a reality. Reason, as we said before, has not exhausted its cunning.

Inasmuch as he was a child of the Enlightenment, Marx retained his faith in Reason. But in his life-long critique of Hegel, he also pleaded that Reason be rescued from the clutches of capital. In the process, he provided the fundamental theoretical means to examine and criticize the historical relation between capital and Reason. And this relationship, as he repeatedly pointed out in the final, mature phase of his work, was no simple process of unilineal development. Correcting many of his earlier formulations, Marx in his last years saw little regenerative value in the depredations of colonialism in Asian countries. And it was in Russia that he saw in 1881 'the finest chance' in history for a country to pass into a phase of socialist development without first submitting to capital and thus 'committing suicide'. Marx was convinced that capital in its global form had reached a stage where it was definitely 'against science and enlightened reason' and he saw even in the 'archaic' resistance of the popular masses in countries still not enslaved by capital the possibility of a new beginning.[3]

Thus, much that has been suppressed in the historical creation of post-colonial nation-states, much that has been erased or glossed over when nationalist discourse has set down its own life history, bear the marks of the people–nation struggling in an inchoate, undirected and wholly unequal battle against forces that have sought to dominate it. The critique of nationalist discourse must find for itself the ideological means to connect the popular strength of those struggles with the consciousness of a new universality, to subvert the ideological sway of a state which falsely claims to speak on behalf of the nation and to challenge the presumed sovereignty of a science which puts itself at the service of capital, to replace, in other words, the old problematic and thematic with new ones.

Notes

1. Act II, Scene 2.

2. G.F.W. Hegel, *Lectures on the Philosophy of World History: Introduction,* tr. H.B. Nisbet (Cambridge: Cambridge University Press, 1975), p.89.

3. See in particular the drafts of Marx's letter to Vera Zasulich, now available in English translation in Teodor Shanin, *Late Marx and the Russian Road* (London: Routledge and Kegan Paul, 1983).

Bibliography

Major Texts

Bankimchandra Chattopadhyay

1. *Baṅkim Racanābalī* (ed.) Jogesh Chandra Bagal, 2 vols. (Calcutta: Sahitya Samsad, 1965).
2. *Baṅkim Racanābalī (English works)* (ed). Jogesh Chandra Bagal (Calcutta: Sahitya Samsad, 1969).

Mohandas Karamchand Gandhi

1. *The Collected Works of Mahatma Gandhi*, 87 vols. (New Delhi: Publications Division, 1958-   ).

Jawaharlal Nehru

1. *Selected Works of Jawaharlal Nehru*, 15 vols. (New Delhi: Orient Longman, 1972-82).
2. *Jawaharlal Nehru's Speeches*, 5 vols. (New Delhi: Publications Division, 1954-68).
3. *An Autobiography* (London: Bodley Head, 1936).
4. *The Discovery of India* (New York: John Day, 1946).

Others

Abdel-Malek, Anouar, 'Orientalism in Crisis', *Diogenes* 44 (Winter, 1963) pp.102-40.

Althusser, Louis, *For Marx*, tr. Ben Brewster (London: Allen Lane, 1969).

Althusser, Louis and Balibar, Étienne, *Reading Capital*, tr. Ben Brewster (London: New Left Books, 1970).

Amin, Shahid, 'Gandhi as Mahatma: Gorakhpur District, Eastern U.P., 1921-1922' in Ranajit Guha (ed.) *Subaltern Studies III* (Delhi: Oxford University Press, 1985), pp.1-61.

Anderson, Benedict, *Imagined Communities: Reflections on the Origin and Spread of Nationalism* (London: Verso, 1983).

Apter, David E., *The Politics of Modernization* (Chicago: University of Chicago Press, 1965).

Bandyopadhyay, Brajendranath and Das, Sajanikanta, *Sāhitya Sādhak Caritmālā*, vol.2 (Calcutta: Bangiya Sahitya Parishad, 1945).

Bhattacharya, Pradyumna, 'Rammohun Roy and Bengali Prose' in V.C. Joshi (ed.) *Rammohun Roy and the Process of Modernization in India* (Delhi: Vikas, 1975).

Breuilly, John, *Nationalism and the State* (Manchester: Manchester University Press, 1982).

Buci-Glucksmann, Christine, 'State, Transition and Passive Revolution' in Chantal Mouffe (ed.) *Gramsci and Social Theory* (London: Routledge and Kegan Paul, 1979) pp.113-67.

————— *Gramsci and the State*, tr. David Fernbach (London: Lawrence and Wishart, 1980).

Carpenter, Edward, *Civilisation: Its Cause and Cure and Other Essays* (London: George Allen and Unwin, 1921).

Chandra, Bipan, *The Rise and Growth of Economic Nationalism in India* (New Delhi: People's Publishing House, 1966).

Claudin-Urondo, Carmen, *Lenin and the Cultural Revolution*, tr. Brian Pearce (Brighton: Harvester Press, 1977).

Collingwood, R.G., *Ruskin's Philosophy* (Chichester, Sussex: Quentin Nelson, 1971).

Das, Sisir Kumar, *The Artist in Chains: The Life of Bankimchandra Chatterji* (New Delhi: New Statesman, 1984).

Davidson, Donald, 'On the very idea of a conceptual scheme', *Proceedings of the American Philosophical Association*, 17 (1973-74) pp.5-20.

Davis, Horace B., *Toward a Marxist Theory of Nationalism* (New York: Monthly Review Press, 1978).

De Barun, 'A Biographical Perspective on the Political and Economic Ideas of Rammohun Roy' in V.C. Joshi (ed.) *Rammohun Roy and the Process of Modernization in India* (Delhi: Vikas, 1975).

————— 'A Historiographical Critique of Renaissance Analogues for Nineteenth-century India' in Barun De (ed.) *Perspectives in the Social Sciences I: Historical Dimensions* (Calcutta: Oxford University Press, 1977) pp.178-218.

Desai, A.R., *Social Background of Indian Nationalism* (Bombay: Popular Book Depot, 1948).

Desai, Mahadev, *The Gospel of Selfless Action or the Gita According to Gandhi* (Ahmedabad: Navajivan, 1946).

Deutsch, Karl W., *Nationalism and Social Communication* (Cambridge, Mass: MIT Press, 1966).

Dunn, John, *Western Political Theory in the Face of the Future* (Cambridge: Cambridge University Press, 1979).

————— 'The Identity of the History of Ideas' in P. Laslett, W.G. Runciman and Q. Skinner (eds.) *Philosophy, Politics and Science*, Series IV (Oxford: Oxford University Press, 1972).

————— 'Practising History and Social Science on "Realist" Assumptions' in C. Hookway and P. Pettit (eds.) *Action and Interpretation: Studies in the Philosophy of the Social Sciences* (Cambridge: Cambridge University Press, 1978).

Dutt, R.P., *India Today* (Bombay: People's Publishing House, 1949).

Fleisher, Martin, *Radical Reform and Political Persuasion in the Life and Writings of Thomas More* (Geneva: Librairie Droz, 1973).

Gellner, Ernest, *Thought and Change* (London: Weidenfeld and Nicolson, 1964).

————— *Nations and Nationalism* (Oxford: Basil Blackwell, 1983).

Gramsci, Antonio, *Selections from the Prison Notebooks*, tr. Q. Hoare and G. Nowell Smith (New York: International Publishers, 1971).

Guha, Ranajit, 'Neel Darpan: The Image of the Peasant Revolt in a Liberal Mirror',

Journal of Peasant Studies, 2 (October 1974) pp.1-46.

————— *Elementary Aspects of Peasant Insurgency in Colonial India* (Delhi: Oxford University Press, 1983).

Hayes, Carlton J.H., *The Historical Evolution of Modern Nationalism* (New York: R.R. Smith, 1931).

————— *Nationalism: A Religion* (New York: Macmillan, 1960).

Hegel, G.F.W., *Lectures on the Philosophy of World History: Introduction*, tr. H.B. Nisbet (Cambridge: Cambridge University Press, 1975).

Hollis, Martin, 'Reason and Ritual', *Philosophy*, 43 (1967), 165, pp.231-47.

Huntington, Samuel P., *Political Order in Changing Societies* (New Haven, Conn: Yale University Press, 1969).

Iyer, Raghavan N., *The Moral and Political Thought of Mahatma Gandhi* (New York: Oxford University Press, 1973).

Joshi, V.C. (ed.) *Rammohun Roy and the Process of Modernization in India* (Delhi: Vikas, 1975).

Kautsky, Karl, *Thomas More and his Utopia*, tr. H.J. Stenning (London: Lawrence and Wishart, 1979).

Kedourie, Elie, *Nationalism* (London: Hutchinson, 1960).

————— (ed.) *Nationalism in Asia and Africa* (London: Weidenfeld and Nicolson, 1970).

Kemiläinen, Aira, *Nationalism* (Jyväskylä: Jyväskylä Kasvatusopillinen Korkeakoulu, 1964).

Kohn, Hans, *The Idea of Nationalism* (New York: Macmillan, 1944).

————— *Nationalism, Its Meaning and History* (Princeton: N.J.: Van Nostrand, 1955).

————— *The Age of Nationalism* (New York: Harper, 1962).

Lenin, V.I., 'What the "Friends of the People" Are and How They Fight the Social-Democrats', *Collected Works* (Moscow: Progress Publishers, 1964), vol.1, pp.129-332.

————— 'A Characterisation of Economic Romanticism', *Collected Works*, vol.2, pp.129-265.

————— 'Critical Remarks on the National Question', *Collected Works*, vol.20, pp.17-54.

————— 'The Right of Nations to Self-determination', *Collected Works*, vol.20, pp.393-454.

————— 'The Socialist Revolution and the Right of Nations to Self-determination', *Collected Works*, vol.22, pp.143-56.

————— 'The Discussion on Self-determination Summed Up', *Collected Works*, vol.22, pp.320-60.

Löwy, Michael, 'Marxists and the National Question', *New Left Review*, 96 (March-April 1976) pp.81-100.

MacIntyre, Alasdair, 'Is Understanding Religion Compatible with Believing?' in Bryan R. Wilson (ed.) *Rationality* (Oxford: Basil Blackwell, 1970).

Marx, Karl, 'The British Rule in India' in K. Marx and F. Engels, *The First Indian War of Independence 1857-1859* (Moscow: Foreign Languages Publishing House, 1959).

————— 'Preface to *A Contribution to the Critique of Political Economy*' in K. Marx and F. Engels, *Selected Works*, vol.1 (Moscow: Progress Publishers, 1969).

Mill, John Stuart, *Nature, The Utility of Religion, and Theism* (London: Watts, 1904).

Paggi, Leonardo, 'Gramsci's General Theory of Marxism' in Chantal Mouffe (ed.) *Gramsci and Marxist Theory* (London: Routledge and Kegan Paul, 1979) pp.113-67.

Pandey, Gyan, 'Peasant Revolt and Indian Nationalism: The Peasant Movement in Awadh, 1919-1922' in Ranajit Guha (ed.) *Subaltern Studies I: Writings on South Asian History and Society* (Delhi: Oxford University Press, 1982) pp.143-97.

Plamenatz, John, 'Two Types of Nationalism' in Eugene Kamenka (ed.) *Nationalism: The Nature and Evolution of an Idea* (London: Edward Arnold, 1976) pp.23-36.

Poddar, Arabinda, *Baṅkim-mānas* (Calcutta: Indiana, 1960).

———— *Renaissance in Bengal: Search for Identity* (Simla: Indian Institute of Advanced Study, 1977).

Porshnev, Boris, 'Historical Interest of Marx in his last years of Life: The Chronological Notes' in E.A. Zelubovskaya, L.I. Golman, V.M. Dalin and B.F. Porshnev (eds.) *Marks Istorik* (Moscow: Institute of History, Academy of Sciences, 1968) pp.404-43.

Rolland, Romain, *Mahatma Gandhi: A Study in Indian Nationalism*, tr. L.V. Ramaswami Aiyar (Madras: S. Ganesan, 1923).

Rorty, Richard, *Philosophy and the Mirror of Nature* (Oxford: Basil Blackwell, 1980).

Rosdolsky, Roman, 'Worker and Fatherland: A Note on a Passage in the *Communist Manifesto*', *Science and Society*, 29 (1965) pp.330-7.

Ruskin, John, *Unto this Last* (London: W.B. Clive, 1931).

Said, Edward W., *Orientalism* (London: Routledge and Kegan Paul, 1978).

Sarkar, S.C., *Bengal Renaissance and Other Essays* (New Delhi: People's Publishing House, 1970).

Sarkar, Sumit, *The Swadeshi Movement in Bengal 1903-08* (New Delhi: People's Publishing House, 1973).

———— 'Rammohun Roy and the Break with the Past', in V.C. Joshi (ed.) *Rammohun Roy and the Process of Modernization in India* (Delhi: Vikas, 1975).

Sassoon, Anne Showstack, 'Passive Revolution and the Politics of Reform' in Sassoon (ed.) *Approaches to Gramsci* (London: Writers and Readers, 1982) p.127-48.

Sen, Asok, 'The Bengal Economy and Rammohun Roy' in V.C. Joshi (ed.) *Rammohun Roy and the Process of Modernization in India* (Delhi: Vikas, 1975).

———— *Iswar Chandra Vidyasagar and his Elusive Milestones* (Calcutta: Riddhi-India, 1977).

Seton-Watson, Hugh, *Nations and States: An Enquiry into the Origins of Nations and the Politics of Nationalism* (London: Methuen, 1977).

Shanin, Teodor (ed.) *Late Marx and the Russian Road* (London: Routledge and Kegan Paul, 1983).

Siddiqi, Majid Hayat, *Agrarian Unrest in North India: The United Provinces, 1918-22* (New Delhi: Vikas, 1978).

Skinner, Quentin, 'Meaning and Understanding in the History of Ideas', *History and Theory*, 8 (1969) pp.3-53.

———— 'Some Problems in the Analysis of Political Thought and Action', *Political Theory*, 2 (1974) pp.277-303.

Smith, Anthony D., *Theories of Nationalism* (London: Duckworth, 1971).

Stalin, J.V., 'Marxism and the National Question', *Works*, vol.2 (Calcutta: Gana-Sahitya Prakash, 1974) pp.194-215.

Tolstoy, Leo, 'The Kingdom of God is Within You', in *The Kingdom of God and Other Essays*, tr. Aylmer Maude (London: Oxford University Press, 1936).

———— *The Slavery of Our Times*, tr. Aylmer Maude (London: John Lawrence, 1972).

Van Dijk, Teun A., *Text and Context: Explorations in the Semantics and Pragmatics of Discourse* (London: Longman, 1977).

Walicki, Andrzej, *The Controversy Over Capitalism: Studies in the Social Philosophy of the Russian Populists* (Oxford: Clarendon Press, 1969).

———— *The Slavophile Controversy: History of a Conservative Utopia in Nineteenth Century Russian Thought*, tr. Hilda Andrews-Rusiecka (Oxford: Clarendon Press, 1975).

Wilson, Bryan R. (ed.) *Rationality* (Oxford: Basil Blackwell, 1970).

Winch, Peter, 'Understanding a Primitive Society', *American Philosophical Quarterly*, 1 (1964) pp.307-24.

Wolf, Ken, 'Hans Kohn's Liberal Nationalism: The Historian as Prophet', *Journal of the History of Ideas*, 37, 4 (October-December 1976) pp.651-72.

Index